HITLER'S U.S. ALLIES

HITLER'S U.S. ALLIES

AMERICANS WHO SUPPORTED THE NAZIS

BY NORMAN RIDLEY

FRONTLINE
BOOKS

First published in Great Britain in 2024 by Frontline Books
An imprint of Pen & Sword Books Ltd Yorkshire – Philadelphia

Copyright © Norman Ridley, 2024
ISBN 978 1 03611 095 6

The right of Norman Ridley to be identified as Author of this work has been asserted by him in accordance with the Copyright, Designs and Patents Act 1988. A CIP catalogue record for this book is available from the British Library All rights reserved.

No part of this book may be reproduced or transmitted in any form or by any means, electronic or mechanical including photocopying, recording or by any information storage and retrieval system, without permission from the Publisher in writing.

Typeset by Lapiz Digital Printed and bound in the UK by
CPI Group (UK) Ltd, Croydon, CR0 4YY.

Printed on paper from a sustainable source by
CPI Group (UK) Ltd, Croydon, CR0 4YY

Pen & Sword Books Limited incorporates the imprints of Archaeology, Atlas, Aviation, Battleground, Digital, Discovery, Family History, Fiction, History, Local, Local History, Maritime, Military, Military Classics, Politics, Select, Transport, True Crime, Air World, Claymore Press, Frontline Publishing, Leo Cooper, Remember When, Seaforth Publishing, The Praetorian Press, Wharncliffe Books, Wharncliffe Local History, Wharncliffe Transport, Wharncliffe True Crime and White Owl.

For a complete list of Pen & Sword titles please contact

PEN & SWORD BOOKS LTD
47 Church Street, Barnsley, South Yorkshire, S70 2AS, England
E-mail: enquiries@pen-and-sword.co.uk
Website: www.pen-and-sword.co.uk

Or

PEN & SWORD BOOKS
1950 Lawrence Rd, Havertown, PA 19083, USA
E-mail: uspen-and-sword@casematepublishers.com

CONTENTS

Prologue ix

Chapter 1	The Background to American Fascism	1
Chapter 2	Friends of the New Germany	27
Chapter 3	William Dudley Pelley and the Silver Legion	53
Chapter 4	The New Deal	62
Chapter 5	Father Charles Coughlin	86
Chapter 6	Berlin takes a Fresh Approach	98
Chapter 7	The German American Bund	110
Chapter 8	The Christian Front	137
Chapter 9	Doing Business with the Nazis	154

Appendix 1 German American Bund Organisation 163
Notes 166
Sources 172
Sources 172
Index 175

It is late, but not too late to save American Democracy if Americans will awaken now!

Elizabeth Dilling, The Red Network, 1934

PROLOGUE

When Lieutenant Colonel Franklin D'Olier a Philadelphia textile millionaire, returned from France in 1919, he led a movement that showed exactly what American fascism might look like. On 15 March 1919, members of the American Expeditionary Forces (AEF), the US military forces stationed in Europe, convened a meeting. In attendance were officers drawn largely from the upper classes, led by Lieutenant Colonel Theodore "Ted" Roosevelt, Jr, the eldest son of the recently deceased former president, Theodore "Teddy" Roosevelt. The movement dedicated itself to fighting for veterans' issues, such as adjusted compensation and disability benefits but an equally significant purpose was to build a national organization as quickly as possible and return home to crush the militant workers' movement they saw as inspired by foreign radicals, and to prevent veterans from being influenced or organized by left-wing political forces. After the recent Bolshevik revolution in Russia and the communist riots in post-war Germany, there was a real and widespread fear that the America working class might become radicalised by communist propaganda and roused to insurrection. This movement, calling itself the American Legion, had its roots deep within the wealthy capitalist echelon of American society and was able to deflect any accusations of being a class-based movement by basing its creed on patriotic 'Americanism' where 'the relationship between masculinity, citizenship and service was deeply engrained among these all-male citizen-soldiers'.[1] D'Olier was elected as National Commander and brought the Legion of First World War veterans back to the US where he dedicated himself to 'fighting every element that threatens our democratic government [and] should the day ever come when they menace the freedom of our representative government, the Legion would not hesitate to take things into its own hands...as the Fascisti of Italy [had done].' A future leader, Alvin Owsley, later went on to say that 'the Fascisti are to Italy what the American Legion is to the United States.'[2]

The Legion had acquired a congressional charter and quickly established itself as an important political force in American life, with powerful supporters in the business community and the press and with organisations in every small town and city giving it a membership of almost one million by the end of 1919. The immediate post-war years saw great industrial unrest in America with more than four million workers involved in three major strikes in 1919 alone resulting in a government crackdown on left-wing organisations. A leading socialist James Maurer described an atmosphere where 'Intolerance was rampant, constitutional rights were flagrantly violated, free speech was throttled, public and labour union meetings were mobbed, labour schools, labour union headquarters, and the offices of labour and progressive publications were invaded by mobs composed of American Legion members.' Ole Hanson, the mayor of Seattle called for the government to 'either hang or incarcerate for life all the anarchists in the country' saying that if they didn't, he would.

What happened next is eerily reminiscent of events that were taking place in Berlin where street violence between right-wing paramilitary Freikorps and communists was commonplace. Events came to a head during the 20,000-strong May Day parade in Cleveland, Ohio in support of Eugene Debs and other left-wing activists who had been imprisoned. The police attacked the marchers, killing four, injuring 200 and arresting some 120 others. Elsewhere violence erupted in Centralia, Washington, where, after a violent confrontation with the revolutionary Industrial Workers of the World (IWW), the First World War veteran and IWW member Wesley Everest was broken out of jail and taken by Legionnaires to a nearby bridge where they lynched him and riddled his body with bullets.

At the first convention of the American Legion in November 1919, delegates passed a resolution praising the actions of Legionnaires in the town of Centralia, Pennsylvania. The historian William Pencak, in his book *God and Country*, sees the Legion at this stage as having appointed itself America's leading anti-Bolshevik organization and in effect the American 'Freikorps'.[3] The Friekorps paramilitaries of Weimar Germany would become the foundation of the Brownshirt and Gestapo organisations in Nazi Germany. Where IWW meetings were planned in Reading Pennsylvania, truckloads of former service men were brought in from the rural district, armed and ready for trouble.

Press reporting of violence between unions and Legionnaires was muted but it had not gone unnoticed by business leaders. Thomas E. Wilson, president of Wilson & Company, one of the largest meatpacking companies in the United States, donated $10,000 to American Legion funds. Following his example other local businessmen chipped in to raise the total to $100,000. Legionnaires spearheaded the attack on socialists, communists, the IWW, and other radical labour and political activists and were being routinely used to break industrial strikes. By 1920 membership of the Legion was, like fascist movements in Europe, mostly made up of white-collar professionals, self-employed businessmen, and other solidly middle-class groups in small town and rural areas. The Legion would go on to play a significant role in the story of fascism in the US.

Chapter 1

THE BACKGROUND TO AMERICAN FASCISM

In its historical epoch in the 1920s and 1930s, fascism had a very real presence in the USA, comparable to that on continental Europe.[1]

There has been a consistent trend in the writing of American history to avoid the term fascist in relation to American far-right movements. Preferring to use terms such as 'nativist' or 'white supremist' writers and politicians have usually decried fascism as a 'fringe alien philosophy' the seeds of which have never taken root in America. Often the term was used by politicians as a term of abuse to denigrate opponents who showed no particular fascistic tendencies whatsoever. When it was taken up by journalists as shorthand for whatever they were arguing against, it is no surprise that the word 'fascist' rapidly lost meaning for the vast majority of the population. Even when someone like the far-tight demagogue, Gerald Lyman Kenneth Smith, was described by his biographer Glen Jeansonne as sharing some of the beliefs of European fascists: racism, anti-Semitism, xenophobia, extreme nationalism, red baiting, authoritarianism, and glorification of war, force, and violence, the writer still does not ascribe to him the epithet 'fascist'. Taking an objective view, however, it is clear that there was a real and recognisably fascist movement in the United States between the wars, comparable to that on continental Europe, even if it failed to break through into the mainstream as a political and social force.[2]

Fascism has clearly recognisable characteristics. It emerges as a political or social movement with a party structure underpinned by middle-class supporters. Its breeding ground is national economic or social crisis and its momentum gets its energy from mob hysteria. A focus for emotional frenzy is found in a scapegoat upon whom is heaped blame for all the troubles and misfortunes besetting the community. Set against this 'social evil' is the image of the true patriot whose hereditary virtues make them naturally superior to all other races and whose heroic mission is to bring stability, enlightenment and culture to the world, by force if necessary.

The nucleus of disaffection is small at first but, if it is to gain traction, learns to reach out to others with propaganda and wild promises that have emotional appeal. Targets for enrolment in the cause generally have existing deep-rooted prejudices to which the carriers of the message can appeal. It may be the industrial magnate's fear of labour unrest, the middle-class reaction to diminishing economic stability or the working man faced with falling wages, degraded working conditions or unemployment. Success or failure of a fascist movement often depends upon the breadth of its appeal across the whole social spectrum. At first the movement seeks to acquire power through legitimate political processes but beyond a certain threshold it will resort to illegal, undemocratic and unconstitutional methods. European fascism had showed that a fully-fledged fascist dictatorship was most likely to arise when a nation has suffered humiliation or was faced with economic chaos and had found voice in a forceful and unscrupulous leader.

Writing in 1935, H. Arthur Steiner saw genuine fascism as having clear manifestations.

- The rejection of democracy.
- A dictatorial technique.
- Repression of individual freedom.
- Repression of organised labour.
- Intense nationalism.
- A reactionary perspective.

Whilst any American fascism would necessarily have its own peculiar features, it would, he says, need to satisfy each of six minimal doctrinal requirements. Steiner looked at each to see to what extent they applied to America in 1935.

The rejection of democracy.
Fascism, he says, is the 'negation of democratic dogma' where the state becomes an organism whose aim, life and means of action are superior to those of a single individual, who loses his significance and identity

and whose individual rights are superseded by obligations to the state. Copious and repetitious constitutional limitations have been placed upon the American state, however, that has enabled it to act only in a greatly restricted sphere.

A dictatorial technique.
While not all dictatorial regimes are fascistic, it is necessarily true that all fascist regimes are dictatorial. Policy is always decided by the state and aligned with the interests of its leadership. It is enforced by a bureaucracy which is responsible only to the head of government, the dictator, who brooks no veto. By definition, fascism restrains individual initiative.

Repression of individual freedom.
In order to avoid disruptive movements, the fascist state imposes extensive restrictions upon the rights of an individual to criticise it. Whilst there had been moves, particularly in California, to restrict membership of any movement designed to overthrow the government, i.e. the communist party, under penalty of imprisonment it is a sign of weakness to have to legislate to that end. In the mid-1930s, Steiner recognised the danger of society growing weaker by failing to protect itself through 'constructive improvement' and continuing down the path of restrictive legislation.

Repression of organised labour.
Fascism in its early stages, as it struggles for a voice within a democratic system, must show an interest in improving the lot of the proletariat as well as the middle classes but once in power it wastes no time in restricting the rights of workers to challenge the interests of their employer. In this respect the American nation had grown up embracing this tenet of the fascist creed and vested interests were in no hurry to change that.

Intense nationalism.
The question of chauvinism is complex and in the economic sphere revolves around the argument for protectionism against free trade and has little to do with broad philosophical principles. Steiner found 'genuine and thoroughgoing' nationalism only amongst 'professionals to whom militarism [is] the very blood of life or among those journalists and politicians who find the stimulation of national consciousness highly profitable'.[3]

A reactionary perspective.

A desire to put the clock back is common to many societies, especially in the older generation, so it is no surprise to find that sentiment prevalent within American society.

While Steiner looks for characteristics of fascism, Robert Paxton, in his book *The Anatomy of Fascism*, prefers to look at exactly what constitutes fascism from the viewpoint of it being a process rather than a formula. He asks what makes a movement fascistic, not from the aspect of do they all wear the same colour shirt, or do they possess a sufficiently charismatic leader but by asking whether or not a political movement makes claims that it alone can solve an overwhelming crisis, whether within the organisation the individual is subordinated to the group and whether the group sees itself as victimised giving it the right to take extra-legal action against its enemies. Fascism exists, he says, even where it does not achieve power and it does not disappear simply because it does not have popular support.

To be clear: there is a distinction between a fascist state and a democratic state in which fascist movements exist. All societies have the potential to experience an upsurge of fascism when the conditions allow. It would be hard to find a modern society in which no fascistic element exists to a greater or lesser extent. When the foundations of democracy are threatened by war, severe economic downturn, natural disaster or plague it is common for society to invest great powers in a strong leadership if it can be convinced that it holds the key to its survival. The danger is that such a leadership, having convinced a big enough section of the community that they hold such a key and taken a tight grip on the reins of power in circumstances that deny or inhibit opposition, might choose to implement an agenda that seeks to smash the old order and closes off all paths towards a return to democratic government. The probability is that they would then use intimidation, violent persecution of all opponents, total suppression of free speech and pollution of the judicial system to hold onto their absolute power for personal aggrandisement or enrichment. Then you have a fascist state.

A fascist movement, on the other hand, has ambition but no immediate means of achieving power. It plots endlessly for weaknesses to exploit, for enemies to blame. It offers simple solutions to complex questions and advocates a programme of radical reform that can only be implemented after grabbing power through violent insurrection. It seeks to impose a regime embodying a pernicious doctrine satisfying the interest of a minority group of vested interests to the detriment of all others. To achieve power, such a movement would have to mobilise violent anti-intellectual mobs ready to blindly follow a charismatic leader preaching bombastic, irrational, and fabricated propaganda. The path from ambition to realisation, however, is harder or easier depending on the severity of any crisis they choose to exploit or the underlying strength of democratic institutions that they would have to overcome to take control.

What would American fascism look like? It would not be logical for it to mimic fascism in other countries. The language and symbols of American fascism, Paxton says, would necessarily have to be indigenous, familiar and reassuring and not appear to be 'exotic' to loyal Americans. American fascism would speak of American heritage and claim to defend traditional American values. The great variety of types of fascism in countries such as France, Germany, Italy and Britain indicated that an American variety would develop under its 'own peculiar stimuli and with its own peculiar manifestations'.[4]

Fascism was still seen as something that had crept into America from abroad but Victor Ferkiss argued that it was deep-rooted in American political traditions such as agrarian-based populism with its anti-Semitic and nationalistic invective against the power of 'money men' and urban institutions. Conspiracy theories claimed that liberal democratic institutions were too weak to stand up to big business and international finance. Yet even he was reluctant to call it fascism, preferring to say that it was simply 'compatible in spirit' with it.[5]

This view was supported on the communist wing by A.B. Magil and Henry Stevens who noted that ever since Warren Harding's presidency of the early 1920s legislative bodies in the US had been losing ground to the executive as the economy was developed in the interests of monopolies.[6] Having seen the gradual concentration of economic power through monopolies the New Deal had introduced the second basic requirement for a fascist state which was expansion of state power. When it came to what fascism in America would look like, their view was that it would have its own peculiarities arising out of its unique situation. Fascism, they argued, would not be a mass movement from below but would come in 'under the radar' by appealing to traditional American ideals such as liberty and freedom and through a long process of whittling down democratic rights. There would be no revolution but an evolution of an idea that Americans could believe in. Believing that they were living out the American dream the people would find themselves ensnared in a web of control that was quite different from that which they had been promised.

*

Outbreaks of right-wing activist movements such as Silver Shirts, Black Legion or Christian American Crusade have been dismissed as incoherent peripheral 'blips' of discontent that in no way resembled fascist movements that were characterised by centralist control. However, it has been argued by Leo Ribuffo that racism and anti-Semitism alongside a general anti-liberalism and anti-leftism, are not aberrations but values that had 'long circulated through American society [that were] widely shared by 'normal' Americans,' but he, also, refuses to ascribe to that trend the term 'fascism'.[7]

So let us examine those movements in the history of America that it might reasonably be argued were fascist. Such movements reared their head in America at least five times in various manifestations between 1830 and the start of the Second World War. Lurking all the time in the background, fascism is described by William S. Bernard as a real and persistent threat like a 'cultural germ, dormant for a while, and then suddenly springing into renewed virulence,' waiting for conditions favourable to its multiplication and spread.[8] Such conditions of social disorganisation might include war, revolution, economic depression or the cultural shocks that resulted from mass immigration.

The first discernible fascist movement in America arose just after its Revolutionary War with Britain with the onset of mass immigration when the country cried out for families to settle the lands vacated by the forced re-settling of native Americans west of the Mississippi river. In 1830, alone more than 25,000 arrivals were recorded, and that rate increased over the following few years causing a backlash of resentment within the native-born population. This was at a time when Americans were involved with inventing a national identity and in the process bringing in a concept of nationality or ethnicity to describe the various culturally distinct groups in the country.

Cultural differences and relatively closed immigrant communities were common but the influential painter and inventor of Morse Code, Samuel F. B. Morse, argued that the country was threatened if minorities with 'certain kinds of cultural characteristics' were enfranchised.[9] Resentment stemmed from the image that native-born Americans had of themselves as a people who had shrugged off foreign loyalties and were developing a cultural landscape based upon loyalty to their new country and a sense that it was they who had created the nation through strife giving them special status. Theirs was an essentially Anglo-Saxon character which set them apart from groups such as

Irish and German immigrants, whose own cultural identity had been forged through resistance to an occupying power. It was not so much a nationalist identity that immigrants from these countries brought but more an allegiance to local groupings within America which they were reluctant to abandon to 'Americanisation'. Much as leaders of immigrant communities held that it was the desire for freedom and fealty to democratic institutions and traditions that made someone American it was the case that ethnicity became a status category within American society.

Native-born Americans had a strong Protestant tradition which found a voice in the revivalist Second Great Awakening, an outpouring of religious fervour with, as a central feature, an emotional appeal to the supernatural. In Massachusetts, in particular, increasing industrialisation had seen an influx of Irish Catholic immigrants which was met with suspicion and resentment by the poor Protestant community. The wealthy, however, exhibited no such prejudice and even sent their daughters, between the ages of six and sixteen, to be educated at the Catholic Ursine Convent in Charlestown near Boston. The convent had originally taken in girls from poor Catholic families but having moved to new premises now provided an education in conventional subjects such as geography and history but also moral philosophy, rhetoric, composition and for an extra fee, French, music and dancing. The convent took in as boarders fifty daughters of wealthy Protestant families who paid handsomely for the privilege, but no attempt was made to instruct the students in the Catholic faith. One pupil, Lucy Thaxter, would later write that she never experienced 'any other treatment than the kindness and sympathy which greeted [her] first entrance there'.[10]

Trouble was never far away but it boiled over on the evening of 11 August 1834. A few days previously, rumours had begun circulating about Sister Mary John who had suffered a mental breakdown two weeks previously and was now believed to be held in the cellars of the convent against her will. Posters appeared in the town proclaiming that 'All Catholics and all persons who favour the Catholic Church are...vile imposters, liars, villains, and cowardly cutthroats.'[11]

When a delegation demanded to see Sister Mary John, the Mother Superior initially refused permission on the grounds that the patient was too ill to see anyone but later allowed one visitor who attested that Sister Mary John was being properly looked after. Nevertheless, protests became more strident and even the local bishop preached a sermon calling on the community to be calm. All to no avail because on the evening of the 11th an angry mob descended on the convent.

They demanded to see Sister Mary John but were refused entry to the convent by the Mother Superior who, according to Lucy Thaxter used 'harsh and abusive language'.[12] The mob reacted with shouting and threats as the nuns led the children out of the building to a safe place. Outside a bonfire was lit in the convent grounds and the mob broke in breaking valuables and throwing out burnables to be hurled onto the bonfire. In a letter written later by Mother St. Augustine O'Keeffe she refers to some of the rioters entering the mortuary chapel where they opened coffins and pulled out the teeth of the dead. Meanwhile the fire had spread to the building which burned to the ground. It is not known if the safe evacuation of the children was known to the rioters.

On the following day, there was public revulsion at the incident but it was widely put about that the fire had been started by a mob from Boston not Charlestown but the leaders of the riot were well known. At a meeting called on the following day, local dignitaries expressed outrage and allocated funds to rebuild the convent. The attack, they said, was a base and cowardly act for which the perpetrators deserved the contempt of the community. Nevertheless, another mob went to Mt. Benedict and lit more fires. Only the presence of troops prevented them from storming a nearby Catholic church. In Charlestown, a shanty town of Irish labourers was burned down.

The mayor of Boston, Theodore Lyman Jr. ordered an investigation which led to thirteen arrests. They were brought to trial before Justices Shaw, Putnam and Morton and charged with arson and burglary. The prosecutor had found great difficulty in finding any witnesses to testify given that notices had been posted in the town to the effect that 'All persons giving information in any shape or testifying in court against any one concerned in the late affair at Charlestown may expect assassination according to the oath which bound the party to each other.'[13]

When the prime defendant John R. Buzzell was found not guilty after a ten-day trial and twenty-one hours of jury deliberation, he said 'The testimony against me was point blank and sufficient to have convicted twenty men, but somehow I proved an alibi, and the jury brought in a verdict of not guilty.'[14] He went to press to express his thanks for the many gifts his admirers had sent him. Only one defendant was found guilty and he was sentenced to life imprisonment. He was pardoned and released after seven months.

*

During the next few years, a number of anti-Catholic 'nativist' parties sprang up, which amalgamated into the Native American

Association formed on 11 July 1837 which had a working-class identity given expression in the rhetoric of upper-class political leaders who conveniently side-stepped issues of class division with appeals to ethnic hatreds in their ambition for political power. Newly arrived immigrants, they said, should enjoy none of the rights and privileges of native-born Americans and should only be allowed to attain such rights after twenty years residency.

Animosity towards Catholics grew along with the rising tide of immigration. The next significant eruption of violence was in 1842 when anti-Catholic riots broke out in New York where churches and institutions were attacked and destroyed. This was closely followed by riots in Philadelphia two years later where nativist protestors came up against government militia resulting in eight deaths. Trouble spread to Baltimore and Louisiana where rioting prompted the government to make significant increases to their law enforcement agencies. The early nativist movement began to lose momentum, however, as a booming economy provided work for all and the underlying fear of immigrants taking jobs from native-born Americans receded.

This huge influx of immigrants which amounted to close to two million between 1840 and 1850 meant that new traditions, habits and practices began to have an effect on American culture. Again, this was resented by a new wave of explicitly Anglo-Saxon and middle-class opposition to foreigners that rose up in 1849 calling itself the Know Nothing movement or the Supreme Order of the Star-Spangled Banner or sometimes, the Sons of the Sires of '76. In order to join, one had to prove American and Protestant ancestry for at least two generations, a requirement that would be echoed in the Aryan regulations of Nazi Germany. The stated aim of the movement was protection of traditional religious and political values, and their methods were crude and violent. Anti-Irish street gangs, calling themselves 'Rip Raps' and 'Plug Uglies', meted out extreme violence to opponents and aften crossed the line of criminality, again in a way that Nazi brownshirts would eighty years later. The first martyr of the cause was William 'Bill the Butcher' Poole, a violent gang leader and prize-fighter who was shot and killed during a bar brawl with immigrants in New York on 24 February 1855. A crowd of 25,000 attended his funeral.

To give legitimacy to street violence, the movement publicised its creed in books such as *A Defence of the American Policy* written by Thomas R. Whitney. In it he said that only those with the proper qualifications deserved full rights. Women's suffrage was abhorrent and unnatural, Catholics were a threat to the stability of the nation, and German and Irish immigrants undermined the old order established by the Founding Fathers. The publication *A Voice to America* openly disseminated racist propaganda claiming that the Anglo-Saxons were the 'dominant race to whom the possession of the continent has manifestly been delivered'.[15] The movement seemed poised to make the breakthrough into mainstream American politics with 8 senators and 104 Representatives in Congress and a strong showing all along the eastern seaboard but just when it seemed to be on the cusp of replacing the Whig Party, it foundered on the question of slavery. It had no coherent policy on an issue that was fast supplanting immigration as the main preoccupation of the masses and as a result the Know Nothings rapidly faded from the political landscape and became an irrelevance in American politics but it had left its mark.

American fascism that long predated the nationalistic European fascist movements, however, was not so easily eradicated and simply lay in abeyance until the next crisis emerged. Even at its lowest point, nativist politics remained lurking in the undergrowth of ethnic and class resentment. This started to bubble up in 1880 when a new and different wave of immigration saw German, English, Irish and Scottish incomers outnumbered by others coming in from Russia, Austria-Hungary and Italy. Between 1870 and 1880 almost three million immigrants entered the country, and this was followed by over five million during the next decade. By 1890, fifteen per cent of the population of America was non-native and the culture shock of trying to assimilate so many new customs and traditions threatened new tensions. The eastern seaboard, accustomed to such pressures seemed to cope reasonably well but it was in the mid-western states where trouble was brewing. Many earlier immigrants, primarily Irish, were sufficiently confident now to move out of the overcrowded and increasingly inhospitable immigrant areas and move west to encroach on settled communities that resented and feared them in equal measure.

On 13 March 1887, at Clinton, Iowa, a council was formed of the American Protective Association (APA), a new anti-foreign movement, to give voice to, primarily anti-Catholic, sentiments claiming that Catholic allegiance was primarily to the Vatican and not the United States constitution. Their scaremongering propaganda claimed that the Vatican was trying to gain control of the United States government. Although the movement started slowly, as a result of electoral defeats it gained traction at one time having as many as seventy weekly newspapers and becoming a national organisation, but it was drawn into a propaganda war over membership and greatly over-estimated its actual support. In the elections of 1896, the APA joined with other organisations on a ticket of restricted immigration, a freeze on public money going to sectarian organisations, barring new immigrants from the franchise and suffered a heavy defeat from which it never recovered.

Nativism was again eclipsed but lived to fight another day. The legacy of the Know Nothings survived in various initiatives and policies aimed at each new wave of immigrants. In 1912, the House Committee on Immigration actually debated the issue of whether Italians could be considered 'full-blooded Caucasians' and whether immigrants coming from southern and eastern Europe might be considered 'biologically and culturally less intelligent'. From the end of the nineteenth century to the first third of the twentieth, Asian immigrants were excluded from naturalisation based on their non-white status. After the First World War a new wave of immigration from war-torn Europe hit American shores but it was the time of the Bolshevik Revolution and communism was rapidly replacing Catholicism in American minds as the main threat to their way of life. On 21 December 1919, nicknamed the *Soviet Ark* (or the *Red Ark*) by the press, the *USS Buford* was used by the Department of Justice to deport 249 non-citizens to Russia from the United States because of their alleged political beliefs.[16]

*

The southern states emerged from the American Civil War a devastated land whose wealth was ebbing away and which had no industry on which to build a modern economy. President Abraham Lincoln had devised a plan to rebuild the south and provide assistance to the four million recently freed black slaves, but when Lincoln was assassinated, the plan sank without trace. Born amidst this turmoil, the Invisible Empire, dedicated to the mission of redeeming the South's pre-war traditions, emerged as part of the craze for secret brotherhoods which swept across the United States in the wake of the Civil War.

Many of the leading white families in the south were humiliated by defeat in the Civil War and feared that radical Republicans in the north wanted to destroy the foundation of their culture, wealth, and power. Poor southern whites, whose only consolation was that, at least, they were better off than the slaves, now found themselves right at the bottom of the social pile with equal status alongside the freedmen and felt resentment towards Black people because of it.

Six well-educated, ex-Confederate soldiers from prominent southern families of Scottish-Irish descent, James Crowe, Richard Reed, Calvin Jones, John Lester, Frank McCord, and John Kennedy started the Ku Klux Klan (KKK) just before Christmas of 1865 in Pulaski, Tennessee. Initially it arose simply so that they might have something to do to alleviate their boredom. The organisation they founded was based on a college fraternity and adopted many of its basic rituals including its name. Ku Klux came from Kuklos Adelphon and they added the Klan for fun and because it harked back to the clans of their forefathers. Members amused themselves by holding secret midnight ceremonies deep in the woods or by parading through the streets of town at night dressed in outlandish disguises. To amuse themselves, they appeared before Black people trying to frighten them by covering themselves with sheets and claiming to be ghosts of the Confederate dead. Word spread across the south and soon copycat groups sprang up all under a loose affiliation to the Pulaski six who now realised that their movement had the potential to become more than just an amusing game for them.

The widespread deprivation experienced by both Black and non-Black people in the post-Civil War chaos had given rise to widespread lawlessness as small bands of White criminals looted plantations. Unskilled, uneducated former slaves were driven by dire poverty to take up petty thievery in order to survive. In response, vigilante groups were organised to hunt down and punish the lawbreakers and this conflict was given further impetus by the growing fear that emancipated slaves would wreak vengeance on their erstwhile masters. These vigilantes would soon become the shock troops of the Klan but before that would happen, the movement had to become politicised.

As the movement transitioned from being a bunch of pranksters and petty criminals to a political organisation it adopted a military flavour. After consultation with politicians at the State Conservative Convention in Nashville, one of the original Klan members, Frank O. McCord, made plans to transform the Klan into a political movement. It would be organized along military lines with a rigid command structure. A Grand Cyclops would lead a local den, or chapter. Above him was a Grand Giant in charge of all dens in a county, then came the Grand Titan and highest in the state was the Grand Dragon. It introduced elaborate oaths of secrecy threatening dire punishment for those who spread details of the order. Its doctrine was built around stopping the national reconstruction process imposed by the north and restoring power to the southern states.

Klan anger was stirred to fury when the government passed the 1866 Civil Rights Act and adopted the 14th Amendment, which decreed that no state should 'deprive any person of life, liberty, or property, without due process of law' and extended full citizenship rights and legal protections to ex-slaves. After President Lincoln's assassination, an unofficial caste system had been introduced that segregated former slaves, effectively re-establishing White supremacy enforced with extreme violence in states such as Mississippi, Florida and South

Carolina. Lincoln's successor Andrew Johnson vetoed the Civil Rights Act on the grounds that the federal government had no jurisdiction to intervene to prevent racial violence but Republicans forced it through. Black people who made up more than a third of the population in the south acquired new freedoms and rights but they were intimidated and quickly disenfranchised through poll taxes and application of literacy tests. White supremacy was reinforced by harassment of Black people with violence and murder and the introduction of oppressive laws all of which was justified by projecting the emancipation of the slaves as the root cause of lawlessness.

The Klan at this time was really just a loose association of autonomous local Klan organisations set up to express 'the discontent, fears and prejudices of the unlettered middle class,' and just one of many others such as the Knights of the White Camelia in Louisiana.[17] This short-lived, overtly racist outfit had been founded by Confederate Colonel Alcibiades DeBlanc in 1867 and quickly gained a fearsome reputation for a reign of terror against the Black population resulting in over 1,000 murders. The Klan was similarly to achieve notoriety with the level of violence that they were prepared to employ to achieve their political purpose. That purpose was not to curb Black lawbreaking which was not a significant issue but to thwart attempts by northern Republicans to mobilise the Black vote in the southern states where the power brokers were mainly Democrats but they had to do it in a way that did not antagonise northern politicians whom they relied upon to finance reconstruction of the southern states and what better way than to cloak their movement in secrecy. Southern politicians chose the Klan as the best means of retaining their political power. Most of the vigilante groups were easily persuaded to hitch their star to the Klan wagon when it became clear that its code of secrecy and practice of disguise would allow them to carry on their reign of terror with impunity.

Membership of the Klan ranged from bankers to lawyers to soldiers to farm labourers. The Klan's main targets were Black people who had joined up with the Republican Union Leagues. There are no official records of Klan activities but it has been estimated by the Illinois Legislative Investigation Committee in 1976 that at least a 1,000 murders were committed by Klan members but aside from that they meted out punishments such as beatings and whippings. Klan membership rose and violence increased. Agents infiltrated into the Klan to gather evidence of wrongdoing were often discovered and murdered and where some were brought to trial, juries invariably acquitted them. Appalled by the level of barbarity and affronted that the American south was becoming tarnished by a growing reputation for racial hatred and abomination, the KKK Grand Wizard, ex Confederate general Nathan Bedford Forrest, moved to have the Klan disbanded in 1869 but Klan-inspired activity continued.

One of the worst atrocities in which the Klan was involved was on Easter Sunday 1873 in Colfax, Louisiana when a mob of Klansmen and Confederate soldiers stormed the Grant Parish courthouse. Following a hotly-contested Louisiana governor's election, southern White Democrats had refused to accept results that put Reconstruction-era Republicans in office. The Democratic leaders called for armed supporters to help them take control of the Colfax Parish Courthouse from legitimate officeholders. The Republicans responded by calling up, mostly Black, supporters to defend the place. On 2 April fighting erupted between the two groups. Then on 13 April more than 300 armed White men, including members of the Knights of White Camellia and the Ku Klux Klan, attacked the courthouse with a cannon. Defenders ran out and the attackers shot them as they fled taking others prisoner but soon they started shooting the prisoners and the indiscriminate killing spread to Black people who had not even been anywhere near the courthouse and the massacre continued into the night. Estimates put the number of defenders killed at around a hundred, half of which were executed after they had surrendered with three White attackers dead also. Some 97 White militia men were arrested and charged with violation of the Ku Klux Klan Act. A small number were convicted but soon released after the US Supreme Court in *United States v. Cruikshank* ruled that the Enforcement Act was unconstitutional. No one was ever arrested by the state of Louisiana.

Meanwhile the government had passed the 15th Amendment giving Black men the right to vote and introduced the Force Bills making it a federal crime to intimidate voters. This was followed by a Congressional investigation into Klan activities. The final nail in the KKK's coffin was the Enforcement Act of 1871, also known as the Ku Klux Klan Act which empowered the president to suspend *habeus corpus*. His motivation was to curb racial violence in the south by giving authority to federal troops rather than state militias and having perpetrators of racial violence tried in federal courts.

By 1877, President Rutherford B. Hayes had withdrawn the last of the occupation armies from the south and local government there was once again in the hands of native-born White southerners that enforced segregation and tacitly condoned intimidation of the Black communities. Southern and border states began restricting the liberties of Black people. A series of 'Jim Crow' laws were passed mandating racial segregation in all public facilities in the states of the former Confederacy. Jim Crow institutionalised economic, educational, political and social disadvantages and second-class citizenship for most Black people living in the United States. The Jim Crow system was underpinned by the belief that White people were superior to Black people in all important ways, including but not limited to intelligence, morality, and civilised behaviour. If necessary, violence must be used to keep Black people at the bottom of the racial hierarchy. Jim Crow etiquette operated in conjunction with Jim Crow laws and demanded that

- A Black male could not offer to shake hands with a White male because it implied being socially equal.
- If Black and White people ate in the same room, White people were to be served first, and some sort of partition was to be placed between them.
- Black people were not allowed to show public affection toward one another in public, especially kissing, because it offended White people.
- Black people were called by their first names. Black people had to use courtesy titles when referring to White people, and were not allowed to call them by their first names.
- If a Black person rode in a car driven by a White person, the Black person sat in the back seat, or the back of a truck.
- White motorists had the right-of-way at all intersections.

In conversation with White people, a Black person must

- Never assert or even intimate that a White person is lying.
- Never impute dishonourable intentions to a White person.
- Never suggest that any White person is from an inferior class.
- Never lay claim to, or overly demonstrate, superior knowledge or intelligence.
- Never curse a White person.
- Never laugh derisively at a White person.
- Never comment upon the appearance of a White female.

Much of the *raison d'être* for vigilante action was fading away but it was opposition from southern communities as a whole, sickened by Klan violence, that brought it to heel and eventually defeated it. Even Klan members slipped away and no longer took part in ceremonies or atrocities. Lack of control from the top had allowed some individual cells, run by ruthless and megalomaniacal local leaders to mete out extreme violence and operate in ways far beyond what most members were willing to tolerate.

The extent to which the KKK was part of a broader fascist movement is open to debate. Richard Steigmann-Gall certainly believes that it was 'recognisably, almost idiomatically American'. Peter Amann saw the Klan's strategy of infiltrating like-minded people into high office rather than imposing them through revolution as decidedly 'un-fascist' but Robert Paxton calls the KKK the world's first fascist movement. 105 Paxton argues that the Klan's penchant for extreme violence, fondness for uniforms and stated ambition to defend 'legitimate interests' against the oppression of a failed state are attributes associated with fascism.

Within a couple of years of the Enforcement Act the Klan had all but disappeared but, having started out as a masked terrorist group devoted to maintaining White supremacy and ensuring cheap sharecropper labour, the Klan had a second manifestation which attracted three to six million members in the 1920s in the northern states with Altoona, Pennsylvania having the largest proportion of Klan members per head of population. It drew inspiration from D. W. Griffith's overtly racist film *The Birth of a Nation* which depicted the southern states as having been victimised by northern politicians and the southern White man as being forced, almost, to submit to race-mixing. The overall message was the southern Whites must be protected from oppression by the emancipated Blacks.

This rejuvenated movement drew its inspiration, in part, from Mussolini's Italy. Klansman Charles Jefferson urged the Klan to follow Italy's example to address the 'vast volumes of discontent' in America while the Klan newspaper *Imperial Night-Hawk* called Italian fascism a 'rainbow of promise' and a 'voice in the wilderness' of human freedom.[18] Similarities between Italian fascism and the KKK were that both used a combination of mass politics, violence and intimidation to whip up nationalist fury and bridge class divides. Both were extremely anti-communist, but also blamed big business for the impoverishment of family-run small businesses.

The spiritual father, founder, and first Imperial Wizard of this second Klan movement was the 'misdirected and impractical dreamer' William J. Simmons.[19] Born an Alabama farm boy, he had marched off to war with the First Alabama Volunteer Infantry and having survived it became a travelling preacher of gospel. During a three-month confined to bed after a motoring accident in 1911, Simmons experienced what he said had been a mystical vision in which he had seen 'a row of white-robed figures on horseback racing across the sky'.[20] He had been to fill in the details of a plan he had developed in his mind to resurrect the old Klan. It was a mysticism that 'no logic or philosophy could reach' and his vision was little more than a personality cult swamped in melodrama, what Charles O. Jackson called 'vague illusions to personal development within unspecified degrees of fraternal mysticism'.[21]

Simmons inaugurated the movement by climbing a rocky outcrop of Stone Mountain in Alabama with some thirty others on Thanksgiving Day in November 1915. There, alongside a granite altar holding copies of the US Constitution, the Declaration of Independence and the laws of the reborn KKK, they set fire to a kerosene-soaked sixteen-foot high wooden cross while Simmons read out twelve chapters of the Book of Romans. This was a completely new innovation that had never been employed by the original Klan. Following this, Simmons drew up a list of rituals and a constitution which he promptly copyrighted in his own name. Like many other secret organisations of the time, the Klan was organized as a secret society and employed an elaborate ritual, secret signs, symbols and handshakes. Simmons also held all rights to sell Klan regalia.

He had been impressed that, on 17 August 1915, a lynch mob had been allowed to murder a Jew, Leo M. Frank, who had been found guilty, on circumstantial evidence, of raping and murdering Mary Phagan, a thirteen-year-old girl. The trial had been sensationalised by the press and the mob had been incensed when Frank's death sentence had been commuted to life imprisonment. Anger was aimed, at first, against the governor John Slaton who declared martial law. Frank was attacked in prison and stabbed by another inmate in the throat but survived. The mob then broke Frank out of jail, drove him over a hundred miles to Phagan's hometown of Marietta where they lynched him. Amid international condemnation, many Georgians celebrated Frank's execution. None of the perpetrators were brought to trial and locals were sufficiently impressed to form the 'Knights of Mary Phegan' as a reincarnation of the KKK and it was on this murderous foundation that Simmons built his new movement. Frank was later pardoned in 1986 when new evidence pointed to an African American Jim Conley as the guilty party.

Nothing much may have come of Simmons' bizarre revelation had he not met a local magazine editor, Jonathan P. Frost, whose publications were filled with racial diatribes. They found common cause and together built up a following but the relationship was short-lived. Simmons had no ambitions to exploit the movement expecting simply that like-minded people would find their own way to his door. It was clear that the two men had different ambitions for the movement and when it dawned on Simmons, wrapped up in his own mysticism, that Frost dwelt in a world more anchored in reality he went to court and had Frost ousted from the movement.

It was only when a local reporter heard about the existence of the Klan that it was exposed to the glare of publicity. Simmons refused him permission to photograph Klansmen in full regalia so the reporter hired stooges, covered them with sheets hiding their faces and published that photograph of them instead. Notwithstanding Simmons' reticence, membership in 1919 had grown to around 4,000. Klan membership became a core qualification for public office in Southern states. Many influential national figures were Klansmen at some point in their lives, including Senator Robert Byrd and the future US Supreme Court Justice Hugo Black.

Simmons had applied for and was granted a charter on 4 December 1918 in Bowden Georgia that culminated in a new organisation calling itself the Knights of the Ku Klux Klan. Simmons adopted rituals and regalia of the old Klan but took it in a significantly different direction on a crusade against 'degenerative forces' that threatened the 'American way of life'.[22] He was, however, too much of a compulsively secretive mystic and dreamer to give coherent voice to his vision in a way that allowed him to appeal to his putative audience which was conservative 'middle America'. For instance, he made no stand at all on the subject of violence as a means to an end and was often enigmatic or contradictory in his pronouncements. He combined exhortations that had religious appeal such as 'I believe in fraternal orders and fraternal relationships ... so that all men might know something of the great doctrine of the fatherhood of God and brotherhood of man,' with a hard-headed commercialism and a 'hocus-pocus mummery' all of which denied him a stable foundation to create a viable doctrine for the movement.[23]

At this point it was perceived as a major threat to the political system with several Senators and Congressmen reputed to be members. It derived its strength above all from ethnic and religious conflict and its policies were invariably adorned with the rhetoric of pure patriotism. Its local branches (klaverns) often bore patriotic historical names such as American Defender, Pride of America or Old Glory.[24] This second manifestation saw the KKK become a mass organization by expanding its enemies list to include Catholics and Jews claiming that America's destiny was as a White Protestant nation. This second Klan's doctrine initially deviated somewhat from that of its predecessor in that it was mainly nonviolent, was not secret, and pursued a highly successful electoral and legislative strategy. It advocated the rights of 'native' labour over immigrants, a return to tradition, military virtues and paramilitary structure, and assumed all the familiar ritualistic trappings of authoritarian movements. Had it existed in contemporary Europe, historians would unhesitatingly have termed it a fascist group on the model of Italy, Spain or Germany. The Klan newspaper *Imperial Night Hawk* called Mussolini's fight to crush communism and anarchy 'an entirely worthy cause' and the Reverend Charles Jefferson of New York referred to the KKK as 'the Mussolini of America'.

Both in its worldview and its dynamic force, the KKK had much in common with German National Socialism and Italian fascism. As well as mobilising working men and women it had particular attraction for the petite bourgeoisie and also enlisted the active backing or toleration of important members of the establishment giving it a measure of legitimacy. Law enforcement agencies were sympathetic and often turned a blind eye to illegal activities, especially violence. In common with other fascist movements, the KKK exhibited a fondness for ritualised activity and public displays of power. Its very visible public activities were geared toward festivities, pageants, and social gatherings packaging its fascistic ideology as traditional small-town values and wholesome fun.

Whilst there were similarities there were significant differences also. The United States had much lower levels of working-class organization and consciousness and the KKK often projected itself as a friend of organized labour which suffered from deep racial, ethnic, and skill divisions in the American economy.

In particular, it exploited the insecurity of native-born, Protestant, White, skilled workers by demonising Black, foreign-born, and radical workers. Membership often benefitted from industrial disputes where strike-breakers from other ethnic groups left some native-born White workers eager to find scapegoats for their misfortune.

Simmons had been shrewd enough to tie the Klan organisation to himself personally as holder of its charter but he was far too involved with his fraternal mystic vision to run the organisation on a sound financial basis. It may well have disappeared in a cloud of insolvency but for the intervention of two public relations executives on the lookout to make money, Edward Y. Clarke and Mrs. Elizabeth Tyler. In 1920 Simmons signed a contract with Clarke and Tyler whereby their Southern Publicity Association would recruit new members for him and get eight of each ten-dollar initiation fee as reward. Clarke now set about raising the Klan's profile by associating it with issues that concerned much of the population of the country such as bloody race riots that had recently erupted in St Louis, Chicago, Illinois and

Houston. Also on the national agenda was the much-feared spread of communism into the country and the massive immigrations of people, mostly Catholics, fleeing a war-ravaged Europe.

Those who had lobbied to bring in Prohibition had been quick to blame Catholic immigrants for the 'saloon culture' that they claimed was rampant all across the continent but especially in the eastern industrial areas where many immigrants lived and worked. On 16 January 1919, the 18th Amendment was ratified which made the production, transport and sale of intoxicating liquors illegal, although it did not outlaw the actual consumption of alcohol. It was soon clear that the law was flouted by criminal gangs and consumption of alcohol continued which led many to call for tougher measures. When the law enforcement agencies proved to be ineffective, the KKK stepped in to lend its support and condemn the Catholics who many saw as the main consumers of alcohol. The Klan began raiding Catholic immigrants' homes, burning down their businesses and planting evidence to use against them. Harvard History professor Lis McGirr believes that 'Prohibition provided the Klan essentially a kind of new mandate for its anti-Catholic, anti-immigrant, White Protestant nationalist mission [and allowed it to] gain a foothold in local communities in the 1920s by arguing that it would clean up communities, it would get rid of bootleggers and moonshiners.' Many people, especially women who were often the victims of the alcohol abuse, were drawn to support the Klan as a result.

Despite success in boosting membership, it was not until the *New York World* published a series of articles focussing on Klan violence that it came to national attention. There was a brief unproductive Congressional investigation before the politicians found something else to focus on but it had given the Klan invaluable publicity. Unfortunately, the publication also uncovered evidence that Clarke and Tyler had been previously indicted for violation of the Mann Act, a law enacted to curb interstate trafficking of women for immoral purposes. Simmons stood by them, however, but many powerful members were appalled by the accusations. Just before the 1922 national convention, Simmons was persuaded to accept a new role in the organisation. He would be given the title of Imperial Emperor, a high-status but powerless largely ceremonial position, where he could spend his days developing his ideas about ritual and cultish practices. In his place they planned to bring in a dentist from Dallas called Hiram Wesley Evans who had recently been appointed to head the propaganda section. Evans had been born in Alabama and moved to Texas as a child with his family. Within the Klan he had been made an 'exalted cyclops' and showed off his credentials by forcibly removing Alex Johnson, a Black bellhop, from the Adolphus Hotel and wrote 'KKK' on his forehead with acid. Evans would later expound his philosophy in a book *The Klan's Fight for Americanism* in which he wrote,

> There are three ... great racial instincts, vital elements in both the historic and the present attempts to build an America which shall fulfil (sic) the aspirations and justify the heroism of the men who made the nation. These are the instincts of loyalty to the White race, to the traditions of America, and to the spirit of Protestantism, which has been an essential part of Americanism ever since the days of Roanoke and Plymouth Rock. They are condensed into the Klan slogan: 'Native, White, Protestant supremacy.' [The] moral breakdown has been going on for two decades. One by one all our traditional moral standards went by the boards or were so disregarded that they ceased to be binding. The sacredness of our Sabbath, of our homes, of chastity, and finally even of our right to teach our own children in our own schools fundamental facts and truths were torn away from us... The Ku Klux Klan, in short, is an organization which gives expression, direction and purpose to the most vital instincts, hopes, and resentments of the old-stock Americans, provides them with leadership, and is enlisting and preparing them for militant, constructive action toward fulfilling their racial and national destiny.... The Klan literally is once more the embattled American farmer and artisan, coordinated into a disciplined and growing army, and launched upon a definite crusade for Americanism![25]

Evans was forthright in his condemnation of the way the Klan had been run before his arrival. In a clear attack on Clarke and Tyler, he railed against the 'sales agents' who had grown rich on their commissions and recruited members who brought little to the movement and had no connection to the 'great mass of Americans of the old pioneer stock'.[26] He also derided the 'stupid and dangerous oratory' of people like Simmons but at the same time acknowledged the 'fundamental truths' that underlay the movement. He was determined to unleash 'one of the most irresistible forces in human affairs; the fundamental instinct of race pride and loyalty.' Evans also brought to the fore, a concept of racial 'whiteness' that, for the first time, stigmatised southern and east European immigrants as alien to the ideal Nordic stereotype.

Simmons realised his mistake and tried to regain control. He still had significant personal sway with the older members and decided to take his case to court to force Evans to stand aside. He lost but the court ordered the Klan to pay him for the use of the charter and regalia he had copyrighted. The court battle had weakened the Klan and divided its members who had been astonished to see the levels of profits that were being made at their expense.

Simmons tried to set up a rival organisation, the Knights of the Flaming Sword, with a few of his old, disgruntled followers but his ineptitude and 'head in the clouds' approach doomed it to failure from the start. His days as a leader of the Klan were well and truly over and he faded into obscurity while Evans went on to as make the front page of *Time* magazine on 23 June 1924.

This was in spite of the fact that less than a year before that date, Evans had led a gathering of 25,000 Klansmen in Carnegie, Pennsylvania, a city of coal mining and steel mills with a large Catholic community and a city administration run by a Catholics. Over 1,000 new members were to be initiated into the movement in a ceremony on 25 August 1923 involving huge burning crosses and a parade through the Catholic areas of the city. Truckloads of timber were brought in to build the crosses which were wrapped in tarred cloth. As night fell, the crowd donned their hoods and fired up their crosses. Bands started up and fireworks were set off as speeches thundered out of the loudspeakers. It was a clear foretaste of the torchlight parades that were to come in the streets of Germany a decade later. The city authority tried to halt the march but thousands of Klansmen armed with guns and clubs forced their way past them to be met by huge crowds of people blocking the streets with lines of trucks. Taking a detour the marchers came to Glendale Bridge which they also found blocked to them and a standoff ensued before the chief deputy sheriff of Allegheny County, John J. Dillon arrived with a few of his officers. He pleaded with both sides to stand back but to no avail. A Klan official, Sam Rich, stood on top of a car to address the marchers and was immediately pelted with missiles from the other side. This roused the marchers to anger and they forced their way over the bridge. They were met with more bricks and stones but the leading marchers were prepared for violence and bludgeoned their way through the crowds up to West Main Street. Gunshots rang out from both sides. Most were fired into the air to scare but one bullet struck Klansman Thomas Rankin Abbott in the head and he died minutes later. The Klansmen started to retreat but many on both sides were seriously injured, many being treated for gunshot wounds but there were no more fatalities. When more deputies arrived to calm things down, hundreds of weapons were confiscated and when the sun rose the next morning it found 'streets strewn with coal, bricks, railroad ballast, cudgels and other weapons including handguns'.[27] The local *Gazette Times* recorded that 'many men dusty, torn and apparently weary, some with unattended wounds, lacerations and bruises' were seen leaving the city.

Meanwhile the search was on for Abbott's killer. A local undertaker Patrick 'Paddy' McDermott was arrested and charged with murder while six other locals were arraigned for inciting a riot. No Klansmen were brought to trial. The county coroner was swamped with conflicting evidence and was unable to reach any conclusion with the result that McDermott walked free. Evans and his fellow leaders publicly eschewed violence but they well knew that for the participants this was awesome entertainment and a break from the drudgery and monotony of everyday life. They quickly realised the propaganda value of the incident and claimed that by publicising it widely in its national newspaper *The Imperial Night-Hawk* as an attack on the rights of innocent Americans to peaceful assembly it would lead to tens of thousands of new members to the Klan. He offered a $2,500 reward for eyewitnesses to the shooting. Abbott's funeral was attended by hundreds of hooded Klansmen who lamented the death of a 'true martyr to the cause'. A Federal judge in Pennsylvania found that Klansmen 'stirred up racial and religious prejudices, fomented disorder and encouraged riots and unlawful assemblies which have resulted in flagrant breaches of the peace, defiance of the law, bloodshed and loss of life.'[28] Abbott's widow persuaded law officers to reopen the case against McDermott and despite no new evidence being offered, he was re-arrested and imprisoned. He would wait for two years in jail until coming to trial when, after hearing much contradictory evidence took forty-seven minutes to acquit him.

Making the most of the publicity, Evans planned another march in the Catholic town Scottdale a week after the Carnegie riot in which another 1,000 new members would be sworn in and another burning cross parade would take place. He was greatly surprised when only a few thousand Klansmen turned up for the parade, none of whom were in KKK hoods. In the event, the march went off peacefully, more like a festival with much food and refreshment taken although it was a time of Prohibition and the drink was, for the most part, non-alcoholic which may have helped to keep the peace. When KKK leaders returned to their vehicles, however, they were shot at by town residents who were met with a hail of bullets in reply. The Armed Klansmen took this as a signal to return to the town and this time intent on mayhem but there were enough state police officers on hand to block their entry. Few Klansmen were willing to confront the police without their hooded disguise.

The Klan's popularity peaked in 1923 and 1924, but the social conditions that once fuelled its growth were fading. Post-war recession was giving way to renewed economic growth although southern states benefitted much less than their northern neighbours. Employers all across the economic landscape were seeing a decline in union membership amongst their work force and left-wing organisations failed to find resonance. The drive for racial equality also foundered as white supremacy kept its iron grip as attested by the failure of the federal government to bring in anti-lynching legislation. As the threats that underpinned white insecurity faded so membership of the KKK dwindled. It still had power and appeal, however. On 8 August 1925, more than 50,000 of its members paraded down Pennsylvania Avenue in Washington, DC carrying American flags. National leaders of the organization wore colourful satin robes and the rank and file wore white, their regalia adorned with a circular red patch containing a cross with a drop of blood at its centre but the movement was all but bankrupt.

The great parade could not disguise the fact that the fortunes of the Klan were now in decline. Exactly why this was so has been a much-debated issue and most historians have seen it as a reaction to its reputation for violence but counter to this is Evans' assertion that the Carnegie violence brought in thousands of new members. It can certainly be argued that it was the excitement associated with violence committed behind the protection of masks that motivated many to join in the mid-1920s. This was substantiated when a bloody confrontation between Klansmen and miners in Lilly, which left three residents dead from gunshot wounds, swelled KKK membership in the region by 100 per cent. Nobody was arrested for the killings and elsewhere in western Pennsylvania, KKK floggings, kidnappings and street violence went unpunished. Things changed somewhat when anti-mask laws were enforced. These had been introduced in New York in 1845 making it illegal to appear in public disguised and armed. This meant that Klansmen could no longer parade and riot without being identified by the law enforcement agencies.

There may well have been much more of a negative effect on membership, also, after David C. Stephenson, the Grand Wizard of Indiana and twenty-two other states, had, only two days before McDermott's trial for murdering Abbott, gone on trial on a similar charge in Noblesville, Indiana. He was found guilty of the kidnapping, rape and second-degree murder of Madge Oberholtzer, whose dead body bore so many bite marks she was described by a witness as looking as if she had been chewed by a cannibal. Sentenced to life imprisonment, Stephenson exposed several leading public figures as being members of the Klan. More damning publicity followed when Evans banished Rich for financial mismanagement and soon afterwards his replacement, W. L. Robinson, was kicked out also for 'defiling [his] office by [having] immoral relations with his stenographer'.[29] Public scandals such as these drove away many who had been recruited by Clarke and Tyler whose always tenuous accord with the KKK's root philosophy was overcome by the embarrassment of association with the discredited movement.

The Klan had always been hampered by the lack of a really dynamic leader and had lacked any sophisticated political strategy both of which were vital if it was to have any longevity as a political force. The result was that even apologists tended to veer away from associating the symbol of Southern chivalry and gentility that had become associated with 'violent, ill-educated second-hand Ford owners'.[30]

*

All fascist movements up until the 1930s had been political and social movements organised along party lines working through legitimate political channels and depending primarily upon the middle classes for support. All had singled out specific groups as scapegoats for the nation's ills and appealed to race prejudice with a message often couched in psychopathic mumbo-jumbo. They had, however, all suffered from a lack of dynamic leadership and the fact that they had been reactive movements to short-lived crises. They had sometimes shown themselves to be, moreover, little more than 'typical American financial rackets' whose primary motive was profit from the sale of uniforms and supplies.[31]

Publications such as the *Awakener* and the *American Quarterly* appeared during the early 1930s to promulgate a doctrine that rejected democratic norms in favour of rule by a 'cultivated few over the many who are assumed to be permanently unable to think and act for themselves'.[32] Such a view was a clear attempt to defend the existing class system against change. State power was to be taken under the control of dominant capitalist forces to preserve the economic order which was the exact opposite of what had happened in Russia during the 1917 revolution where state power had been usurped to decimate it. This 'highbrow, dress-shirt type of fascism' was doomed, however, because any movement based on such a blatant philosophy was going to lack a popular base. On its rise to power, any fascist movement must disguise its ultimate goal behind promises of power and plenty and a general improvement in the prospects of its putative supporters.

Nevertheless, as an indication of the lengths to which an elite would be prepared to go to achieve to take unconstitutional action to realise its ambitions in this direction, the case of Smedley Darlington Butler is instructive. Butler, a highly decorated ex-marine, known to his men as 'old gimlet eye', had been approached by a group of wealthy industrialists in 1934. These backers planned to instal him as a dictator after launching a military coup. While those implicated, such as J. P. Morgan, ridiculed the 'Business plot', a Congressional Committee reported that although 'no evidence was presented... to show a connection... with any fascist activity of any European country... [t]here was no question that these attempts were discussed, were planned, and might have been placed in execution.'[33]

Chapter 2

FRIENDS OF THE NEW GERMANY

> Americans of my age and generation had been accustomed to see the best intellectuals in our country go to Germany for education...thousands of houses had German girls for governesses for their children...tens of thousands of families had German relatives...the bonds between the two lands were so deep we could not regard what happened in Germany with indifference.
> Hugh Wilson, US Ambassador to Germany 1938[1]

The first wave of German immigration began just after the end of the Napoleonic wars when harvest failures in Europe led to widespread hardship threatening a collapse of the social order. Later creeping industrialisation threatened the livelihoods of the many small farmers and artisans, mostly from the Rhine valley, who had long been the backbone of the German economy. When they arrived in the US these people settled mostly in small rural locations where communities had linguistic affinities and where cultural heritage was treasured. Although numbers were small at first, a pattern was established, and migratory bridgeheads were created to which others would follow. In this way it may be argued that such migrants were not relocating to embrace the new but were doing so in order to preserve the old. During the latter half of the nineteenth century, it had been agricultural labourers and factory workers and their families who made up the bulk of emigrants. These tended to settle in urban areas like Chicago, New York and Philadelphia where the bulk of employment opportunities lay.

There was another much smaller group who emigrated around 1848 and who would go on to play a disproportionately large part in creating the image of the German American. These were from the educated middle classes and integrated into American society on a level that gave them greater impact on and influence within the American establishment. They were not slow to criticise their new hosts. American society they said, 'measures the value of a human being only on the basis of income' and admitted they would 'feel more comfortable here if there were more paintings, better drama, and less religion'. They would also bring with them a sort of elitist Germanness that grated with the previous immigrants who had gone to America to get away from all that. Another important issue around the 'forty-eighters' was their growing pride in the growth of German industrial power in their native land and its burgeoning importance in European politics after Bismarck's unification of Germany into a nation state in 1871.

As early as 1883, the first US festivals were held to celebrate German Day and three years later the first German American Historical Society, GAHS, was formed in Baltimore. Just after the turn of the century, the National German-American Alliance (*Deutsch-Amerikanischer Nationalbund*, NGAA) was formed which brought together hundreds of small German immigrant groups with a stated ambition to protect its members from 'nativist' attacks and to promote good relations between the US and Germany. Run largely by the educated middle classes, the NGAA organized cultural events and financed a variety of historical publications outlining the achievements of German immigrants. It is unfortunate that the somewhat elitist NGAA leadership showed disdain for low culture and failed completely to engage with the German working class leaving them largely alienated from NGAA programmes. This inevitably accelerated their integration into American culture.

*

When the First World War broke out, propaganda stories in the English press about German atrocities in Belgium and the sinking of the passenger ship *Lusitania* in which 197 Americans died, made life very uncomfortable for German Americans who became subdued and disinclined to parade their ancestry. Then when the US entered the war in 1917 German ethnic nationalism came under severe pressure to remove itself from public scrutiny. Many took on American citizenship to show their loyalty to their new country and abandoned any habit they may have had to converse in their native tongue. Vigilante groups were quick to pounce on any who showed disloyalty by questioning the American war effort. Readership of German American newspapers declined sharply. The teaching of German was eradicated from the school curriculum and in Iowa, it became punishable to speak German in public. Facing accusations of disloyalty to the US government, the NGAA was disbanded in 1918.

German Americans had first been targeted during the First World War by German intelligence services as a means of furthering political goals, but these efforts largely foundered in the face of concerted US government anti-German policies. With the signing of the Treaty of Versailles after which Germany lost substantial territory and population, attention in Berlin turned towards restoring German national pride and standing by reaching out to Germans beyond the Reich's borders to awaken their ethnic consciousness (*Deutschtum*) and add their political weight to German efforts to reverse the depravations of Versailles. It would be a long hard struggle to restore German Americans to what had previously been a respected place in American society. The feelings of many were encapsulated in the words of Paul Schultze who had lived and worked in Philadelphia since 1892 when he lamented that the German immigrant was now looked on as a mere cipher who was called a troublemaker when standing up for his rights. Another German immigrant, Käte Küchler, had arrived much later in New York but she, also, felt like 'only a foreigner and a German one at that.'[2]

It was not uncommon for Germans who had perhaps not fared as well as others in the New World to decry what they perceived as abandonment by the Reich and it was not unreasonable to think that it was the most ardent Nazi-sympathisers who had resisted Americanisation who made up the majority of them. It was amongst this section where appeals to Germanness would be most likely to bear fruit. Others, who would also be inclined to look over their shoulders to their ancestral homeland, felt what would later be moulded into the sentiment *Amerika verpflichtet, Deutschland verbunden* (obligated to America, tied to Germany).

It was really only after the crushing ignominy of the Treaty of Versailles that Germany developed a concern for 9,000,000 members of German minorities in those regions that had been stripped from them. Even during the Weimar years, there had been a concerted effort to encourage these communities to continue to regard themselves as Germans rather than adopt the nationality and customs of their new countries. Germans who lived in the US, however, were somewhat different in that they had arrived there voluntarily, and many had eagerly assimilated into the cultural 'melting pot'. There would be approximately 1,600,000 German-born Americans in the

US by 1930 who had joined many millions more American-born of German descent.[3]

Weimar looked to 'cultural diplomacy' (*Auswärtige Kulturpolitik*) to combat the decline of German power and elevated it by systematic state-funding to become an important feature of German foreign policy. It wasn't much to compensate for the loss of its traditional assets such as a strong economy, a large army and reliable allies but it was a start. The estimated 25,000,000 ethnic Germans who lived outside the Reich (*Auslanddeutsche*) were envisaged by the German Foreign Minister, Gustav Stresemann, as being required to 'shape the politics of the foreign state [in which they reside] in a way that is beneficial to the German Empire [and] serve as mediators for the proliferation and understanding of German culture and German world view amongst the people of their state'.[4]

Approximately 430,000 German immigrants arrived in the United States between 1919 and 1933 to join the more than five million who had come before them and it was within this section of American society that the German intelligence agencies hoped to extend their influence. Few of those recruited from these ranks had any political experience or understanding of whatever role they might be called upon to play but there were more than a few who were motivated to give it a try. The sheer number of German migrants was enough to convince the Germans that they could recruit sufficient numbers of competent activists from within them to avoid having to train and infiltrate professional agents from Germany. Enthusiasm was no substitute for competence, however, and relations between the German intelligence agencies and organisations of German Americans would be far from smooth.

At first it was ardent Nazi supporters in the US who, without any organised plan, began recruiting agents in a somewhat haphazard fashion without due regard for the fact that many immigrants were developing an affinity for their new home. While most had escaped Germany because of its dire economic plight to find work in the US a large percentage of the young especially saw it as a temporary relocation and retained an ambition to return to Germany when work prospects there improved. They would generally live in German-speaking communities and find employment among other German immigrants making little or no effort to integrate into American society. It was this group that retained strong emotional bonds to the *Volksgemeinschaft* (German worldwide community). It was they who saw themselves as the front-line fighters for the Nazi cause and were the ones most likely to respond to overtures for cooperation with the Nazis but, because of their resistance to integration they were ill-equipped to be of much use.[5] Many had, however, made a great effort to assimilate into US society and it was a fatal error of judgement by the German intelligence agencies that they did not fully appreciate the way that American culture encouraged and accelerated that process. Neither did they understand until it was too late that the fanatical minority of activists separated by 3,000 miles of ocean would be hard to control.

The example of Georg Durrschmidt encapsulates what must have been the experience of many. He had been a First World War veteran and arrived in the US with his wife and two children in the early 1920s, finding accommodation in the Queens district of New York and employment at Bell Laboratories. Despite the fact that he had become naturalised and was integrating successfully into American society where there were so many German churches, clubs, and amusement facilities, he still had strong emotional links to his home village of Zwickau in Bavaria and missed the intimacy of a closely-knit community.

In 1926, another one of these post-war immigrants, Edmund Fürholzer, who had been involved with an extreme right-wing organisation in Bavaria, the *Reichslandbund,* turned up penniless in the Yorkville district of New York often called Germantown. This was a predominantly German-speaking section of Manhattan where Fürholzer met kinsmen who, like him, had been enraged by what they saw as the unwarranted and pernicious terms of the Treaty of Versailles that had stripped Germany of much of its eastern provinces and imposed crushing financial war reparations. Whilst not overtly political, they reserved a significant measure of venom for the German politicians, whom they believed to have betrayed the armed forces by agreeing to an armistice in 1918.

Together with his new friends, Fürholzer started up a German language newspaper *Deutsche Zeitung* through which they could give vent to their anger and frustration. It had competition, however, from the very popular and well established *Illustrierte Zeitung* and struggled to survive as a going concern until 'Colonel' Edwin Emerson stepped in to support it financially at which point it was emboldened to call itself 'A Fighting Paper for Truth and Right – A Bridge between the United States and Germany.'

Born in Dresden in 1869, Emerson had arrived in America with his family as a child and went on to graduate from Harvard in 1891 with a BA degree. Reputedly one of Theodore Roosevelt's Rough Riders during the Spanish-American War, he went on to report on the Russo-

Japanese War of 1904–05 when he was captured by the Japanese. Later he worked as a journalist on the *Boston Post* and the *New York Evening Post*. During the First World War, he covered the Balkans for the *Washington Post* where he was captured by the Turks and handed over to the Germans. Whilst in captivity, he had been impressed by propaganda denying Germany responsibility for starting the war and, under German supervision, began an English language newspaper that was distributed to English PoWs showering them with more pro-German propaganda. It is said that he was personally acquainted with Field Marshal von Hindenburg. When this 'soldier of fortune, mediocre author and fairly competent war correspondent' returned to the US he became a vocal critic of the terms the Germans had been forced to accept at Versailles and lived at 215 East 15th Street with an office at Room 1923 at 17 Battery Place which was the address of the German Consulate General.[6] He wrote a number of books including *The Adventures of Theodore Roosevelt*. Under his patronage, the *Zeitung* published articles condemning the 'criminals' who had led Germany to defeat in the war and other articles railing against the menace of communism. Free copies were distributed to German American organisations but got a mixed reception from them. There is speculation, but no proof, that the newspaper was given a measure of financial support by the German Consulate.

The *Zeitung* carried two separate and distinct types of articles. On the one hand it promoted positive propaganda about the new Germany and on the other it warned of a backlash of 'nativism' that would target immigrants as 'agents of a foreign power' before taking steps to deport them.[7]

Fürholzer now approached the New York State Republican Committee in a bold attempt to inveigle it into an unofficial liaison with the German American community. If they would care to invest $20,000 in the *Zeitung* the paper would undertake a concerted campaign in support of the Republican candidate, Herbert Hoover, in the upcoming presidential election. Given that the election was only weeks away at the time, the committee saw no benefit for them in such a deal and turned Fürholzer down. Despite its continuing precarious finances, the newspaper survived albeit with low circulation long enough for its small band of loyal supporters, many of whom had joined the New York City unit of the overseas National Socialist German Workers' Party (NSDAP) to see the emergence of Nazi power in Germany in January 1933. Fürholzer had even written to Hitler in 1930 suggesting that he be made the American correspondent of the German news service Transocean, which later became the *Deutsches Nachrichtenbüro*.

The post-war immigrants differed from their earlier counterparts primarily in their bitter reaction to defeat in war and Versailles. Many had crossed the Atlantic seeking work or escape from a nation on the brink of economic and political chaos. Many of those who had arrived before 1914 had assimilated into American life and saw themselves as Americans but beneath that still retained a cultural identity that gave them an emotional relationship with Germany. Despite the efforts of the US government to create an American culture binding all the different nationalities, they still harboured a desire to retain links with the land of their ancestors.

For the German Americans this had meant hundreds of clubs and societies (*Vereine*) and in Germany, a range of organisations were created within the Foreign Office (*Auswärtiges Amt*) and, later, by the NSDAP, concerned with the problems, interests, hopes, fears and ambitions of German groups outside the Reich (*Auslanddeutschtum*). These were small and relatively insignificant organisations and a large proportion of them simply ceased to exist when they failed to live up to NSDAP expectations after 1933.

One group that survived and thrived, however, was the German Foreign Institute (*Deutsches Ausland Institut,* DAI), created in Stuttgart in 1917 to counter French and British propaganda aimed at weakening German trade relations. At first it had restricted itself to maintain contact with Swabian Germans living abroad but was later expanded to cover all Germans. The DAI won the approval of Hitler and expanded under the Nazis. It was funded through the Ministry of the Interior and a number of private business donations but, by its very nature, could not avoid being employed as a tool of diplomacy.

It was while Hitler was in jail, only a few months after the Beer Hall Putsch and during one of the lowest points in the NSDAP's history, that the first Nazi organization in the United States emerged. Newer immigrants were drawn to organisations such as the National Socialist Teutonia Association (*Nationalsozialistische Vereinigung Teutonia*), more usually called the Free Society of Teutonia or the Teutonia League. It was founded in the industrial powerhouse of Detroit, with its large German population, on 12 October 1924 by the 'old guard Nazis' Alfred Ex, Frank von Friedersdorff, and the brothers Gissibl, Peter, Andreas and Fritz. Fritz was the driving force despite having only arrived in the US aged twenty, in December 1923. Like several other German immigrants of the time who would go on to play a part in German American societies, he claimed to have fled Germany after marching with Hitler in his abortive Beer Hall Putsch of November that same year. It was a chaotic time in Weimar Germany and the NSDAP was still small and in its embryonic stage so it is reasonable to assume that the US movement was operating very much under its own direction when trying to create a Nazi movement on American soil. Gissibl would make his mark early for being able to raise funds for the Nazi cause in a society that was significantly more affluent than Germany in the mid-1920s. Hitler, himself, wrote on more than one occasion to personally thank Teutonia groups for their financial contributions to NSDAP funds.

The Teutonia League was initially little more than a social club whose meetings often ended in heavy beer drinking sessions and the hearty singing of rousing traditional German songs, but the movement held extremist political views, similar to those of the paramilitary wing of the German Nazi party (*Sturmabteilung*, SA). The Society never had extensive membership but its significance was that, apart from its fund-raising, it nurtured many of what would become the leadership backbone of future German American organisations. In 1926, it changed its name to the National Socialist League of Teutonia at which point all members were urged to join the NSDAP.

Another young, energetic and talented Nazi party member, the nineteen-year-old Walter Kappe had arrived from Germany on the *SS Orduna* in 1925 to become one more important and influential member of the Teutonia League. At the age of seventeen, Kappe had left the University of Gottingen to join the ultra-violent, far-right paramilitary Freikorps, in which he served for some nine months as a member of the illegal 'Black Reichswehr'. He would soon also join the newly formed Nazi Party. Kappe would boast of having taken part in the Hitler Beerhall Putsch but so did many Nazis who emigrated to the US after 1923. June 1925 found Kappe working at a farm implement factory in Kankakee, Illinois but once he found his feet in the new land, he got a job as a journalist on the Chicago *Abendpost* newspaper. Among the other staff he gained a reputation for 'slanting' stories to exaggerate certain features and was generally treated with caution given that he was prone to petulance and arrogance, especially when drunk. Often he would tell people that he was from a family of Prussian 'Junkers' aristocrats which was innocent enough but when he began posting crudely offensive anti-Semitic articles the management had seen enough of him and he was fired. Josef (Sepp) Schuster, who had been born near Dachau in Germany was another who claimed to have taken part in the Beerhall Putsch. Here was someone else who would have a major impact on the fortunes of the National Socialist League of Teutonia after his arrival in 1927, at the age of twenty-three.

The society now published a somewhat crude, illiterate and poorly edited newspaper *Vorposten; News of the German Freedom Movement in the United States* that promised to 'tell the truth about Germany', a country it claimed was now in the hands of Jewish Bolsheviks.[8] Evidence suggests that the society was not so much motivated by a desire to bring National Socialism to America as to enthuse Germans living in America, especially the post-war arrivals, to prepare themselves for a return to the Reich at some future date and join the Nazii Party there. Meanwhile, they raised funds that were sent to Germany to help fund the NSDAP.

*

Kurt G.W. Lüdecke was born into a wealthy family in Berlin in 1890 but the death of his father saw the family fall on hard times. He found the most productive way of providing for the family was by defrauding and swindling, mostly women, as he travelled all across France, England and the United States in the years before the outbreak of the First World War. He avoided conscription due to a minor medical condition and spent the war working in a psychiatric hospital in Heidelberg. At the university there he attended lectures on racial theory given by Professor Alfred von Domaszewski that led him onto the path of anti-Semitism.

After the war he got work as a purchasing agent travelling to South America and Mexico where, by nefarious means, he acquired a passport in the name of Conrado Lüdecke.

Soon he was back in Berlin selling ex-military surplus. It was a lucrative business since the Treaty of Versailles had barred Germany from having a military air force so there was a great deal of material to trade with countries like Sweden which had a large aircraft manufacturing industry. Having made a small fortune in a very short time, Lüdecke invested in art and went to the United States to promote an exhibition of German paintings. This did not go as well as he had expected and so he returned to Berlin where he joined up with the National Socialists after attending a rally and hearing Hitler speak. In 1922, he went to Munich and plotted with the right-wing paramilitary organisation, the *Bund Bayern und Reich,* to overthrow the local government there. In Munich he had become more involved with the NSDAP and gained favour with Hitler who sent him to Italy where he was granted an audience with Mussolini as an 'official representative [of Hitler] in the kingdom of Italy'.

The arrest and imprisonment of Hitler after the abortive Beer Hall Putsch barely slowed Lüdecke's progress and he went again to the

United States in 1924 this time on a fundraising trip for the Nazi party, which he claimed was on the direct orders of Hitler. He had little success in this regard among the disparate German American organisations he contacted in the US but hoped for better results when he met Hiram Evans, Imperial Wizard of the KKK and his acolyte Milton Elrod. The Klan was on an upward trajectory politically at the height of its influence and power and well-endowed with funds. Lüdecke hoped to persuade Evans to part with some of his money to support a like-minded outfit to his in Germany but he was disappointed here also. The fragmented nature of German American societies he encountered seemed to him to have great potential but little organisation. If his fundraising mission was doomed to failure there was no need to assume that his whole trip was. If the five million Germans spread amongst German American communities were better organised, the potential for fundraising within them would be greatly enhanced. This transition, however, would initially require funding in the opposite direction. Political links with the Klan might convince Berlin to support his idea. The Klan itself boasted many congressmen, senators, and judges in its ranks.

Unfortunately for Lüdecke, he was unable to progress his ideas very far when his globetrotting was halted in 1924. On a trip to Germany, he was brought before a Munich court charged with blackmailing one Frau Martha Behn. Found guilty, he spent a few weeks in jail before returning to the US Once there he set off on a round of lectures on the political situation in Germany to promote his ideas but rather than raise funds, he left a trail of debts and unpaid bills wherever he went. At the end of 1924, he went to Chicago to help increase the circulation of the pro-Nazi newspapers, *Der Stürmer* and the *Völkischer Beobachter* just at the time that the Gissibl brothers were forming the Teutonia League. Lüdecke had been only one of a number of people sent directly by the Nazis to the United States to be the party's eyes and ears there. Others such as Sepp Schuster, Paul Themlitz, Hermann Schwinn, Karl Sprecht, and Heinrich (Heinz) Spanknöbel travelled all across the continent at the same time sending back reports on what they found. These men would play a vital role in aiding the expansion of the Teutonic League.

Lüdecke had not been impressed with what he saw in America. The German American groups he came across seemed to him to be uncoordinated and lacking political direction. What they needed above all else was leadership by someone like himself. Despite being somewhat piqued at not having been given a leadership role where he would have the chance to do something about that, he publicly expressed confidence in leaders such as Gissibl and Kappe but agreed with their feeling that they were getting insufficient guidance and support from Germany. As late as 1930, Gissibl was still berating the party back in Germany and asking 'What is the intention of the Reichsleitung in relation to [membership] of the NSDAP?'[9] Lüdecke was also disgruntled over the appointment of Dr. Hans Nieland as head of the NSDAP Foreign Department (*Auslandsabteilung*) a position that he coveted for himself. Lüdecke had failed to find success as a fundraiser but the reasons for that may have been down to his own profligacy and financial incontinence. The US was, in fact, becoming a reliable source of contributions to NSDAP funds through membership fees and Lüdecke was never slow to see opportunities where money was circulating. He watched with envy as Nieland creamed off two thirds of all Teutonia fees to finance his own office and used his position of influence to promote his favourites.

Lüdecke played his part when the Teutonia League established its own newspaper, *Der Vorposten,* spreading its virulently anti-Semitic and pro-Nazi viewpoints throughout America. The paper carried a swastika on the masthead and carried many references to Hitler. Printed in German and selling for ten cents, it was no more than a partial success at best. Lüdecke set up a link with the German editors of the *Völkischer Beobachter*, which, by 1929, would become a well-established partnership between the two newspapers. He was also instrumental in establishing the *Swastika Press* a large publisher that printed numerous anti-Semitic propagandistic works, including the *American Guard*, in order to spread the Nazi ideology throughout the whole of the US Bookshops in Boston and New York were inundated with Lüdecke's pro-Nazi publications along with books, smuggled into the country by German sailors working for the North-German Lloyd-Hamburg American Steamship Company, with titles such as *Handbuch der Judenfrage, Das Programme der N.S.D.A.P.,* and *Reich un Kirche.*

Lüdecke married a twenty-eight-year-old librarian, Mildred Coulter, in Detroit on 13 June 1927. In the few years following, he travelled freely between Germany and the United States until he was arrested by the Gestapo in July 1933 on charges relating to yet more blackmail. He spent a year in Oranienburg concentration camp without coming to trial before persuading his captors to allow him to go under guard to Berlin to plead his case before Alfred Rosenberg. He had no difficulty in evading his guards during an overnight stop in the city and fled to Switzerland.

Before long, Lüdecke was in Paris and, according to the German Embassy there, was planning a trip to the US on a Czech passport. When he did arrive there in September 1934, he found himself hauled up to give evidence before the Special House Congressional Subcommittee on un-American Activities Authorized to Investigate Nazi Propaganda and Certain Other Propaganda Activities, usually referred to as the McCormack-Dickstein Committee. This annoyed new Nazi Minister for Propaganda, Joseph Goebbels, who was anxious to avoid bad publicity especially given that he was plagued by persistent rumours that his wife Magda had been in a relationship with Lüdecke at some point in the past.

Unable now to return to Germany, Lüdecke set out to make a name for himself as a writer and published a book *I Knew Hitler* in 1937. This brought him a modicum of fame which encouraged him to apply for American citizenship. A judge saw things differently, however, calling him 'a cheap politician and a hanger-on and would have stayed in Germany if the Nazis had offered [him] a job'.[10] Then when Germany withdrew his German citizenship, he found himself a 'foreign-born resident' in America. The day after the Japanese attack on Pearl Harbor, Lüdecke was arrested and interred on Ellis Island where he remained throughout the war. He was deported back to his home country in 1948 where he died in 1960.

*

By the end of 1932, American and German anti-Semitic connections were well-established but despite gaining plaudits from Goebbels for their contributions, the Teutonia League ran up against significant opposition and seems to have ceased to exist at some time during March 1933. Lüdecke had tried to tempt the rudderless membership into a new party, which he called The Swastika League, under his leadership but Gissibl made his own pre-emptive move by creating the Friends of the Hitler Movement and tried to have it designated as the official Nazi organ in the United States. NSDAP members outside Gissibl's organisation, especially those in New York, were having none of it, however, and were successful in having their cell chosen to represent the Nazi party in the United States under the title *Nationalsozialistische Deutsche Arbaiterpartei Orstgruppe New York* also called *Gauleitung-USA* or Gau-USA. Gissibl was furious to see America's Nazi power base relocate to New York, but he was powerless to oppose the move. The city was already home to the American branch of First World War Veterans, the Stahlhelm and the United German Societies of Greater New York (UGS). However, he bided his time and six months later sent his acolyte, the violent, foul-mouthed and impetuous, Heinz Spanknöbel to investigate rumours of internecine strife within Gau-USA which proved to be true but before Gissibl could exploit it for his own benefit, the disintegration of Gau-USA was averted by the appointment of a new leader, Paul Manger. The recovery was short-lived, however, as the Great Depression bit deep into Gau-USA fund-raising creating another crisis. Gissibl saw his chance by rescuing the movement from financial meltdown. He transferred his allegiance to Gau-USA and advised his followers to do likewise and was rewarded with joint leadership of the movement along with Spanknöbel, who proved to be an even more ruthless and wilier operator than Gissibl.

Spanknöbel was born in Hamburg, Germany, and had been ordained as a minister in the Seventh Day Adventist Church in Wurtzenburg in 1920. Little is known about his arrival in America but US immigration record D.L. 55830/8 shows that his sister Martha arrived on the *SS Columbus* on 7 Dec 1925, to join her brother, Karl, at 5192 St. Clair Street, Detroit. At that time, she was single, aged 22 and had two brothers and two sisters in the US Unfortunately, she was not well and suffered a mental breakdown being admitted to the Detroit Receiving Hospital on 5 April 5 1926. On 14 August the same year, she was deported back to Germany on the *SS Lützow* on the ground of dementia praecox. Spanknöbel presumably was one of the brothers that was living in the US before Martha's arrival. He is known to have worked briefly at the Ford Motor Company in Detroit in 1929 and had worked for the Herbert Hoover campaign in the 1932 presidential election but his irascible nature ensured that he was not particularly popular with his fellow German Americans.

When Franklin D. Roosevelt won, his administration became extremely concerned about the effect of Hitler's government on American-German trade and security of the vast American investment in Germany but within the United States population as a whole there was little anti-German sentiment except within the Jewish community. In response, Goebbels and German Finance Minister Hjalmar Schacht launched a massive public relations initiative through the Carl Byoir and Associates public relations firm in Manhattan. Those roped in to boost the Nazis image were Colonel Emerson, the poet George Sylvester (Swastika) Viereck, the industrialists Willi von Meister and Adolf Scheurer and the propagandist Frederick Franklin Schrader. They began by publishing, through MacMillan, a book entitled *Germany Speaks* which dealt with the Nazi attitude to Jews.

Emerson soon became frustrated at having to work with others, especially Manger, whom he thought useless, and branched out by forming the Friends of Germany funded by the German Nazi Party. His aggressive uncompromising character was evident by the way this new grouping held large mass meetings, policed by local paramilitary thugs where bitter attacks were made against Jews and Catholics The meetings were well attended by visiting officers and sailors from German ships docked in New York, but the sentiments volubly expressed saw a wave of resentment against German Americans sweep across the city.

Aping the internecine rivalries that riddled the German Nazi Party, rivals sprang up to challenge Manger with party squabbles making the local newspapers on a daily basis. In Germany, Hitler was concerned at the bad publicity that was nullifying all public relations exercises and tried to calm things down by appointing Ernst Wilhelm Bohle as leader of the *Abteilung für Deutsche im Ausland*, the Nazi organisation for Germans abroad which was to have a significant part to play in future events. For his part, Goebbels recalled Emerson for a dressing down and a crash course in the subtler forms of propaganda.

*

The election of Hitler to the German chancellorship in January had obviously done little to promote harmony between competing Nazi supporters in the United States with several splinter groups breaking away from Gau-USA to promote their own brand of fascism. In this Spanknöbel saw his opportunity and made his bid for power. He had returned to Germany on the *SS Europa* on 26 April 1933 but returned on 2 July on the same vessel. While in Germany he had a meeting with Rudolf Hess, Hitler's second-in-command at the NSDAP whom he impressed with much exaggerated Gau-USA membership figures for which he naturally took the credit. Spanknöbel's account of the meeting is at odds with the version later put out by Hess. He claimed that Hess gave him personal written authorisation to go back to the US and create a new, more structured German American organisation that would better promote the NSDAP agenda.

Spanknöbel returned to the US with a swagger claiming friendships at the highest level in Berlin where he had been given full authority from Hess to knock the US movement into shape although in support of this he could only offer verbal assurances and a letter signed by someone called Schmeer.[11] He secretly plotted against Manger with Kappe and Schuster to bring Gau-USA and Emerson's Friends of Germany together. There is some evidence from newspaper reports that this had taken place as early as April but there was no official recognition of a new organisation until, at a convention in Chicago on 28 July 1933, Spanknöbel announced the first official Nazi movement in the United States, the Friends of the New Germany (*Bund der Freunde des Neuen Deutschland*, FONG) with himself as the first American führer although he eschewed that title in deference to Hitler and simply called himself the *Bundesleiter* with Gissibl as his deputy. Swastikas were proudly displayed, and the Horst Wessel song provided the soundtrack. Kappe was appointed Press and Propaganda chief of the movement.

It did not go unnoticed by other groups that Spanknöbel was inclined to stamp his authority with extreme violence. One employee of the Hapag-Lloyd Shipping Lines, Frederick Mensing, who had dealings with Spanknöbel at this time recalled that he 'had a rather dominating personality, and it did not seem very wise to argue with him'.[12] Mensing would also tell the McCormack-Dickstein inquiry that he was instructed to tell all company employees in the US that they had to join FONG or they would forfeit their German citizenship. At the same time, the head of the NSDAP in the US, Gestäftsführer Hans Strewst told its members that Hitler had ordered the dissolution of the Nazi Party in America and advised all members to sign up with FONG. Branches of the Friends were also set up at this time across the border in Canada in Toronto, Montreal, Winnipeg and Vancouver.

Many American Nazis fell into line and signed up to the new movement, but some refused and threatened to cause trouble. Spanknöbel's response showed that during his short trip to Germany he had learned a thing or two about enforcing party discipline. He created a fighting force under the command of Sepp Schuster based on the SS storm troopers calling it the *Ordnungsdienst* (OD). It was enough to persuade dissidents to join up or go away and stop being a nuisance.

One of the features of FONG were anti-Semitic rallies staged in areas close to where Jewish communities lived often resulting in violent street clashes. Jews were left in no doubt that, given the opportunity, FONG would develop tactics similar to those being employed by the Nazis against Jewish communities in Germany but not everyone took it that seriously. Law enforcement agencies and even wealthy well-established Jewish business houses, not entirely unused to such events, looked on the violence as an arbitrary and transient reaction to what was happening in Germany and hoped it would soon pass. Attention was focussed more on events in Germany with organisations such as the United Front Organisation against German Fascism organising fundraising drives to help Jews to leave Germany and a boycott of German goods was inaugurated to try and influence the American government's response to anti-Semitism there.

More violence erupted on 31 September 1933 when FONG organised a meeting at Schwabenhalle in Newark to celebrate the eighty-fifth birthday of German President von Hindenburg. Fritz Gissibl and the German Consul Hans Borchers were to speak. Supporters turned up wearing swastikas and gave the stiff, outstretched arm Nazi salute when the meeting started. Jewish gangs had prepared for the meeting. They threw stink bombs into the crowded room and attacked the people with iron bars as they rushed out. Clearly the Nazis were not going to be allowed to operate with impunity.

It is worth noting that while the Nazi-style salute was gaining notoriety as a symbol of fascism it was virtually indistinguishable from the Bellamy salute that Americans, especially schoolchildren, had been required to give when reciting the Pledge of Allegiance. It was replaced in 1942 by the 'hand over heart' salute.

Firmly in control, Spanknöbel set about supplementing the *Deutsche Zeitung* with another party newspaper *Das Neue Deutschland* with money from the German consul Otto Kiep. Both now carried English translations of Hitler's speeches. Emerson, who still held the allegiance of his Friends of Germany organisation, was not to be so easily outmanoeuvred, however, and he remained more or less untouchable by Spanknöbel, who needed to keep his followers onside. He was unable to overcome Spanknöbel's endorsement by the German consulate, however, and bad feeling between the two men persisted. Spanknöbel tackled the issue with his usual cunning and proposed a deal to Emerson whereby he would be offered virtual joint leadership of FONG if he allowed his Friends of Germany movement to amalgamate with it. Surprisingly, Emerson accepted which meant that he could no longer challenge Spanknöbel from without and would be accused of fomenting divisions if he made trouble within.

Emerson was no fool, however, and calculated that Americans would reject an American political party led by someone who was a member of a foreign agency such as the NSDAP and he was now ideally placed to take over when Spanknöbel's position became untenable. Emerson encouraged Spanknöbel to become more erratic by spreading his wings and reaching out to Americans who had pro-German sympathies but no German heritage. Furthermore, he stood by as Spanknöbel courted old and well-established German American organisations who were clearly not pro-Nazi. Spanknöbel even approached the Jewish Ridder brothers Viktor and Bernard, publishers of the *New Yorker Staats-Zeitung und Herold* and tried to browbeat them into printing pro-Nazi propaganda. He brandished before them what he claimed was his signed authorisation to act for the German government with respect to matters involving Germans and German Americans in the United States. The Ridders were in no mood to be dictated to by an upstart and threw him out.

Nothing daunted, Spanknöbel turned his attention to the UGS where he packed a meeting with Schuster's OD thugs chanting anti-Semitic slogans. The meeting was sufficiently intimidating to see representatives of four Jewish groups walk out. Those remaining voted to appoint Spanknöbel to the UGS board of directors but not enough for it to agree to allowing the German flag with swastika to be unfurled at the upcoming German Day celebrations. At the next UGS meeting, Bernard Ridder was booed out of the hall when he tried to make an objection. The entire board, apart from Spanknöbel resigned and a motion was carried to hold a meeting at the Manhattan Armoury on Lexington Avenue. Despite vociferous opposition from Jewish War Veterans the authorities refused to cancel the meeting saying it would be unconstitutional to do so and it went ahead under a swastika flying from the mast of an American government building. Buoyed by this success, Spanknöbel now ordered his OD men to paint swastikas on a number of New York synagogues including the prestigious Temple Emanuel. Press coverage was entirely negative for the UGS and their activities came under the scrutiny of the McCormack-Dickstein Committee. The New York Democrat and chairman of the House Immigration Committee, Samuel Dickstein, had already been alerted by the increasing level of street violence and accused the German Consulate of bringing provocateurs and propagandists into the country. The committee had been set up at his suggestion but, aware that his being a Jew might make it appear that his grievance was personal, he allowed John W. McCormack to lead so as to avoid any unnecessary accusations of Jewish control of the process.

Spanknöbel called another meeting at Schwabenhalle, 593 Springfield Avenue, Newark, to rally opposition to the McCormack-Dickstein Committee but already his leadership was being called into question. One of his own FONG officials wrote to Kappe calling him an 'inflated notorious swindler'.[13] Kappe was an ardent Nazi and had spent years trying to encourage sympathy for the cause amongst German Americans. He had been given responsibility for FONG's intelligence section (*Bundnachrichtenstelle*). Through this he had links to German Military Intelligence, the *Abwehr*, and was instrumental in setting up a network of informants within the German American community and also in other pro-fascist groups in the US It was probably through Kappe that Berlin was informed about Spanknöbel's disruptive style. The level of concern shown in Berlin was clear when Bohle was urged to restrict his organisation's political activities in the US.

Spanknöbel's Schwabenhalle meeting went ahead with large numbers of uniformed OD men in attendance as security against attack. This time, the opposition was boosted with members of other anti-Nazi clubs and organisations making around a thousand protestors in all. The hall was packed with some 800 people and a huge swastika was draped across the stage behind the speakers. Again, the meeting was broken up with stink bombs. Expecting a violent attack, the OD contingent tried to get Spanknöbel out through the crowded hall. Fifty policemen who had been outside dived in to stop the fighting that had broken out as the meeting hall emptied but the mayhem was so intense that another 150 were called up before order was restored.

When Mensing travelled to Germany he had meetings with Bohle and Hess, who denied giving Spanknöbel the sort of authority he claimed. Mensing made clear to them also that the US Justice Department had started asking questions about who exactly was behind FONG and how much control the NSDAP had over it. Spanknöbel had already caused a stir by telling the German Embassy in Washington that it was his intention to bring all German societies under the control of FONG. Probably as a result of Mensing's disclosures, the *Auswärtiges Amt* issued a memorandum on 16 October 1933 which became known as the October Directive. Its main points were,

- Only citizens of the Reich could be Nazi Party members.
- No Nazi Party member was to become active politically in the US.
- Spanknöbel was to be removed from a position of power in the German American community.
- Leadership of FONG was to be constituted exclusively of American citizens.

The Directive proved to be something of a damp squib, however since its conditions were somewhat vague and there was no follow-up to ensure compliance. All except for the central purpose, that is, which was to get rid of Spanknöbel. The Newark city mayor and government agencies now went on the attack. Spanknöbel was charged with being an unregistered agent of foreign nations and threatened with deportation. Before a warrant could be served, however, he went into hiding then left the country on 29 October 1933 on the *SS Europa* back to Germany claiming that he 'could not bear the thought of being tried by Jewish judges'.[14] New York's Jewish leaders made sure that Spanknöbel's embarrassment got maximum press coverage. He would go on to serve in the German army during the war when he was captured by the Soviets and never returned. While Spanknöbel had overreached himself in terms of his power grab, he had at least created a nationwide structure that his successor could work with.

*

Hess was not impressed. He had wanted a strong American pro-Nazi movement with an entirely German-affiliated membership outside the NSDAP. Goebbels also made clear his disappointment at Spanknöbel's heavy-handed tactics which were sure to alienate German Americans rather than encourage them to rally to the Nazi cause. Hess and Goebbels may well have agreed on objective but did not entirely agree on method, however. While Hess wanted to boost American support for Germany through politics, Goebbels, not surprisingly, preferred insidious propaganda across a broad front.

The *Auswärtiges Amt* called on FONG to confine its activities to the non-political sphere and only allow membership to German nationals and to give it credibility, the leadership would be restricted to those with American citizenship. The latter condition had been clearly the result of Congress taking a close look at FONG. There was still a difference of opinion over whether an overtly Nazi organisation on American soil with strong American roots would create diplomatic problems or strengthen ties between the two countries and squabbling between the various German agencies competing for control of ethnic Germans abroad did not allow for a coherent strategy to emerge. Eventually Hess forged some sort of consensus but refused to sanction Spanknöbel's preferred successor, Ignatz Theodor Griebl, even though he was a naturalised American citizen of German birth, an officer in the United States Army Reserve and a personal friend of the German Consul in New York, Dr Hans Borchers. Griebl was a member of the German cultural organisation, the Steuben Society, and had been actively working for the Gestapo since arriving in the US as a recruiting agent for contacts within the armament industries. He was popular within the German American community but had an unfortunate reputation with the American press as a man not slow to use his fists in an argument and was a fiery speaker at Nazi rallies. In 1934, he had given a speech to 20,000 German Americans at a swastika-clad Madison Square Garden on German Day where his fiery rhetoric had been rapturously received. Both Griebl and his wife had been called up to testify before the McCormack-Dickstein Committee the adverse publicity from which forced his resignation as assistant clinical surgeon at the Harlem Hospital in New York.

The NSDAP choice was Gissibl, who had been waiting in the wings for his time to come, despite the fact that he was still a German national. He had tried to resign his NSDAP membership but the party had refused to accept it. He was not going to get an easy ride, however. There was no shortage of ambitious men hoping to step up and take on the leadership: Ernst Hanfstaengl, Lüdecke and Kappe were all preening themselves ready to launch a bid but back at the German Foreign Institute in Stuttgart, they were looking to disband FONG altogether. Both Gissibl and Griebl now claimed leadership of FONG with Griebl counting on a hard core of Spanknöbel supporters and threatening to split the party again. Gissibl went into action in the best Nazi traditions. He began a smear campaign against Griebl that proven sufficiently venomous to see his rival ousted in short order. Pushed aside from FONG leadership, Griebl would go on to play a quite different role for the Nazis in the murky world of espionage.

Gissibl now set about defining the strategy and purpose of FONG. An eleven-page document, *das Neue Deutschland -Was geht es uns an?* sent to the NSDAP press office in Berlin, outlined a strategy to counter the 'lies' printed by the 'eastern Jewish' press and give an 'objective view' of Hitler's Germany. The consciousness of German Americans was to be stimulated to understand the racial-political responsibilities they had towards their ancestral homeland. This document was to become the bedrock of FONG ideology until at least 1938.[15]

By the end of 1933, FONG was running out of steam. It had not recovered from the Spanknöbel debacle and, despite coming up with a written mission statement, its leadership lacked confidence and direction. Unwilling to see the movement flounder, however, Emerson and members of the German consulate intervened and arranged meetings between FONG and the German American Business League (DAWA) that had been formed to get round the Jewish boycott of German-made products. FONG grasped the opportunity to ingratiate itself with the many New York lower-class and middle-class business owners and present itself as defenders of their rights. A letter they sent to President Roosevelt called the boycott insulting, humiliating and racially discriminating to loyal Americans. To the faithful, FONG newspapers announced that German Americans would no longer 'conform to the dictates of the dominant Jew-ridden Anglo-Saxon culture.' We are and remain Germans, the editorial said, 'Germans in America.'[16]

FONG's message was loud and clear not just to post-war immigrants but to all Americans of German ancestry. It is quite possible, it said, to be a good American and also a good German but, increasingly, the American press and Dickstein saw NSDAP demands that FONG members work within guidelines laid down in Berlin as incompatible with American interests.

Walter Kappe, who had been appointed as head of the US Defence and Reconnaissance Department of the NSDAP was now chief propagandist for FONG and editor-in-chief of *Deutsche Zeitung*. He spared no effort to brand Dickstein as the *bête noir* and urged all German Americans to seek protection under FONG that was the only organisation prepared to protect them from a 'Jewish [and communist] pogrom' to come. The 'Black card' was also brought into play where Black activists were characterised as pawns in Jewish and communist plots and were consequently targeted by the same vicious propaganda.

For his part, Dickstein identified FONG members as 'social outcasts, thugs and misfits'. Actual membership details are scarce and tell us little. We are left to make estimates based on flimsy details which, for instance puts the number of FONG members who were also members of the NSDAP in the low hundreds.[17] Many post-war immigrants, however, were young men who had lived through the German revolution of 1919–1920 when communists were crushed by the brutal Freikorps paramilitaries. They had been endlessly subjected to propaganda blaming international Jewry for starting the war and widespread, malicious and unsubstantiated accusations that the German army had been betrayed by the politicians who had capitulated to the Allies just at the moment when Germany was about to seize the initiative on the battlefield. Many could not help but bring their prejudices with them and whilst they may not have been hard-core Nazis, the FONG message of restoring German prestige against the machinations of Jews and Bolsheviks who wanted to keep Germany on its knees resonated with them.[18]

Dickstein's investigations, dubbed the 'Jewish Inquisition' by the Nazis was making headlines and causing much discomfort in Berlin, however. Nazi interference in American political life was deeply resented and it was now a question, seriously debated within the highest levels of the Nazi leadership, of whether it was expedient to continue with its activities there or withdraw its support for FONG completely. There had been serious misgivings about continuing in this area after the Spanknöbel affair and it was now accepted that the choice of an overt Nazi like Gissibl as his successor had been a mistake but to remove him now would be an act of weakness and could be exploited by Dickstein as an admission that Gissibl was a Nazi puppet. Berlin was reluctant to completely abandon any hope of building an American Nazi movement and chose to sidestep the issue by toning down FONG activities there instead by ordering it to dissociate itself from the NSDAP.

That did little to reverse the bad publicity that FONG was getting in America with membership starting to fall off at an alarming rate. As a consequence of this trend, FONG tried to distance itself from Nazi Germany and seek to create an essentially American Nazi movement, but Gissibl refused to stand down and make way for an American-born leader. In Berlin, FONG was starting to look like a liability. Hanfstaengl was instructed by Hess to read the riot act to Gissibl and bring him into line.

In no uncertain terms, he put pressure on Gissibl to promote Reinhold Walter, a naturalised American of German birth who was not a member of the NSDAP. Powerless to resist this pressure coming directly from Berlin, Gissibl agreed and allowed Walther to become the official public face of FONG but he was certainly not prepared to let him take over the reins of full *Bundesleiter*. The two men disagreed on many fundamental points. Gissibl wanted to retain strong links with, and take directions, from Germany with the ultimate aim of giving the movement full NSDAP credentials but Walter had a much more US-oriented approach. Having got Hess's backing, Walther was equally stubborn and refused to play second fiddle to Gissibl so the fuse was laid and required only a match to light it. In May 1934, displaying his new-found credentials, Walter struck it by gathering anti-Gissibl dissidents in an attempted coup to remove Gissibl completely from FONG but Gissibl was too much of an old plotter himself not to see the warning signs and outmanoeuvred Walter by removing him from office before his plot could gain momentum.

When the McCormack-Dickstein Committee began its investigations, Dickstein had been quick to rouse public anger by dramatizing and overplaying the dangers of Nazi infiltration into the American way of life with exaggerated claims. American public opinion was further incensed when Hitler authorised the Night of the Long Knives murderous purge of his rivals in Germany on 30 June 1934. In the US, public disquiet was growing about just what kind of administration was developing in Germany as Nazism began to tighten its grip.

Gissibl could see that his close connection to the NSDAP was harming FONG's chances of growing support and, fearing new moves to unseat him, he chose his own candidate to take on the titular leadership of FONG while he, hopefully, would continue to pull the strings in the background. At a FONG convention at the end of June 1934, on a stage draped with American and German flags alongside pictures of Hitler and Roosevelt, in a move that won wide support from the floor, Gissibl publicly resigned his office and recommended that Hubert Schnuch replaced him. Schnuch, an American citizen, had been born in Aachen and served with both the German army and the Freikorps before moving to the United States in 1923 where he joined the Teutonia Association. In 1931 he was awarded a Bachelor of Philosophy degree from the University of Chicago and had gone on to gain a PhD from Yale in 1934.

If his appointment was meant to calm anti-FONG sentiment, it was less than successful when, weeks later he was called to appear before the McCormack-Dickstein Committee and made a number of egregious anti-Semitic remarks in the full glare of press scrutiny. Gissibl had made another grievous error of judgement and was forced to make sure that Schnuch was kept out of the public spotlight thereafter. Gissibl had also manoeuvred two of his old comrades, Sepp Schuster and Walter Kappe into positions of influence. Nevertheless, news that FONG was now under the control of an American citizen had legitimised the movement to some extent and this was further boosted by a growing sense among German Americans that Dickstein was deliberately rousing anti-German sentiments in the country to further his own career. Together these factors had the effect of increasing membership by drawing in new German American recruits who, rightly or wrongly, felt that they needed the protection of some sort of fellowship in case US public opinion turned hostile towards them.

Berlin continued to be concerned about events, however. Hitler had become involved after reading reports of a deterioration in German American relations and wanted to know to what extent that was as a result of FONG activity. Hess told him that such reports were exaggerated but that 'any overt efforts made in the United States [on behalf of FONG] were entirely pointless.'[19] Gissibl did his best to divert criticism by closing a Madison Square Garden rally on 6 October with the 21,000-audience giving a rousing rendition of the Star-Spangled Banner.

The unexpected growth in FONG membership had encouraged internal moves to oust Gissibl, moves that may or may not have been instigated from Berlin after Hitler's intervention. Anton Haegele, a naturalised American who had been appointed deputy leader at the Chicago convention, headed a move to wrest control from Gissibl by calling him a traitor and accusing him and Kappe of embezzling funds. He rallied Gissibl's opponents, including the influential president of the pro-Nazi Steuben Society, Theodor Hoffmann, whose personal animosity towards Gissibl was well known. He had written to Hitler in 1934 to express his view that as long as the Friends were controlled by Reich Germans it would be detrimental to German-US relations. Berlin took his opinions on board at the time but felt that some level of support for FONG from Berlin was essential to prevent the total collapse of their US strategy and continued to give Gissibl its qualified backing. In mid-December, Haegele, supported by Walter, Ludwig Glasser, Gerhard Procht, Werner Brink and Theodor Strohlen stormed into the building at 305 East 46th Street in New York and managed to get control of the FONG's printing presses but Schnuch's people had barricaded themselves into the editorial and business offices in the same building. Haegele served an eviction notice on them as fighting broke out on the streets of Yorkville between the rival factions. Haegele launched an attack against Gissibl by publishing a manifesto entitled *The End of the Bund's Mismanagement*. 'The misrule of the Schnuch faction,' it said, 'smells to the high heavens. It placed in peril the very existence of the Friends of New Germany.'[20] Haegele's putsch did not have huge support from the wider membership, and he needed to generate momentum to give the impression of control but he suffered a major setback when he failed to bring Schuster and his OD thugs onside which made taking over the national headquarters in Yorkville well-nigh impossible. Neither was Haegele likely to get much support from the DAI in Stuttgart. Moschack told the German consul, Oskar Schlitter that he had never even heard of Haegele who, by now, had printed more newsletters claiming to have taken over the leadership of FONG. Under the headlines *The End of a Misrule* he published a newsletter announcing the 'Self-Liquidation of Schnuch, Kappe, Gissibl and Co.' and claimed to be in complete control of both the *Deutscher Beobachter* and the New York branch of FONG. The Gissibl faction came out fighting with their own edition of the *Deutscher Beobachter* announcing that the revolt had been crushed. It was difficult for the members to know exactly what was going on. Jewish communities, however, feared that any change favouring the Haegele faction would mean a revival of the faltering DAWA and a resurgence of anti-Semitic activity.

Gissibl and Schnuch called a meeting at the New York Turnhalle attended by 1,000 people, on 20 December 1934. In attendance to maintain order were 200 men in uniforms bearing the swastika insignia. Small groups who tried to shout down the speakers were unceremoniously removed from the hall. Schnuch took the stage and accused Haegele of doing Dickstein's work for him by breaking up the Friends movement. It was agreed to ban Haegele from taking any actions in the name of FONG. The American press revelled in the disharmony. After the meeting, the *New York Times* ran a headline

'NAZIS TO "PURGE" THE LEAGUE HERE; Friends of New Germany Decide to Expel Haegele Group of insurgents'.[21] Haegele responded in early January 1935 claiming to have ousted Gissibl and Schnuch and renamed FONG as the American National Socialist Bund (*Bund Amerikanischer Nationalsozialisten* BANS).

Essentially Haegele's point had been that FONG was far too much under the control of Berlin and its leaders in the US and Gissibl, Kappe and Schuster, were obsessed with their own aggrandisement. The movement would be better served by playing down its Nazi credentials and replacing 'the German agents, Gissibl and his clique' with a leadership that was visibly and doctrinally American.[22] As it stood, FONG was battling against the realities of US public opinion. The Dickstein's committee, which had now been granted $30,000 funding by Congress, had made much of the movement's links to the NSDAP which in turn had raised the level of concern of the US authorities who believed that many of the new members were being infiltrated to intensify the pro-Nazi character of the movement. Gissibl had not been blind to this and had, in fact, belatedly tried to loosen FONG's ties to the NSDAP but could only go so far since it still relied to some extent on financial support from Berlin.

Haegele's coup was never able to generate enough support from the membership and foundered leaving Gissibl hanging onto power, but the rebellion had laid bare the dissention within FONG ranks and opened a rift that would not be easily bridged. Dickstein's report of February 1934 attacked NSDAP involvement in US affairs through FONG and other organisations and started to create a sense that America was being subjected to malicious interference from Berlin. The sheer size of the FONG movement, or at least the perceived size, was threatening to raise the level of anti-German sentiment in the US and was becoming a corrosive issue in US-German relations at government level. At a time when Berlin was making great efforts to develop a good relationship with Washington, US public opinion, encouraged by the press, was sliding towards hostility. This happened also to be when the press was making much of the Butler coup attempt and the Dickstein Committee's report of February 1935 wasted no time in accusing the NSDAP of interfering in internal US politics. It called customs officials who testified that they regularly intercepted propaganda material that crews of the Hapag-Lloyd passenger liners, such as the *SS New York* and *SS Hamburg*, had tried to smuggle in through New York.

Theodor Hoffmann made an urgent visit to Berlin to complain to Hitler personally about the young German Nazis immigrants whom, he said, were the root of all the trouble. Bohle rejected this view and urgently tried to counter Hoffmann's criticisms by saying that Hoffmann was just piqued that FONG seemed to be getting too powerful and eclipsing his own organisation, the Steuben Society. Bohle was supported by Luther at the US Embassy whose view was that breaking with FONG completely would be 'extremely undesirable'.[23] Despite high level support from the DAI, time was now running out for FONG which Berlin saw as becoming a liability and a hindrance in efforts to establish good relations between Germany and the US In the eyes of many it had become synonymous with thuggery and subversion. In German diplomatic circles its activities were condemned as 'conspiratorial child's pal'.[24] Hess had seen enough of 'the predominantly hostile attitude towards the New Germany which has become established…in the press' and set about dissolving FONG.[25] He called for the resignation of all German nationals from the movement by the end of 1935 and the immediate repatriation of leaders of FONG who were also members of the NSDAP. Bohle went further and ordered the immediate resignation of all NSDAP members, whether German or American nationals, from the movement and called on it to refrain from all political activity. Dickstein could hardly believe his luck when he got hold of a copy of this instruction that indicated the numbers of ideologically motivated and politically active Nazis that had been in the FONG membership.

Kappe would be one of the more strident Nazis who would be obliged to return to Germany in 1937 where he was appointed head of the press department of the German Foreign Institute and later, together with Gissibl, founded the American-German Comradeship. As a counter-intelligence officer, Kappe would go on to lead Operation Pastorius in 1941, in which German sabotage groups were to carry out attacks on American industrial centres after they had been dropped off on the east coast from U-boats. The operation was a complete failure with all eight agents arrested, six executed and two receiving prison terms. Kappe was killed in action on the Eastern Front in 1944.

Chapter 3

WILLIAM DUDLEY PELLEY AND THE SILVER LEGION

> You are hereby cordially invited to attend another meeting of patriotic, Christian citizens who believe there is a very urgent need for united action on behalf of our Government.[1]

'The time has come for an American Hitler,' said William Dudley Pelley while campaigning for the United States presidency in 1936 as leader of the Christian Party under the banner of 'For Christ and the Constitution'. He went on to say, 'When I'm president...I'll do away with the Department of Justice [and form] a Christian government.' The party's manifesto called for disenfranchisement of Jews and limitations placed on their rights to employment.[2] When the votes were counted, he had won 1,598 against Rosevelt's 27,757,333. All of his votes came in Washington which was the only state where he had been able to get on the ballot.

Pelley had been born into a deeply religious family in Lynn, Massachusetts in 1885. During his childhood, he later said, he had been 'perpetually hungry, shabbily dressed [and] non-too-happy'. An impoverished childhood and a lack of formal education, however, did not prevent his taking up a career in journalism when he edited and published *Philosopher Magazine,* a vehicle for his 'smouldering Bolshevism [and the] fearful storm of hatred and despair' that he felt. He grew up to be a 'slender, distinguished-looking man' and later went on to become a police reporter with the *Boston Globe* in his late twenties.[3] As well as his journalistic career, Pelley wrote fiction sufficiently good to win two O. Henry Awards. His most successful was one of his earlier books entitled *The Toast of Forty-Five* whose themes were blood ties and

Christian sacrifice. His religious connections saw him selected by the Methodist Centenary and the Rockefeller Foundation for missionary work in Japan and Korea at the height of the Russian Civil War. Soon afterwards, he travelled all across Siberia working for the International YMCA and sending back reports to the *Saturday Evening Post* of Allied intervention against the Bolshevik forces. When he returned to the United States, he wrote articles for *Sunset Magazine* and *World Outlook* giving his personal views on the communist revolution full of references to 'Christian white men' which he saw as superior to the Asian races he had encountered on his travels.

Despite his success as a writer, Pelley was heavily in debt when he moved to southern California and set up the Pelley and Eckels Advertising Agency in 1928 hoping to commercialise his obvious literary talents. These also saw him taken on by Warner Brothers as a screen writer for famous actors of the day such as Tom Mix, Lon Chaney and Hoot Gibson. Two of his books were made into films with religious themes depicting a 'common man' who would rise up to lead the nation.

It was at this time, while he was living in Altadena that he claims to have had what he called an 'ecstatic interlude', a transformational experience and a revelation. It was similar to one he claimed in his autobiography to have had as a child. In that one, he says that he was sitting on a hilltop outside East Templeton when 'a corner of the veil of Eternal Mortality was flashingly lifted'.[4] According to an article, *My Seven Minutes in Eternity*, which he wrote for the *American Magazine* in 1929, in his second 'hypo-dimensional' experience he had died and gone to heaven for seven minutes. While he was there he met with God and Jesus, who instructed him to undertake the spiritual transformation of America. He later claimed that the experience gave him the ability to levitate, see through walls, and have out-of-body experiences at will. He was endowed with the ability to 'unlock hidden powers' within himself and was chosen to give inspiration to the whole human race.

Moving to Asheville, North Carolina in 1930, and, supported by a wealthy backer, he founded the Galahad Press and the short-lived esoteric women's Galahad College at the Asheville Women's Club building on the corner of Sunset Parkway and Charlotte Street, the names deriving from his fascination with medieval legend. Students were taught a 'superior form of Christianity and Christian economics'. Modules taught both in the college and as correspondence courses included Ethical History, Spiritual Eugenics, Social Metaphysics, Christian Philosophy, Educational Therapy and Cosmic Mathematics. In April 1931, he founded the League for the Liberation (Fraternity of the Liberation) and established a Church of the Christian Democracy offering a weekly service of talks on spiritual identity and morality.

He published a book entitled *No More Hunger* in which he described his theories of Christian Democracy loosely based on Mussolini's Italian corporate state. Christianity, he said, must be protected against the evils of 'modern educational institutions [supported by] the modern barbaric state'.[5] It was an irrational plea to go back to the pre-war days before the waves of immigration from southern and eastern Europe had crossed the Atlantic.

Working late in his office on the evening of 31 January 1933, Pelley received a copy of the local newspaper reporting on the elevation of Hitler to the Chancellorship of Germany. In his biography, he wrote that 'I looked at the lines. I read them again. I sought to comprehend them. Something clicked in my brain!' He had long admired Hitler for his opposition to 'the Jewish menace' and the news of his success sparked a reaction in Pelley's mind akin to those of his spiritual revelations. At that moment he conceived the idea of the Silver Legion of America, later called the Silver Shirts and claimed that it was all part of his divine revelations.

He described the Silver Legion as '[preparing] a great horde of men nationally to meet the crisis intelligently and constructively. Every Silver Shirt must...be in a position to join with tens of thousands of similarly enlightened Christians and preserve the form of constitutional government set up by our forefathers. If this [means] using force...very well then, it means force.'[6] It had a militaristic structure of national commander, field marshals and general staff.

The Legion was incorporated on 19 March 1934 in Delaware. Membership of the Silver Shirts, which included both men and women, stretched across the whole continent and while there are claims that it may have been more than a million it is more likely that it never rose above 15,000. Membership fees were set at $1, all of them going into his Pelley's personal bank account which he declared to the IRS as personal income.[7]

In an unscheduled appearance before the House Committee on Un-American Activities (Dies Committee) in 1940, Pelley would testify that Colonel Edwin Emerson offered him $10 for each German he enrolled into the Silver Shirts saying that he had sufficient resources to cover 15,000 new members which means, assuming that his offer was genuine, that he had access to significant funds. Where they were coming from is open to speculation.[8] Members of Pelley's Legion were largely drawn from struggling and retired middle-class businessmen, clergymen, lawyers and skilled workers in the Midwest and West Coast whose lives had been thrown into turmoil by the Great Depression. They were predominantly white and of Anglo-Saxon, German, northern European, and Protestant ancestry. There had been a significant KKK presence in the Seattle region since the mid-1920s into which Pelley tapped for his support there. The movement's symbol was a scarlet letter 'L' featuring prominently on its flags and uniforms, which included black boots or leggings and Sam Brown belts. Initially the movement was funded by George B. Fisher of Crowell Publishing ($20,000), Sarah C. Scott ($10,000) and Dr John S. Brinkley ($5,000). A weekly magazine, *Liberation*, was published, declaring itself to be a 'Journal of Patriotism and the Higher Fraternity', alongside a weekly newspaper *The Silver Ranger*. Articles were heavily biased towards anti-communism, anti-Semitism, and extreme patriotism.

Pelley, described as a short man with a magnetic personality, intense eyes, striking facial hair and a clipped Van Dyke goatee, now spread the word travelling across the continent giving lectures and making speeches expounding his religious and political beliefs that borrowed from Pythagoras, the Manicheans, William James, the Rosicrucians, Pyramidology and Madame Blavatsky. His message was that a cataclysm was approaching, a notion that appealed to Christian fundamentalists, in which the Jews and Communism would ultimately be defeated in a final battle that would bring in a new Christian Commonwealth. His revelations, he said, were supported by secret prophesies foretold in the design of the Great Pyramid in Egypt. Pelley, however, did not go as far one of his acolytes who predicted that 'When we eliminate Communism and Jews from the United States it will not be with ballots, but with guns, wading in blood.'

In 1933, Pelly had recruited an exiled Estonian aristocrat, Paul von Lillienfield Toal to act as liaison between the Silver Legion and Nazi government.[9] Toal worked as an executive for the *Norddeutscher Lloyd* shipping company and acted as a courier. Pelley would provide information about the political situation in America and Toal would take out advertising space in the *Liberation* paying up to ten times the going rate. Toal also made recommendations about who might be promoted in the Silver Shirts and organised parties on board *Norddeutscher Lloyd* cruise ships to which Pelley and Emerson were invited.

Toal was evidently known to the US authorities who, alerted by Pelley's subversive activities, brought Toal before the McCormack-Dickstein committee on 9 July 1934. Thereafter Toal, now exposed, played very little part in Pelley's operations.

The movement began to get noticed by the press. *Harper's Magazine* published an article by Johan Smertenko in November 1933 in which he accused Pelley of scapegoating Jews for the economic depression. The *New Republic* followed up with a piece on fascist groups singling out the Silver Shirts as 'dangerous' and an organisation that 'needed watching'.

A meeting on 10 March 1934 attended by Pelley, Emerson and Royal Scott Gulden, the leader of a revolutionary organisation called the Order of '76 discussed the merger of Gulden's movement with the Silver Shirts. Gulden's strategy had been to get people into places which would provide access to important information. Already only a week previously, in Room 830 of the Hotel Edison in New York, Pelley had met Sidney Brooks, head of the research bureau of the International Telephone and Telegraph Company who, because of his position, was a confidant of Republican Senators and Congressmen and consequently was privy to many state secrets. At this meeting they had also discussed the merger of the Order of '76, of which Brooks was a leading member, with the Silver Shirts. Brooks had, in fact assumed his mother's maiden name to disguise the fact that he was the son of Colonel Edwin Emerson. Documents clearly show that Brooks was in frequent contact with the German Consulate General.

Bad publicity may well have been a factor in the closing down of the Galahad Press that filed for bankruptcy in April 1934. Under the full glare of publicity over the collapse, Pelley was hauled up before a grand jury to face sixteen charges including selling stock in the press without first registering its sale with the state, advertising stock for sale with prior knowledge that the Galahad Press was insolvent and diverting $100,000 of its funds for his own personal use. When his correspondence was subpoenaed, it revealed that many of his correspondents were 'poor, uneducated, neurotic, elderly women' and 'lower or middle class Anglo-Saxon[s] who lived in urban areas of the Middle West'.[10]

*

Marine Corps intelligence had infiltrated two marines, Virgil Hayes and Edward T. Grey, into the Silver Shirts and it was their testimony, laid before a Congressional investigation in Los Angeles, part of the McCormack-Dickstein Committee, that prompted the *New York Times* to run with the headline 'Arms Plot Is Laid to San Diego Nazis' on 8 August 1934. Hayes testified that W.W. Kemp of the Silver Shirts had offered him money to purchase a range of guns including pistols, shotguns and rifles from two corporals at the North Island naval base in San Diego. He and Grey had gone on to teach other members street fighting and proficiency in the use of small arms. When Grey testified he told of a plot to capture San Diego City Hall by force in May 1934 while the Communists were staging a May Day celebration. 200 armed, trained Silver Shirts, led by Willard W. Kemp and Donald Niswender, would converge on the city from the outskirts. It was an ill-conceived and futile plot but it showed that the Silver Shirts were ready to contemplate violent insurrection as a means of grabbing power.

The Grand Jury found Pelley guilty and sentenced him to two years imprisonment and a $10,000 fine, suspended on condition of good behaviour. Pelley called it political persecution because of his 'personal admiration for, and moral support of, that great and wise man who at the present writing dominates the German nation and had caused it to take the first great step towards the accomplishment of those aims that appeal to me strongly as a political philosopher'.[11]

Once Roosevelt's New Deal started to lift the American economy out of its gloom, many of Pelley's supporters began to acquire a measure of financial stability which inevitably made them less inclined to support radical political movements. Membership of the Silver Shirts nose-dived and this, combined with Pelley's own financial difficulties, left the movement struggling to maintain credibility. Pelley sidestepped this impasse by founding a new party in December 1935 based in Seattle. His new Christian Party, however, came up with the same old dogmas of 'Down with the reds and out with the Jews.' His ambition was to lead the 'intellectually handicapped multitudes' in a crusade under the banner of 'Christ or Chaos'. To this end he declared himself a candidate for the Presidential election with Kemp as his running mate. To his audiences he said 'the time has come for an American Hitler and a pogrom. When I'm President, I'll incorporate the Silver Shirts into a combination of Federal army and police force. I'm going to do away with the Department of Justice entirely. I am calling on every Gentile in these prostrate United States to form with me an overwhelming juggernaut, ... for Christian government.'

His campaign was a dismal failure and for a time he faded into obscurity despite producing a stream of publications notable for the high quality of their presentation. He was obviously still getting financial backing from somewhere. After a respite, Pelley found new energy and was gratified to find that his rhetoric was warmly received in Minneapolis. The city had the dubious reputation of being one of the most anti-Semitic cities in the country. Discrimination was rife with Jews routinely denied work and housing as well as membership of service clubs. He sent one of his aides, Roy Zachary, to the city in the summer of 1938 to launch a membership drive. Two Silver Shirt private meetings followed in quick succession, on 29 July and 2 August at the Royal Arcanum Hall to which many leading business leaders and professionals were invited. It did not seem to have deterred his audience that Zachary was, at the time, under investigation by the Secret Service for threatening to assassinate President Roosevelt. News of these meetings set off alarm bells just at the time that Henry Ford was being presented with the Grand Cross of the German Eagle by the German vice-consul in Detroit, Fritz Hailer. It became known that Zachary was firing his supporters up to launch an attack on the headquarters of Teamsters Local 544, the organised labour movement in the city. A local newspaper, the *Minneapolis Labor Review,* quoted him as calling for 'Vigilante bands to raid the headquarters of Drivers 544, declaring that the time for the ballot was passed and the only way to deal with the unions was to raid their headquarters and destroy them'. The Teamsters were not easily intimidated, however. Thay had led a major strike in 1934 in which violence had played a very big part. They responded to the Silver Shirts threat by forming a Union Defence Guard (UDG) made up of war veterans and others experienced in strike violence. The UDG set up its own fund-raising activities to buy weapons.

Pelley came to Minneapolis in September to address a rally at the Calhoun Hall. Before he arrived there, however, UDG men gathered outside the packed hall causing those inside to leave and disperse. There was no violence, the threat was sufficient. Pelley, upon hearing about this confrontation took the next train out of town. There were no more attempts to hold public Silver Shirt meetings in Minneapolis.

A local reporter, Eric Sevareid, took a close interest in Pelley's resurgence and began his own investigation. He spent many 'hair-raising evenings in the parlours of middle-class citizens' listening to their condemnation of Jews and their praise for Hitler. His editor was impressed and ran a series of articles deriding these people as 'ridiculous crackpots who were befuddling otherwise upright citizens'.[12]

Reaction was immediate, vitriolic and totally unexpected. Sevareid was threatened by telephone and letter to the point where he became concerned for his family's safety. Even at work he was assailed by 'odd characters, fuming and bridling, [marching] to my desk in the city room, and demanding to know whether I was a Christian or a Bolshevik'. The pastor of the biggest Baptist church in the city pointed him out to the congregation as he sat with his wife during a service calling him 'a foolish cub reporter'.

Pelley had long been in the sights of the House Committee on Un-American Activities (HUAC) and, in 1939, they eventually issued a summons for him to appear before them. At first, he could not be found but continued to have his articles published in the *Liberation*. Then he filed a multi-million-dollar suit against the HUAC for defaming and falsely incriminating him which was a brave move considering that he was still on parole for his 1935 conviction. In October 1939, an arrest warrant was issued in his name by the Superior Court of Buncombe County. David Mayne, one of Pelley's associates was despatched to seek him out but bizarrely he chose instead to forge Pelley's signature to a number of letters implicating Martin Dies Jnr the HUAC chair in a plot to protect the Silver Shirts. To avoid further trouble and to make clear that he had no hand in Mayne's extraordinary scheme, Pelley showed up in the HUAC offices on 6 February 1940.

For three days he answered questions and made front page news in all the national newspapers. He had obviously spent a great deal of time working out how he was going to present himself to the committee. He made every effort to ingratiate himself with the committee and separate himself from the image he had been associated with for so long. His excessive cooperation actually became an embarrassment. He was described by one observer as having jumped on the committee's lap like an unwelcome dog.

After the third day, he was dismissed but spent the next few months vigorously trying to block attempts to have him extradited to North Carolina. That was no help when he was arrested in Connecticut on 4 April and charged with twelve counts of sedition by publishing material whose purpose was the 'dissemination of false statements with intent to interfere with the operation or success of the military or naval forces of the United States or to promote the success of its enemies; and obstruct the recruiting or enlistment service of the United States by distributing certain publications to persons eligible for military service'. After a month-long trial it took a jury just three hours to find him guilty on eleven counts and the judge sentenced him to fifteen years in the federal penitentiary in Terre Haute, Indiana. He was released after serving ten. With the war in Europe now in full swing, the Authorities were in no mood to be lenient with the man who had once proclaimed himself to be 'America's Hitler'.

*

Meanwhile the HUAC explored further the links between the Silver Shirts and Nazi Germany. They called Dorothy Waring who had been infiltrated into the 'Order of '76' and acted there as Gulden's secretary. She later became Pelley's personal secretary also. She described to the committee how Pelley would carry two guns wherever he went, one on his hip and the other in a shoulder holster. Pelley would boast to her that the Silver Shirts would one day march on Washington and take over the government when he would be made dictator. Their guns, Pelley said, were procured by Gulden from the Winchester and Remington arms companies.

The difficulty that is often encountered when examining events of the past is in the need to take a contemporary perspective. Given what we know now, the threat from Pelley seems to have been taken rather more seriously than it deserved. His organisation was small, and it is assumed that there was no significant fascistic tendency in the wider community but events in other countries had shown that populations harboured significant right-wing sympathies that remained dormant until events gave them respectability and created conditions for them to proliferate. Pelley had connections to other small right-wing movements some of whom had supporters in prominent positions and might have been in a position to draw them together into a single movement. Many members and supporters of these groups were men whose resort to violence was by no means restrained and if that violence had been directed against sections of the community against which there was already widespread prejudice it might have enjoyed a certain level of tolerance from the law enforcement and judicial agencies. Pelley and his acolytes certainly missed no opportunity to nourish such prejudice where it existed. Whether or not he had the charisma and personality that fascist movements require of their leader is an open question but he did have connections to the Nazi regime in Germany through people like Toal and Emerson and there is no doubt that Berlin was ready to throw its weight behind him if events had turned out differently. If, for instance, Britain had been forced to come to terms with Germany after the debacle of Dunkirk and the Luftwaffe onslaught during the Summer of 1940 the political climate in the US, already isolationist, might well have evolved into one more amenable to cooperation with the Nazis rather than confrontation. If that had become the case, then Pelley's links with Berlin would have been of much more importance. What might have flowed from that scenario is open to speculation.

Chapter 4

THE NEW DEAL

What America needs is a Mussolini.[1]

In his book *Fascism and the World Economy*, Walter L. Goldfrank postulated that the emergence of fascism anywhere in the world was determined by the level of capitalist development in each nation. In his view it was those countries that had some degree of advanced capitalism but remained dependent on more powerful nations as centres of production and investment capital, that made them uniquely susceptible to fascist movements. In the case of Germany, it was their dependence on American bankers after the First World War which explained how the Wall Street crash and the Great Depression caused the German economy to collapse and drove German capitalists into the arms of Hitler and National Socialism.[2]

After the First World War, Germany was far more dependent on US finance capital than was even Great Britain. It had been only massive American loans and investments that kept the Weimar Republic afloat, but a year before the 1929 crash, American financiers were already reining in their investments in Germany to pour their capital into the Wall Street bubble. The result was a sharp rise in German unemployment figures. As the economic crisis got worse in the early 1930s, the Nazis surged in popularity from their lower-middle class, Protestant base to attract Germany's ruling classes who had begun to see National Socialism as their only hope against the threat of political collapse and socialist revolution.

In the US, the driving force of fascism came from the capitalist class itself, fixated on protecting the wealth and power it had gained during the boom years of the 1920s. They defended themselves against the threat of communism by crushing organised labour and, along with the support of reactionary terrorist groups such as the KKK promoted the doctrine of '100 per cent Americanism'. In Germany, fascism had found its natural base in the lower middle class and a power structure founded on terrorist ultra-nationalism.

The expanding American capitalist economy, whose mantra was 'monopoly', during the 1920s had a distinct imperialist character but this was faltering as the Great Depression hit. Contracting markets threatened unemployment and democratic institutions found themselves at a loss as to how to respond as the financial powerhouses curbed investment in a bid to preserve their assets and promoted profit over human life. Germany, whose institutions were less deeply rooted in democratic tradition than those of America, had responded to the international crisis by embracing a one-party state which crushed all opposition. Leaders of industry and finance in America would not find such a solution quite so easy to achieve.

In his acceptance speech for nomination as the presidential candidate for the Democrats in the summer of 1932, the Governor of New York, Franklin D. Roosevelt said, 'I pledge you, I pledge myself, to a new deal for the American people.' With the famous words 'The only thing we have to fear is fear itself', this policy started to take shape in the first weeks of his presidency and set out to address the problems the Great Depression posed to America by implementing what became known by his own phrase as the 'New Deal'.

National output had fallen by one-third from 1929 to 1933 and thousands of banks had collapsed, taking households savings with them. Unemployment was as high as fifteen million. Two months into Roosevelt's presidency, the *New York Times* reported that the atmosphere in Washington was 'strangely reminiscent of Rome in the first weeks after the march of the Blackshirts, of Moscow at the beginning of the Five-Year Plan.... America today literally asks for orders.' In his book, *Three New Deals: Reflections on Roosevelt's America, Mussolini's Italy, and Hitler's Germany, 1933 – 1939,* the cultural historian Wolfgang Schivelbusch argues that, as a consequence, there are surprising similarities between the economic responses to the crisis of Roosevelt, Mussolini, and Hitler.

Capitalism had failed, that was clear and created one of the two important scenarios that lead to an increase in state power, internal crisis and an external threat. Neoclassical monumentalism is seen as an essential characteristic of Nazi propaganda to express state power and authority but it was not less evident in the government sponsored architecture of 1930s America. While Mies van der Rohe and Albert Speer were giving the Reich the Tempelhof Field and the Haus der

Kunst the US government was building the Gallatin County Court House and the Library of Congress annexe which rivalled them for grandeur. New Deal projects such as The Tennessee Valley Authority stand alongside German autobahns and the reclamation of the Pontine marshes outside Rome as showcases displayed the vigour and vitality of a strong centralised government.

Schivelbusch is clear, however, that we should not go too far and that a great many characteristics of Nazism were absent from America during Roosevelt's New Deal but claims that there were areas of convergence among the New Deal, Fascism, and National Socialism where all three were seen as undermining the basic tents of classic Anglo-French liberalism. Fascism and communism are alike in that they both, at heart, seek to create a strong, orderly, disciplined state and a planned society. Others expressed similar views. Roosevelt's adviser, Rexford Tugwell, praised Mussolini's 'necessary' actions. Roosevelt himself professed admiration for Mussolini who responded in kind while the German *Volkisher Beobachter* praised the US president for adopting 'National Socialist strain of thought in his economic and social policies [and] the development of an authoritarian state [where] collective good is put before individual self-interest'. In his inaugural address, Roosevelt had also said 'I shall ask the Congress for...broad executive power to wage a war against the emergency, as great as the power that would be given to me if we were in fact invaded by a foreign foe.'[3] He certainly had the charisma and popularity to suggest that he had all the attributes required of the leader of a centralised, corporate state.

At a time when the word fascist was commonly regarded as no more than a particular type of moderately authoritarian government, it was no surprise to see ex-president Hoover, an opponent of the New Deal, in 1933 call it a 'fascist regimentation' of society and a decade later to say that it had set up an 'uncanny' parallel with the regimes of Hitler and Mussolini.

So what was there in Roosevelt's New Deal that warranted such criticism? He tackled banking reform laws to allow credit to flow into the economy again. He set out emergency relief programmes through a Social Security system that provided pensions for seniors and support for mothers with children. Work relief programmes created jobs for ten million workers and agricultural programmes saw farm prices stabilised. Hundreds of thousands of new roads, bridges, and tunnels; city halls, libraries and post offices; hospitals, schools and auditoriums; dams, water works and sewage systems; and airports, parks and military installations were built.

All this had consequences for the power structure. Democratic controls were increasingly transferred from the legislature to the executive and followed the pattern of economic power as political power became more concentrated. The President of the United States was given enormous discretionary power over vast funds that were made available to him. Over the course of three years, he created a plethora of agencies to administer these funds.

- AAA (Agricultural Adjustment Administration)
- CCC (Civilian Conservation Corps)
- CWA (Civil Works Administration)
- FDIC (Federal Deposit Insurance Corporation)
- FERA (Federal Emergency Relief Administration)
- FSA (Farm Security Administration)
- NRA (National Recovery Administration)
- NYA (National Youth Administration)
- PWA (Public Works Administration)
- REA (Rural Electrification Administration)
- RFC (Reconstruction Finance Corporation)
- SEC (Securities and Exchange Commission)
- SSA (Social Security Administration)
- TVA (Tennessee Valley Authority)
- WPA (Works Progress Administration).

There ensued what some have called a government by bureaucracy, but it went further than that because the real economic power rested with the dominant economic forces active in each situation. When it came to allocation of funds it was the most powerful financiers and industrialists who actually made the decisions. This concentration of political and economic power and its discretionary use of such vast resources was a clear move towards the domination of the political landscape by the incumbent political party and intensified the relationship between political and financial power in the country.

In 1933, the United States and Nazi Germany had faced the central problem of how to stimulate industrial recovery and there were striking similarities in their approach. Both initially were confronted with arguments for inflation versus deflation and central planning versus free enterprise. German industrialists wanted to crush the labour unions and reverse Weimar's move towards greater democracy and believed that they could achieve this through control and manipulation of the Nazi movement. Its bourgeois middle classes, however, whilst sharing the hostility towards the unions also wanted to curb the power of the banks and urged the breaking of monopolies and were, in the main, enthusiastic supporters of the Nazis. In the United States, there were no such clear-cut divisions or motivations but the government was bombarded with plenty of conflicting advice.

Corporatism was advanced as one solution. The central concept was for industrialists and workers to act together under state supervision, within a planned economy, in such a way as to cut down on waste and labour disputes. Workers were supposed to share equally in the decision-making process but employers were unlikely to embrace that idea with any enthusiasm. This model was already being experimented with in Portugal and Italy and those developing theories to underpin a new American initiative were enthusiastic about it. The Germans adopted this wholeheartedly in 1933 but only after Hitler had curbed trade union power which really gave power to the capitalists. In both the United States and Germany there were strong arguments that saw corporatism as illegal and unconstitutional but, in both, the leadership cited national emergency as sufficient reason to consider it.

At first, both German and US governments came under the influence of powerful big business lobbyists. In German, the bankers' friend Hjalmar Schacht won out against the more socialist Gregor Strasser and Gottfried Feder and in America, the voice of large corporations was heard most clearly above the din. Under growing Nazi pressure, corporatism slowly gave way to totalitarianism where every aspect of life came under the control of the party but in both countries, the process would evolve to give priority to the interests of big business.

There were those in the mid-1930s who saw the shadow of fascism falling across the United States and many business leaders were beginning to feel threatened by Roosevelt's New Deal which seemed to give him almost dictatorial powers. In order to get sufficient support to pass his progressive legislation, Roosevelt had been forced to compromise with Democrats of the southern states, who controlled all of the committees that would have to approve it, but in doing so he was forced to turn a blind eye to the Jim Crow system that reinforced racial injustice there by ceding power to state authorities at the expense of the federal agencies. The rewriting of history where the southern states had fought the Civil War to preserve their rights against northern aggressors rather than to preserve slavery was gaining momentum.

In her 1934 book *Do We Want Fascism?* the historian Carmen Haider, who had been to Italy to study fascism there, argued that the impetus for fascism in the US would come from within the capitalist class and would not require a distinct party, as in Italy and Germany but that it could easily arise within the two-party system and create 'a dictatorial form of government exercised in the interests of capitalists'. Their motivation would be to crush organised labour.[4] The New Deal, she argued, had temporarily saved the capitalist order but only highlighted the perennial conflict between capital and labour. While the National Recovery Administration had set regulations concerning production quotas and commodity prices, it had surrendered to big business the power to implement them. The NRA actually did little to reform the system of monopolies but still the capitalists grew increasingly resentful of government intervention. Millions of workers, meanwhile, were emerging from the worst effects of the Great Depression but found their living standards stagnating and looked to alternative political solutions to improve their lot.

What the NRA experiment had shown to the capitalists was that the State could be used to reorganize the economy in their own interests which lessened their opposition to state intervention per se. The downside for them, however, was that the NRA's success would depend on public works to increase employment and boost consumption, and this would inevitably lead to higher wealth taxes. Industrial growth would be reduced if capital was reallocated to restoring purchasing power to workers all of which would substantially increase the risk of inflation but because of their controls, the capitalists had the power to introduce a collective form of capitalism in the place of traditional American individualism. This, argued Haider, would essentially amount to a fascist state in which violence might erupt in the form of state control of the workers if they should resist what would inevitably become an oppressive system for them. All that was missing was seizure of power through middle class support and the marshalling of this lay with the fascist movements such as the Silver Shirts and the KKK. All that was needed was a sufficiently crippling social and political crisis during which discontent would be manipulated. Republicans would be able to count on the support of reactionary Democratic elites to oppose Roosevelt and the New Deal coalition and allow fascism to take root without disturbing the two-party system. Haider says that 'it would be an insult to their intelligence to think that they could not take care of a movement of discontent and direct it into party action.'[5]

One consequence would probably be the formation of a new left opposition which the fascists would tar with the brush of communism and outlaw it to give them an internal enemy to galvanise their supporters against. Between two such diametrically opposed movements, the middle classes would be reduced to impotency and irrelevance. The political war against Roosevelt's New Deal would then start in earnest. The reactionary wing of the capitalist class would take over the Republican Party which in turn would take control of Congress.

In 1935, a year after Haider's book came out, the Marxist economist Lewis Corey agreed with her that any middle-class movement toward fascism would inevitably be exploited by big business and finance capital. In his book, *The Crisis of the Middle Class*, he argued that reduced industrial output and rising prices had deepened the crisis of America's small business owners and increased unemployment for office clerks, managers, accountants, lawyers, teachers, engineers, public officials, and others. This, he said was driving the middle class to abandon its old democratic ideals blaming labour for its predicament and thereby throwing itself 'into the consuming fires of fascism'.[6]

The middle class, once the flagbearer for liberty, individualism, and bourgeois democratic ideals, would be driven to extremism but they were far too disparate to ever unite in a common cause. Whilst they all wanted to save capitalism from the threat of socialism, small merchants and farmers opposed corporate monopolistic power while managerial and supervisory staff employed by large-scale industry and finance were supportive of it. Corey believed that the two sides would be manipulated by propaganda to unite to crush the labour unions and, caught between monopoly power and socialist revolution would embrace fascism, just as it had in Europe. He summed up his analysis of the situation as 'out of the middle class leaps the monster of fascism: the class that once waged revolutionary war on authoritarianism now provides, in a final desperate struggle for survival, the ideology and mass support for a new authoritarianism determined to destroy all remnants, and the very concepts, of liberty, equality and democracy.'[7] In the event, neither Haider nor Corey were proved right but their arguments pointing directly at the capitalist ruling class as the driving force of American fascism indicate how febrile the mood was in the mid-1930s and how easily things might have turned out differently.

Writing in 1934, also, Roger Shaw likened the New Deal to Italian fascism and accused it of employing 'fascist means to gain liberal ends'.[8] Tracing the roots of fascism, he goes back to Napoleon Bonaparte who, he says, made one of his first tasks as combatting the class struggle inaugurated by Robespierre which he did with aggressive nationalism and focussing France's attention on foreign foes of Austria and England. This was an important aspect of fascism but it was nothing without a revolutionary economic system to go with it. This is what he equates with the 'corporate state' under which labour is crushed and employers become stringently regulated.

Looking at Italian fascism, Shaw recognises both the 'spirit of fascism' which is on the side of vested interests and the 'mechanics of fascism' which oppresses labour and capital equally. He saw the NRA as a clear adaptation of the measures taken by the Italian state. This act effectively fixed wages and prices, established production quotas, and placed restrictions on the merger of companies into alliances. It was a form of industry self-regulation and represented an attempt to regulate and plan the entire economy to promote stable growth. Roosevelt was effectively using the mechanics of fascism to counter the spirit of fascism. The New Deal had riven American society along class lines by pitting the interests of capital, which instinctively opposes economic restrictions of any kind, and those of the working class beset by insecurity and anxiety about the stability of their social and economic status.

It is not the 'self-conscious fascist movements' such as the KKK setting themselves up as self-styled patriots and saviours, Shaw says, who are the true American fascists. That title belongs to the bankers, industrialists and mine-owners who alone had the power to raise private armies, Pinkerton detectives, factory police, vigilantes and massed strike-breakers if the need should arise. They did not see themselves as fascists, however, which was a name reserved for foreign movements. History, Shaw goes on to say, 'records very few cases of a pacific surrender of economic privileges by the possessing order of society'.[9]

Although initially these forces did not openly arraign themselves against Roosevelt's New Deal they saw it as deeply threatening to their interests with its lavish borrowing to finance its plans and the curbs imposed upon their freedom to act. Such a revolutionary economic measure would inevitably have many problems both in planning and implementation which would give them ample ammunition with which to attack and restrict it, they just had to be patient. In 1934, it was Shaw's conclusion that Roosevelt would have to 'look to [his] laurels, seek the maximum of efficiency, and keep [his] powder dry'.[10]

In the November 1933 issue of *The Atlantic*, Max Ascoli wrote, 'In certain quarters it is asserted that Mr. Roosevelt's "New Deal" is nothing other than the first stage of an American movement toward fascism [and that] the economic structure of the country is rapidly being moulded upon the fascist pattern.' The Nazi *Völkischer Beobachter* was an enthusiastic supporter of the early New Deal measures saying, 'Roosevelt's adoption of National Socialist strains of thought in his economic and social policies' was compatible with Hitler's own dictatorial *Führerprinzip*. It lauded the New Deal as a development toward an authoritarian state based on the 'demand that collective good be put before individual self-interest'.

The Führer himself said '[the] moral demands which the President places before every individual citizen of the United States are also the quintessence of the German state philosophy.' Roosevelt, like many Americans at the time, was a huge fan of Mussolini whom he called an 'admirable Italian gentleman'. One of his advisers called Italian fascism 'the cleanest ... most efficiently operating piece of social machinery I've ever seen'.

One of Roosevelt's advisers, General Hugh Johnson, who was in charge of the NRA, a vast scheme for delegating governmental authority to private cartels, was clear that there had to be maximum freedom for business to formulate its own rules with a minimum of government supervision and was very forthright when saying 'cooperation with the president was completely voluntary but exceptions would not be tolerated because the will of the people was behind FDR.' Johnson had never hidden his admiration for Mussolini and may well have gone on to champion ever more fascistic policies had he not been ousted in 1934 for egregious misbehaviour.

It must be remembered that in 1933 fascism was not yet a dirty word. Pro-New Deal propaganda was relentless. The NRA logo, a blue spread-winged eagle holding lightning bolts in one claw and a gearwheel in another, echoed the fascist and National Socialist symbols of the era. The NRA, fascist, and Nazi brands, while visually distinct, nonetheless had both strategic and aesthetic similarities serving the same purpose, to engage citizens and exclude the opposition. In his book *As We Go Marching On* John T. Flynn argued that the New Deal had put itself into the position of needing a state of permanent crisis or, indeed, permanent war to justify its social interventions, just like the Nazi regime had been born in crisis and lived in crisis. Enemies, he said, were 'an economic necessity for us'.[11]

The Great Depression had struck almost simultaneously across the industrialised world and all affected countries responded to it contemporaneously. Faced with the same global conditions it is interesting to look at how the United States reacted and compare that with how Germany did. The two countries were moving in different directions politically in 1933 when they both got new leaders, but their problems and putative solutions were strikingly similar. Both rejected classic, free-market liberalism in favour of a strong corporate state that stressed the importance of order, discipline, and planning.

The public works programmes introduced by Germany in 1933 were much more ambitious than those in Roosevelt's New Deal, that had focused more on direct relief initially, and consequently unemployment in Germany had fallen quicker. They had prioritised subsidies to private industry, tax rebates and stimulated consumption. Roosevelt had backed away from his early support for the Civil Works Administration fearing that it was costing too much money. It was only later in 1935 that this policy was revived under the Works Progress Administration and Public Works Administration.

Both administrations set up work camps, run on semi-military lines, designed primarily to keep young men out of the labour market. In the United States it scooped up all unemployed, unmarried men ages 18–25 and, as Roosevelt put it, got youth 'off the city street corners'.[12] The American Civilian Conservation Corps programme was run by the military and incorporated strict discipline to instil in the young people what its civilian director Robert Fechner called 'patriotism [and] good citizenship'. The CCC was to run from 1933 through until 1942 and the six month's experience gained by each of the three million young men who passed through its camps gave them experience of military life that would stand them in good stead when the war came and, at the same time, gave the army a great deal of experience in handling civilian recruits. The camps were located in the countryside where the work was primarily concerned with conservation and the development of natural resources. It is worth briefly looking at similarities and differences between the CCC and the Hitler Youth camps.

Created as early as 1922, the *Hitlerjugend* movement, including the League of German Girls and the Hitler Youth, began as a recruiting station for young aspiring future members of Hitler's paramilitary organisation the *Sturmabteilung* (SA). It was quite a small, unimportant organisation up until 1933 when Hitler came to power and rejuvenated it with the leadership of Baldur von Schirach. When children reached the age of ten, they were given a 'racial purity' test and, if successful would be recruited to the *Deutsches Jungvolk* and three years later would move up to the *Hitlerjugend*. Membership was mandatory for all who passed the test. All would undergo intense Nazi indoctrination and become a member of the party when they turned eighteen. The Nazi Party had completely changed the education system to place less emphasis on academic subjects and more on physical training. As one participant, Johannes Köppen, put it 'You suddenly felt like something you had never been before, an important person with an essential task.' Another, Werner Gottshau said 'I was thrilled. I was truly enthusiastic… In three years as a soldier, I was still half a Hitler Youth boy.'

Both countries developed youth camps as manifestations of their ideologies as social practices of conduct and control and indeed, youth movements in a number of western countries had emphasised the concept of nationhood and citizenship. As well as places of recreation freedom from the normal constraints of everyday life, they also entailed a measure, greater in Germany that in the United States, of normalisation and discipline aimed at moulding youth as governable subjects infused with ideology and allegiance to the nation state.

It is interesting to note that the German model, which had originated as a movement aimed at freeing youth from everyday constraints had evolved into one with clear paramilitary connotations whereas the American model had started out as the pseudo-military practice of boy scouting but ended up by encouraging the individuality of free self-governing citizens. Despite this American angle it can be seen that both movements involved a regime where individuals were coerced into acting in highly regulated ways making them more governable subjects.[13]

Before 1935, the New Deal had focussed on revitalising the business and agricultural communities and regulating the nation's financial institutions in order to avoid a repetition of the 1929 crash. This had the effect of stabilising the American economy to some extent but there had not been any real economic recovery or significant reduction in the levels of unemployment. Roosevelt persuaded Congress to move beyond the limited federal jobs programmes that were created in 1933 and 1934. They approved a massive spending bill to create the WPA through which it was hoped to create three and a half million new jobs.

Emphasis now shifted to measures designed to assist labour and other urban groups through relief and recovery schemes. This 'Second New Deal' was intended to help stabilize and rebuild the economy, especially its nonbanking sectors. In their sights were banking, the stock market, and labour unions.

Opposition to the New Deal came from both the political left and right. As the Great Depression continued to take its toll and especially given the increasing unemployment rate, Roosevelt's near-unanimous support began to crumble in 1934. A group of conservative Democrats, Republicans, and business leaders believed that certain aspects of the New Deal were an unconstitutional overreach by the federal government and searched for ways to oppose it. However, others saw it as a failure from the perspective of its having not gone far enough in mobilising the power and resources of the federal government to address the issues of poverty and inequality.

THE NEW DEAL

*

In the summer of 1934, there emerged a conspiracy to take over the government in a fascist coup. Gerald C. 'Jerry' MacGuire, a Wall Street stockbroker at the firm of Grayson M-P Murphy & Co of 52 Broadway was at the heart of it. *The New York Post* described MacGuire as 'short, quite heavy with a bullet-shaped head, close-cropped and bright blue eyes'.[14] At the beginning of July 1933, MacGuire and another man, Bill Doyle, arranged to meet a highly decorated First World War hero, the retired US Marine Corps Major General Smedley Darlington Butler at his home. Butler had served in several major world conflicts, including the Spanish-American War, the Philippine-American War, the Boxer Rebellion, and the First World War. During his time in service, Butler became known for his bravery and relentless leadership in battle, and he was rewarded with several distinctions, including multiple Medals of Honor, an Army Distinguished Service Medal, the Marine Corps Brevet Medal, and a Navy Distinguished Service Medal. After his retirement, he had become a popular public speaker telling tales of his long and remarkable military career. Before taking to the lecture circuit, Butler had spent some years in the 1920s as Philadelphia's director of public safety taking a hard line against vice and protection rackets operated by corrupt police officers. In many ways, he was far from an ideal choice for the mission MacGuire had planned for him. During his many talks, he was scathing about the way in which he believed that wars were 'conducted for the benefit of the very few, at the expense of the very many' but it was on behalf of these 'very few' that MacGuire was seeking him out now.[15]

MacGuire and Doyle turned up to Butler's home in a chauffeur-driven limousine, introduced themselves as army veterans and explained that they were concerned about the way that veterans of the American Legion like them were being treated by the government over the payment of First World War bonuses. The bonuses were not officially payable until 1945 but many veterans were unemployed and starving and had formed a 'Bonus Expeditionary Force' to demand early payment. A demonstration in 1932 had turned into a riot and had been broken up by troops led by General Douglas MacArthur using what the Legion called 'unnecessary, criminally brutal and morally indefensible' methods.[16] The Legion was a cause to which Butler was known to be sympathetic.

Would Butler be willing, they asked, to go to the American Legion convention in Chicago and make a speech on their behalf? Butler would not. He had not been invited and he had no interest in going.

MacGuire then tried to irk Butler and rouse his indignation by telling him that his name had been put on a 'distinguished guest' list but crossed out by White House staff when the list had been submitted to the President for approval. Butler did not rise to the bait, however. He would later say that he had 'smelled a rat' and thought he was being used as some sort of pawn in a game he didn't understand. MacGuire now suggested that Butler could attend the convention as a delegate from Hawaii. Butler scoffed at the idea and would not entertain going into the convention 'by the back door'.

The meeting ended but MacGuire came back a few days later with a revised plan. Butler was to gather together 200 or 300 veterans and go to the convention as part of the audience. A special train would be laid on to take them. Butler wanted to know where the money was coming from to pay for all this. 'Friends' was all MacGuire would say but he produced a bank deposit book showing a balance of over $40,000. The men would then be scattered around the convention hall and, at a given signal, would start clamouring for Butler to go up and make a speech. 'A speech about what?' Butler asked. MacGuire then showed Butler a prepared speech about the merits of returning to the gold standard. 'I don't know a damned thing about gold,' he replied.[17]

Butler was sceptical but intrigued and wanted to know how two veterans had access to a limousine and such a lot of money. He agreed to another meeting at the beginning of August. When MacGuire told him that the plan was financed by a number of wealthy businessmen, Butler was sure that these kind of people had no interest in the veterans' cause which raised further doubts in his mind. He challenged MacGuire saying that the 'dumb soldiers' of the Legion had only ever been used by big business interests as a strike-breaking force. MacGuire then admitted that he was acting purely on behalf of his backers and was being no more than 'a businessman'. He advised Butler to do the same.

After a pause of another month, MacGuire again approached Butler in his hotel room in Newark whilst Butler was attending the Twenty-Ninth Division Convention, but Butler had not changed his mind. MacGuire threw down a bundle of eighteen $1,000 bills on the bed for 'expenses'. Butler knew how easy it was to trace such bills if he ever tried to spend one and now definitely thought that he was being set up but he was keen to find out who was behind the plot and asked to meet some of the financial backers.

MacGuire duly arranged Butler to meet a banker called Robert Sterling Clark whom Butler had known some thirty years previously when they had both served in China during the Boxer Rebellion. Clark had inherited a fortune and was renowned for being a bit odd. The two men met a week later in New York when they discussed the contents of the speech Butler had been asked to give. It urged the convention to pass a resolution calling for the government to bring back the gold standard. Butler thought it was a bit far fetched to think that soldiers would get animated over complicated economic issues like that and realised that the Legion was again being manipulated and exploited by big business for its own interests. If the Legion adopted the gold standard resolution then the capitalists could use that alongside the widespread discontent over the bonuses to threaten the government with insurrection by an already disgruntled body of war veterans. Clark told Butler that he was worth about $30,000,000 and was prepared to spend half of it to save the other half. Butler was not sure how his speech or a return to the gold standard fitted into that idea.

Again, Butler turned down the invitation to go to the Chicago convention. 'What the hell does a soldier know about the gold standard?' he asked Clark.[18] Butler says that Clark then backtracked and seemed to lose enthusiasm for the scheme seeing how bluntly Butler had rejected it.

When the convention voted, a motion to bring back the gold standard was carried despite Butler not showing but there was no such resolution passed in support of the veterans' bonuses. MacGuire did not give up on Butler, which was odd given that the resolution that had been passed had, up until that time, been the prime reason for Butler's involvement. The next time the two men met, MacGuire proposed that Butler have his picture taken alongside Governor Al Smith at a soldiers' dinner in Boston and make a speech there for which he would be paid $1,000. MacGuire said that after that he would take Butler around the country speaking to veterans' gatherings to 'see if we cannot get them to join a great big super organization to maintain the democracy'. 'You have got some reason for getting at these soldiers other than to maintain a democracy,' Butler replied and turned MacGuire away hoping it would be the last he saw of him.[19]

When Butler heard from MacGuire again, it was through postcards from all corners of Europe where he was travelling with his wife and children. Butler assumed that Clark was paying for the trip and that it was all part of a bigger scheme set up by MacGuire to scare Clark and trick him into giving him money. He was at least partly correct since MacGuire would later testify that he made this trip on the back of a $10,700 gift from Clark. Butler considered it none of his business if Macguire was exploiting Clark's wealth but in August 1934, a year after the first meeting, MacGuire came to see him again. He told of how he had been abroad to study how different European governments had treated their war veterans. He was in Italy for two months seeing what an essential part veterans played in Mussolini's administration and how well they were rewarded for it. He went to Germany also to see how the Nazis were setting up their paramilitary groups outside the regular army structure and he looked at a fascist organisation in Holland, based on the lines of the SS and led by a man named Mussiat that caught his attention, but it was the *Croix de Feu*, a veterans' organisation in France of some 500,000 men that had most impressed him as being the one that any US movement should base itself on.

The whole fascist movement in Europe is patriotic, MacGuire said because the communists will wreck the nation unless the soldiers save it. His backers had come together to save the American people from forces which were threatening to bring misery, starvation, and disaster to the common people. It was a movement aimed at opposing those who devalued honest dollars by creating fictitious money and paid for it by confiscatory taxation of the savings of one hundred and fifty years of Americanism. This unsound money would see wasteful expenditure in the creation of businesses and government agencies that would compete with and destroy business in which the public has invested its funds.

Butler wanted to know who would pay for it. MacGuire told him that the funding came from an organisation called the American Liberty League. Membership of this League included John J. Raskob, the former chair of the Democratic Party, former New York governor Al Smith, Alfred P. Sloan of General Motors, J. Howard Pew of Sun Oil Company, and Sewell Avery of Montgomery Ward, JP Morgan, Jr, who had secured a $100m loan to Mussolini's government, Irénée du Pont, Robert Sterling Clark of the Singer sewing machine fortune, and the chief executives of Goodyear tyres, Bethlehem Steel, Birds Eye and General Foods all of whom were appalled by Roosevelt's New Deal.

The American Liberty League had been set up under its first chairman, Jouett Shouse, and included all those who MacGuire said had helped finance the coup. The constitution of the League claimed to protect 'defend and uphold the constitution of the United States ... to teach the necessity of respect for the rights of persons and property as fundamental to every successful form of government ... teach the duty of government to encourage and protect individual and group initiative and enterprise, to foster the right to work, earn, save, and acquire property, and to preserve the ownership and lawful use of property when acquired'. Its backers were determined to make Roosevelt protect 'sound money against inflation'. The Agricultural Adjustment Act was, to them, a blatant move towards fascist control of agriculture. And the 1935 Social Security Bill foreshadowed the 'end of democracy'. Roosevelt said the League upheld two of the Ten Commandments pertaining to property but said nothing about 'love thy neighbour'.

Roosevelt had to find another way of financing his New Deal that was costing a huge amount, MacGuire said.[20] The situation in America now demanded similar measures to those in fascist Europe since Roosevelt's government was in danger of financial meltdown with all the money being poured into government bonds to finance the massive public spending programme. State control of the economy was only one short step away from communism in the view of MacGuire's backers. The president was going to need all the support he could get and it was up to Butler to step up and lead the movement on the ground. Macguire assured Butler that Roosevelt was one of the monied classes and he would know which way to jump when the time came but he was a sick man and needed someone to take some of the weight of his office off his shoulders. There was a conversation about how a transfer of power might happen but the plan was for the president to hand over to the vice-president who would then step aside to allow a third man, the Secretary of State, to take over.

A few weeks later, Butler contacted Paul Comly French, a reporter for *The Philadelphia Record* and *The New York Evening Post* who agreed to interview MacGuire on 13 September 1934 in the offices of Grayson M-P Murphy & Co. in New York. MacGuire told him that the country needed a fascist government to save the capitalist system from communists who want to tear it down and wreck America. Half of the American Legion and the Veterans of Foreign Wars would follow General Butler if he would announce the plan that he had in mind, MacGuire said. He told French about his trip to Europe and how he had got enough information to set up a fascist organisation in the US All it needed was a leader, a dictator, a man like Butler. They would use Roosevelt and then get rid of him. There was a plan, that he had seen operating in Germany, whereby all the unemployed men would be put into enforced labour camps. Another economic crash was coming and the Legion would be ready to act.

Butler reported the conspiracy to J. Edgar Hoover at the Federal Bureau of Investigation (FBI), who told Roosevelt. In November 1934 a special session of the McCormack-Dickstein Committee was called to investigate the alleged conspiracy. In its final report, the Committee stated that there was 'evidence showing that certain persons had made an attempt to establish a fascist organization in this country' but it omitted the names of the financial backers which many have suggested meant that Roosevelt made a deal not to bring charges against them if they backed off from opposing his presidency. When the American Liberty League failed to make its mark in the 1936 election its financial backers faded away and the movement collapsed.

On 29 January 1935, the left-wing reporter, John L. Spivak wrote an article in *The New Masses* entitled 'Wall Street Fascist Conspiracy' in which he accused the McCormack-Dickstein Committee of suppressing evidence during the investigation into the Butler affair. In particular Spavik stated that,

- The Committee did not call Butler to testify until it was forced to do so when the *New York Post* and the *Philadelphia Herald* threatened to go public with stories about his involvement.
- When Butler was called he testified in secret session and much of his testimony was not released to the press.
- The Committee failed to call Felix Warburg of the Warburg Bank of Manhattan to explain how a Nazi agent was employed by them and account for the bank's heavy investments in the German economy.
- The Committee failed to call Grayson Mallet-Prevost Murphy, a director of Morgan's Guaranty Trust Bank and several Morgan-connected corporations who was known to have been involved with the American Liberty League. (As early as 1903, President Theodore Roosevelt had employed Murphy for secret assignments, including planning US military interventions. After the First World War, Murphy headed the American Red Cross in Europe, which he used to develop a network of informants in European governments along with 'Wild Bill' Donovan who was later director, Office of Strategic Services. In 1919, Murphy was one of the twenty elite US officers who met in Paris with the guidance of J.P. Morgan & Co. to found and finance the American Legion.)
- The Committee had called an employee of the Hearst Group but after a secret meeting with Roosevelt he declined to appear.
- The American Liberty League was actually named by Butler.
- The Committee failed to call representatives of the Remington Arms Company who it was claimed supplied the weapons to the plotters.
- When MacGuire was called to testify not a single question was put to him about the American Liberty League

Spivak had a meeting with McCormack where he referred to a copy of Butler's full testimony that he had got hold of legally. McCormack refused to carry on with the interview and promised to provide a written reply to a list of questions Spivak presented him with. Pending a full response to Spivak's queries, McCormack wrote to him. Of this reply Spivak said 'I read it over five or six times [and] I still don't know what he is talking about.' When Spivak told Dickstein about the meeting and the list of questions he had given McCormack, Dickstein appeared angry and told Spivak that he had been told nothing about the allegations of involvement by Wall Street and had he been, he would have had no hesitation in calling Murphy, Morgan and Warburg to testify.

All through the hearings, under McCormack's guidance, Dickstein had concentrated on pursuing issues of NSDAP, and particularly, communist involvement. It was only the threat of publication about Butler that the authorities behind the hearings allowed him to be called. Spivak believed that there had been powerful reasons for the emphasis on communism apart from trying to steer the Committee hearings away from the Wall Street involvement in the plot. The Wall Street backers pursued a double agenda of limiting any reference to their participation that might encourage anti-Semitism and of crushing the growing communist influence in the US economy. The Committee hearings, Spivak, believed, were used to bring pressure on the government to bring in laws to restrict, and even outlaw, left-wing organisations.

Spivak got a meeting with Dickstein where he was able to ask a list of questions as follows.

Q. A real investigation of fascist movements in this country would have to take in a study of powerful financial groups and their motivations? Dickstein nodded cautiously.

Q. Then why didn't the committee investigate the financial tie-ups to determine the motives behind such groups as the American Liberty League?
A. Well we didn't have the time or the money or we would have.

Q. What was left out of the Butler story?
A. We confined our activities to evidence permissible in court. We didn't go into the details because it was hearsay.

Q. Why wasn't Grayson M-P Murphy called?
A. We didn't have the time...if we had the time, I would have no hesitation going after the Morgans.

Q. You had Frank Belgrano, commander of the American Legion, listed for testimony. Why wasn't he examined? (He had been listed to appear before the McCormack-Dickstein Committee but after a having a private conversation with Roosevelt, his name was removed and he was never called.)
A. I don't know. Maybe you can get Mr. McCormack to explain that.

Q. Why weren't the names of the Jewish concerns whose money…was used for anti-Semitic propaganda made public?
A. I never saw them…we had so much stuff, I haven't had chance to read all the reports. I wasn't at the Chicago hearing.

Q. And McCormack wasn't at the Chicago hearing either. Then who issued orders not to have those names made public?
A. I don't know.

Q. Why wasn't Felix Warburg questioned as to how the Nazi agent F.X. Mittmeiter got a job in the Bank of Manhattan?
A. I don't know.

Spivak followed this with a second article a week later in which he detailed the various connections between all the organisations implicated in what he called the Wall Street Fascist Conspiracy. His analysis shows how various fascist organisations such as the Crusaders and the American Liberty League were financed by Wall Street capitalists. The Crusaders had been set up to campaign for the repeal of prohibition. It had been financed by the capitalists who thought that the public sale and government taxation of alcohol would transfer the burden of taxation from business to consumers. The League proved to be an efficient and productive movement achieving its objective and its backers decided to keep it in play to lobby against organised militant labour.

The choice of Butler to be the public face of the coup was not a unanimous choice amongst the capitalists who plotted it. He was very much a compromise candidate but nevertheless, he was a spectacularly poor choice. Either the plotters hadn't been listening to what he was saying on his lecture tours or they thought his popularity with the veterans was worth persevering and that if they threw enough money at him he would play along. Who knows what might have happened if they had chosen a different candidate or if they had been more sophisticated and compelling when laying out their case to

Butler. Revolutions can start with a small but fierce flame that finds an incendiary cause and explodes in a moment of chaos. In the US in 1934 there had been widespread poverty and deep resentment, a large force of disgruntled ex-soldiers, capitalists willing to throw millions of dollars into bringing down the president. All it lacked was guile and a figurehead. Macguire and Butler were the wrong people at what might have been the right time.

Writing in the magazine *Common Sense* in 1935, Butler said

> 'I spent 33 years and 4 months in active service as a member of our country's most agile military force – the Marine Corps.... And during that period I spent most of my time being a high-class muscle man for Big Business, for Wall Street and for the bankers. In short, I was a racketeer for capitalism.'

*

Soon after the MacGuire plot had hit the headlines, three men had gone to Louisiana to try and persuade a charismatic politician called Huey Long to join a crusade. One of these men was Philip Cortelyou Johnson, a supremely gifted architect who had used his personal wealth to set up the Museum of Modern Art's Department of Architecture in 1932. Johnson had been born into wealth and had travelled widely in Europe to indulge his fascination for modern German design at the Bauhaus with Walter Gropius, Paul Klee and László Moholy-Nagy. It was there in the early 1930s that he had heard Hitler speak at a Hitler Youth rally in Potsdam and was immediately drawn to him. 'You simply could not fail to be caught up in the excitement of it, by the marching songs, by the crescendo and climax of the whole thing, as Hitler came on at last to harangue the crowd [and] all those blond boys in black leather,' he told a friend. His privileged background and social elitism had given him a profound disdain for democracy which had led him to study the works of Friedrich Nietzsche. In Paris he found the French state had 'lack of leadership and direction' which he blamed on it being controlled by Jews. The American correspondent, William Shirer, who later met Johnson in Poland during the German invasion would note that the German authorities in charge of the press correspondents gave him paid special attention but Shirer found him talkative and frenetic saying that 'none of us can stand the fellow.'[21]

In 1934, Johnson together with his friend and colleague, the second man, Alan Blackburn came under the spell of the third Lawrence Dennis, a fascist ideologue who offered 'a revolutionary formula for the frustrated elite'. Dennis had been born in Atlanta, Georgia in 1893 to an African-American mother, his father's race is not known. Under America's rigidly enforced codes of racial supremacy at that time, the 'one-drop rule' meant that any child of a mixed-race relationship was deemed to be Black, regardless of their complexion. Dennis grew up to be a famous child preacher among Black American congregations at first but later to a wider audience. Then at some point, he cut his family ties so that he could attend the prestigious school of Exeter, and then Harvard, as a White man.

Under Dennis' mentorship, Johnson and Blackburn reinforced each other's extremist views. The two men resigned their posts at the Museum of Modern art declaring that they were abandoning art for politics and launched what they called the National Party (the Young Nationalist Party). It had no policies or doctrine other than a vague assertion that it was merely a group of young men interested in 'direct action' in politics, who believed in a totalitarian state and leadership in place of democracy.

The man that Johnson and his associates saw Long as ' the best example of the nearest approach to a national fascist leader' and a man who attracted devotion and loathing in equal measure. Long was perhaps the most famous demagogue of the whole interwar period. Although not seen as having had a fascistic philosophy, he was renowned for punishing all those who thwarted him with 'grim, relentless, efficient vengeance' and he had reshaped and centralised the state of Louisiana into a government by unilateral control, with no room for legislative or judicial checks. He gave orders to judges, and they submitted to his demands to offer no legal impediment to his actions. His dominance of the militia, the election officials, and the tax-assessing bodies effectively destroyed local government and suspended normal parliamentary procedures in the manner of Hitler and Mussolini. It was, however, a weakness, that he tended to pander to the passions and prejudices of the masses rather than to their reason.

As the first southern politician not to appeal to racists, he had rallied working-class support by speaking out against the wealthy elites of Louisiana where he had been governor in 1928. With his motto of 'Every Man a King', his administration financed infrastructure projects, improved education and set up charity hospitals but as he did so, he built up a ruthless political machine and created for himself what his critics saw as a personal fiefdom gaining almost complete control of all branches of Louisiana's government. When conservative opponents tried to have him impeached, he outmanoeuvred them and doubled down on reinforcing his power base. After death threats, arson attempts, and a drive-by shooting at his New Orleans home, Long beefed up his personal security and surrounded himself with armed bodyguards from the state police.

Opposition hardened when he won a seat in the Senate but refused to relinquish the governorship to his deputy Paul Cyr with whom he had fallen out. Cyr went to a Justice of the Peace and took the oath of office as governor, stating that Long had vacated the office as soon as he was elected to the senate and that he was automatic choice to replace him. Long called out the National Guard, the state police, and the highway police who circled the governor's mansion and the governor's office to prevent Cyr from entering. Alvin O. King, one of Long's acolytes was installed in place of Cyr.

As a senator, Long proposed a 'Share our Wealth' programme to bring in a $30 pension for retirees over sixty years old, free college education, bonuses for veterans, and a 30-hour work week to increase employment. These schemes were seen by his opponents as designed only to win votes but they were wildly impractical with no chance of being implemented. He became very critical of Roosevelt's New Deal arguing that it did not go nearly far enough to alleviate the suffering of the poor and unemployed. 'Nothing that has been done up to this date,' he said in a radio speech on 23 February 1924, 'has taken one dime away from these big fortune-holders; they own just as much as they did, and probably a little bit more; they hold just as many of the debts of the common people as they ever held, and probably a little bit more; and unless we, my friends, are going to give the people of this country a fair shake of the dice, by which they will all get something out of the funds of this land, there is not a chance on the topside of this God's eternal earth by which we can rescue this country and rescue the people of this country.'[22]

In the summer of 1935, he announced his intention to run against Roosevelt, whom he had volubly supported in 1932, in the 1936 presidential election, standing as an independent and promising to run the country on the same lines as he had run Louisiana. Johnson tried to convince Long that he could electrify his campaign by projecting him into living rooms across America using a new propaganda device, the Visomatic which combined gramophone records with photographic images. He even designed a 'grey shirt' to be worn by Long's followers when they congregated or held rallies and a flying wedge as the faction's symbol. Long may have been uneasy with Johnson's flamboyant manner and extravagant suggestions which might have threatened the sensibilities of a man long used to being the guiding light of his own destiny. What might have come of any cooperative venture the four men might have conjured up all became academic, however, on Sunday 8 September 1935. at 21.20 hours as Long was walking down the corridors of the Capitol Building in Baton Rouge returning from a meeting at which he had been able to curb the powers of a long-standing opponent, Judge Benjamin Pavy. On three separate occasions earlier in the evening, Pavy's son-in-law, Dr. Carl Weiss, had tried to speak to Long to plead the judge's case but Long had refused to listen. Weiss was a 28-year-old ear, nose, and throat specialist from Baton Rouge, the father of a three-month-old son and had dined that day with his wife's family. What happened next is open to speculation.

What is certain is that Weiss approached Long one more time at 21.20 hours. One version of the story has it that Long insulted Weiss who was enraged and struck him in the face. There followed a hail of gunfire from Long's bodyguards who later claimed that Weiss had fired first. Weiss fell dead and Long fled the scene only to collapse in a nearby stairwell. He was rushed to hospital where he was operated on. A serious medical oversight had left a gunshot wound to his kidneys untreated and he died some forty hours later. At the inquest into his death, it was noted that a .38-calibre bullet had been removed from his body but the gun that Weiss had kept in the glove compartment of his car was a .32-calibre. The fact that no .32-calibre bullet was found at the scene or in Long's body does not mean that one was not fired, however, and there is one report which says that two wounds on Long's body were indicative of entry and exit wounds caused by a .32-calibre bullet. Two of Long's bodyguards who were present later claimed Long was shot by accident and that Weiss' gun had been taken from his car and planted by his body after the shooting. It is also significant that insurance company investigators recorded Long's death as accidental, not murder, when they authorised the payment of $20,000 to his widow.

An autopsy carried out on Weiss' remains after he had been disinterred in 1991 showed that he had been shot from the front seven times, three times from the right, twice from the left, and twelve times from behind. The implication is that Weiss was killed in crossfire. According to ballistics expert Lucien C. Haag, a .38-calibre bullet found in Weiss' skull should have had enough energy to exit the skull indicating that it may well have passing through another body first. Damage to bones in Weiss' arms suggest that he was in a defensive posture with arms raised before him when he was shot.

*

By 1937 Roosevelt had recognised the dangers inherent in his New Deal programme. He acknowledged that it had given too much

Hiran Wesley Evans, Imperial Wizard of the Ku Klux Klan from 1922 to 1939

The Firebrand Radio Evangelist, Father Charles Coughlin

The radical Louisiana politician, Huey Long, who was murdered on 10 September 1935

Wanted poster for William Pelley

The Nazi Ignatz Theodor Griebl, a leading member of the Friends of New Germany

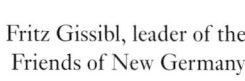

Fritz Gissibl, leader of the Friends of New Germany

Friends of New Germany Rally on 6 October 1935

The bootlegger and anti-Nazi battler Abner 'Longie' Zwillman

Anti-Semitic anti-Roosevelt handbill issued by the American White Guard in California.

Becky Poole holds one of her daughters. Her Catholic husband, Charley, was killed by the Black Legion vigilantes in 1936

Fritz Kuhn Leader of the German American Bund

Fritz Kuhn meets Adolf Hitler at the 1936 Olympic Games

American nazis marching down East 86th Street, New York on 30 October 1939

Young Bundists welcome the Camp Sigfried Special

Isadore Greenbaum beaten by stormtrooper at a German American Bund rally on 20 February 1939

Some of the 'Brooklyn Boys' charged with conspiracy on 5 April 1940

power to the capitalists. 'The liberty of a democracy is not safe if the people tolerate the growth of private power to a point where it becomes stronger than their democratic state itself. That is fascism... ownership of government by an individual, by a group, or by any other controlling power.'[23] The government saw that an explosion of cheap money was threatening to derail the whole New Deal programme and ordered the banks to double their reserves and so reduce the amount of money available in the economy. During the winter of 1937–38, unemployment rocketed back up to 20 per cent, industrial production fell by 32 per cent and the country was plunged into another financial crisis.

Neither was Roosevelt himself above criticism. He had tried and failed to add more justices to the US Supreme Court in an effort to obtain more support for New Deal legislation. His interventionist moves to raise taxes, expand the welfare state and increas regulation of the economy had long been bones of contention with conservatives while criticism from the left centred on the powers he had given to the capitalists to administer the New Deal policies. The most damning criticism, however, was his bid for a third presidential term which broke with the precedent set by George Washington. He would go on to win a fourth election in 1944 shortly before his death. He was not the first to try for a third term, however, but the first to succeed. In 1944, the Republican candidate, Thomas Dewey, said a potential 16-year term for Roosevelt was a threat to democracy. In a speech in Buffalo on 31 October 1944, he said, 'four terms or sixteen years is the most dangerous threat to our freedom ever proposed.' In February 1951, the 22nd Amendment to the US constitution said 'No person shall be elected to the office of the President more than twice, and no person who has held the office of President, or acted as President, for more than two years of a term to which some other person was elected President shall be elected to the office of the President more than once.' Since then, there have been attempts to repeal it but none has got very far.

Chapter 5

FATHER CHARLES COUGHLIN

> It is his aim to replace the American democracy with a regime patterned after Hitler's Germany.
> Samuel Dickstein[1]

One man most often associated with fascism in America in the 1930s was the 'silver-tongued [and] golden-voiced' Catholic priest, Charles Edward Coughlin.[2] Between the years 1926 and 1942 he was a man with significant political power in the United States. He would become the first American demagogue to achieve international fame through the medium of his radio broadcasts. His 'Golden Hour of the Shrine of the Little Flower' and his incendiary weekly newspaper *Social Justice* reached tens of millions of homes railing against the political elite with a message describing American society as being controlled by 'atheistic Marxists [and] international financiers'. His coded anti-Semitism blamed Jews for everything from the Great Depression to the Second World War. He was the first of what would become a long line of media evangelists with his heady brew of religion, politics and entertainment. Millions of confused and discontented Americans, suffering the effects of economic hardship, tuned into his broadcasts every week comforted by his reassuring words and promises of better things to come. By exploiting his status and popularity, he formed a grassroots lobbying movement called the National Union for Social Justice (NUSJ) and then later transforming it into a political party which he called the Christian Front.

Like Pelley's Silver Shirts, Coughlin and his followers would become some of the most violent anti-Semites of the Great Depression era. While Pelley's mobs had counted among their number many violent Ku Klux Klan activists and thousands of nonviolent sympathizers, Coughlin's Christian Front would be seen to include one of the most organized alleged terrorist cells of the decade. Both Pelley and Coughlin hid behind a cloak of religion to shield their real purpose which was the violent overthrow of the democratically elected government.

Civil unrest was in the air in July 1932 as the economic downturn started to bite deep into American society. The government had been rocked by the 40,000-strong Bonus Army that had momentarily occupied the lawn outside the White House before being driven off by tanks and their camps burned to the ground. The out-of-work war veterans, many of whom were American Legionnaires, and their families had come to Washington to demand cash redemption of their service bonus certificates and were fired on by the police for their trouble. Two died from gunshot wounds.

The nation was threatened, Coughlin said, by an insidious conspiracy of international bankers and world communism. He called for 'a re-awakened America…that stands 100 per cent for Americanism, an America that will have no patience either with Nazism or Communism [an America that stands for] Christian nationalism.'[3] The necessary reforms to realise this were many and not particularly revolutionary in themselves but each seemed to address the concerns of a number of different segments of public opinion which gave it wide appeal.

Born in Hamilton Ontario in October 1891, Coughlin's ultimate political ambitions would be thwarted by his Canadian birth. Brought up by a doting overprotective mother, Coughlin was a mediocre student but he graduated from the University of Toronto and went on to be ordained as a Catholic priest in the Basilican Order on 29 June 1916. Coughlin later became assistant pastor at St. Augustine's Church in Kalamazoo in 1923. Returning from a visit to Rome he was assigned the unenviable task of building a Catholic church at Royal Oak, a northern suburb of Detroit, in the heart of KKK territory, an area noted for anti-Catholic sentiments. Named in honour of St. Thérèse de Lisieux, this Shrine of the Little Flower was to be 'a missionary oasis in the desert of religious bigotry'.[4]

Funded by a $100,000 loan, a brown-shingled wooden church was built on an empty plot in 1926 which, despite serving a parish of little more than two dozen families, had a seating capacity of 600. Repaying the loan with such a small congregation was one of the first great challenges of Coughlin's professional life. He found himself barely able to survive except for charitable food donations from his pitifully small congregation. Then he hit on the ruse of inviting the Detroit Tigers and

New York Yankees baseball teams to attend mass and when a crowd of thousands turned up to see them, the famous and hugely popular Babe Ruth took change of the collections which brought in some $10,000. Coughlin also made a point of ingratiating himself with local motor car manufacturers Fred and Lawrence Fisher who became significant financial supporters of the Shrine. Another important contact he made at the exclusive Detroit Athletic Club was the ultra-right-wing Eddie Rickenbacker, a First World War Flying Ace and investor in a radio station Radio WJR that was housed in the 'Golden Tower' building owned by the Fisher brothers. Coughlin now came up with an idea that was to be the making of him.

He had sufficient confidence in his own ability as a preacher to ask his Bishop Michael Gallagher for permission to approach George A. (Dick) Richards, the 'tyrannical and terrifying ruddy-faced entrepreneur with an imperious style of management' who owned Radio WJR, with a view to making radio broadcasts. The broadcaster was struggling to survive hanging on by virtue of an advertising contract with Richards' Buick dealership. Coughlin and Richards hit it off straight away and soon gained a reputation as a 'bawdy and fun-loving pair' whose 'locker-room expletives' aften left onlookers shocked.[5]

Coughlin's radio career began innocently enough with a weekly broadcast known popularly as 'The Children's Hour' in which he told biblical stories to children. When Coughlin made his first broadcast on 17 October 1926, he was by no means the first to give radio talks on religious subjects but his popularity meant that he was the first to become a regular contributor. Within weeks he was offering the first broadcasts of Catholic religious services and 'stood on the brink of a new career, one for which there were no precedents and no rules of conduct'.[6]

To a very great extent, Coughlin created an electronic congregation of millions in which each listener felt a personal bond between them and the voice on the radio. His popularity soared due in no small part to his

> voice of such mellow richness, such manly, heart-warming confidential intimacy, such emotional and ingratiating charm, that anyone tuning past it almost automatically returned to hear it again.... Warmed by the touch of Irish brogue, it lingered over words and enriched their emotional content. It was a voice made for promises... A beautiful baritone ... his range was spectacular. He always began in a low rich pitch, speaking slowly, gradually increasing in tempo and vehemence, then soaring into high and passionate tones.... His diction was musical, the effect authoritative[7]

Listeners were enrolled into membership of the Radio League of the Little Flower for a dollar per person per broadcast and were assured of remembrance in the daily Mass offered at Calvary Hill Jerusalem. As an example of Coughlin's unique approach to fund-raising, deceased persons could also be enrolled for the same price. Coughlin's biographer Donald Warren writes that 'the dollars flooded in and were carried in gunnysacks over to the bank.'[8] Those who did not have radios were kept updated by those amongst their family and friends who had. Almost imperceptibly, religion began to meld with politics in his weekly talks and Coughlin's personal opinions took centre stage. With a backing of soothing organ music, and spiritual discourse, he started attacking left-wing politicians he didn't like. When the Great Crash of 1929 sent the economy spiralling downwards, Coughlin's audience turned to him for comfort and reassurance in a world where individuals felt abandoned and isolated and no longer trusted the government to look after their interests.

Despite his enormous popularity, Coughlin became frustrated that he could not ground his philosophy on a specific foundation. He was drawing enormous energy from his audience but needed to redirect it to be able to feel its total power. The answer came to him on the first day of the new decade when he railed against the Soviet Union for abolishing the trappings of Christmas. He saw that the menace of atheistic communism threatening the basic customs and traditions of Christian festivals and belief brought together the various themes of his rhetoric into a single message of a nation facing the corruption and degradation of its cherished values of family life. His paranoid political tirades were now called 'The Hour of Power' and in them he began to appeal to the basest fears and hatreds of his audience. He had even won over many KKK members to his side.

The 'purple poison of Bolshevism' was now the rallying call and the response was overwhelming. Mail and money poured in to protect America from what his audience perceived as a Moscow-funded communist-inspired social revolution. Within weeks, Coughlin was asked to give testimony to the House Special Committee to investigate Communist Activities in the United States. Often referred to as the Fish Committee, this body was looking into both Nazi and communist domestic infiltration. 'I think by 1933, unless something is done, you will see a revolution in this country,' Coughlin told them. Then, bizarrely, he went on to tell reporters outside that 'there is a movement [threatening] to take down our Stars and Stripes and put up an international flag ... and that movement is headed by Mr. Henry Ford.'[9] This latter swipe at Ford as a supporter of communism was apparently because he had contracted to build tractors for the Soviet Union.

One year later, Coughlin delivered what proved to be one of his most significant talks blaming 'international financiers' which by now had become a euphemism for Jewish bankers and the 'Hebrew' Karl Marx for the Wall Street Crash. It had been the Treaty of Versailles with its crippling reparations imposed on Germany that had flooded money markets in the United States and led to low interest rates, irresponsible borrowing, stock market speculation and inevitable economic catastrophe. The response was almost overwhelming. A small army of almost 100 clerks were needed to cope with all the mail that was cascading into his church. Panic seemed to spring up in both the Catholic Church and the government. Huge political pressure was now put on Coughlin to drop his political diatribes and stick to religion. CBS who broadcast his talks made it clear that if he did not comply, they would take his weekly talks off the air.

If it was indeed pressure from the White House that forced CBS to censure Coughlin it would seriously rebound on them. Within a very short time, Coughlin had set up a network of his own radio stations all across the east coast and the mid-west. His broadcast on 12 February 1932 was a direct attack upon the personal integrity of President Hoover calling him 'the banker's friend, the Holy Ghost of the rich, the protective angel of Wall Street'.[10] Indeed, Coughlin boasted that his criticism of Hoover was a contributing factor towards the ending of his presidential career.

Franklin Roosevelt had been Governor of New York when he had correspondence with Coughlin over the CBS affair but was now the Democratic candidate to challenge Hoover for the presidency. It was suggested that he might want to reach out to the huge numbers of Catholic listeners of Coughlin's radio shows but he was warned that the priest was 'difficult to handle and might be full of dynamite'.[11] The two men met in the spring of 1932 when Coughlin seemed willing to support Roosevelt's campaign but Roosevelt could see that Coughlin would need to be treated with some circumspection.

Coughlin addressed the Democratic National Convention in Chicago with a ringing endorsement of Roosevelt and assured the candidate that he would work with him 'in harmony'. The arrangement worked well and Roosevelt duly won the election but Coughlin had got carried away with his own importance and now felt that he could give the new president advice on how to run the country. His broadcasts began to contain veiled hints that he was now an important member of Roosevelt's advisory team. He boasted to his friends that he had helped to write the inaugural presidential address. Evidence suggests that Roosevelt, unwilling to alienate Catholic voters, publicly tolerated Coughlin, who was a frequent visitor to the White House, but privately found him a nuisance and took little notice of his opinions and suggestions.

If the White House thought that they could just potter along with this charade, keeping Coughlin's audience on their side with no price to pay, they were soon disabused of that notion. Coughlin's arrogance and self-importance drew him into a very public dispute over a looming crisis concerning the Guardian Trust, a large Detroit Bank, that was having serious liquidity problems. In his 26 March address, Coughlin called the banking community a 'den of forty thieves'. The banking newspaper *Detroit Free Press* retaliated by claiming that Coughlin's slanderous accusations were exacerbating the problem.[12]

The war of words broke out of its confines a few days later when the newspaper went on the offensive with a front-page article accusing Coughlin's Shrine of the Little Flower of using donations sent in by the millions of listeners to gamble on the stock market. 'The "sinister insidiousness of the radio" it claimed was undermining civilisation with "poison" from all manner of "evil". Coughlin was quick to play the martyr. He accused the banks of plotting to jam his radio broadcasts but his next one went ahead as planned to blame the *Detroit Free Press* of persecuting him for having "dared to defend the poor". With commendable modesty, he said, "I have done less by far than the patient, loving Master Who scourged the moneychangers from the temple. ... Whom they crucified because the high priests of compromise framed Him with fake witness."[13]

During a Congressional hearing on the banking crisis, Coughlin was called on to testify. He framed his testimony in such a way as to suggest that he had been given privileged information by 'reliable sources in Washington' concerning the banks financial position. He infuriated ex-President Hoover by dragging his name into it, suggesting that it had been his lack of financial acumen that had contributed to the crisis over the Guardian Trust in the first place. Neither was Roosevelt's administration happy that Coughlin had implicated them but they tried to keep out of it not wanting to alienate Coughlin's supporters.

The dispute had given Coughlin even more publicity and introduced him to a nation-wide audience as a defender of the poor but eventually the invective subsided and the dispute faded away. It was not all good news for Coughlin, however. The accusations of misusing funds had done harm to his reputation and there was a lingering suspicion that he had been set up by Roosevelt to attack the banking community that was lukewarm about presidential plans for reviving the economy with a massive injection of public funds.

Coughlin now used his newfound status to give the nation the benefit of his opinion about all manner of political issues. He attacked the Treasury Secretary Henry Morgenthau Jnr. for protecting 'Federal reserve bankers and international bankers of ill repute' over a debate about abandoning the gold standard.

In 1913 the gold standard had been built into the framework of the Federal Reserve and the law required the Federal Reserve to hold gold equal to 40 per cent of the value of the currency it issued and to convert those dollars into gold at a fixed price of $20.67 per ounce of pure gold. The Federal Reserve, therefore, needed a stock of free gold sufficient to satisfy redemption requests that might occur in the near future. It could increase the stock of free gold by increasing interest rates, which encouraged Americans to deposit in banks and encouraged foreigners to invest in the United States. This took money out of the economy causing deflation.

During the financial crisis of 1933 there was a drain of gold out of the Federal Reserve, some of it flowing to foreign nations who feared a devaluation of the dollar. In March 1933, the Federal Reserve Bank of New York suffered such outflows that it could no longer honour its commitment to convert currency to gold. In the summer of 1933, Roosevelt suspended the gold standard and, in the autumn, devalued the dollar. It was hoped that this reflation of the economy would reduce debt levels and stimulate business activity. Then in 1934, Roosevelt signed the Gold Reserve Act which transferred ownership of all monetary gold in the United States to the US Treasury and prohibited the Treasury and financial institutions from redeeming dollars for gold.

Coughlin's criticism of Roosevelt's Treasury Secretary jolted the president into a public rebuke by saying he resented Coughlin's interference. The febrile relationship between the two men was reaching breaking point. When Coughlin later went on the record claiming that he had White House backing for an attack on those who opposed the president's monetary policy, he had clearly gone too far. Roosevelt's people now saw Coughlin as 'an awkward, imbalanced, and even seriously unsettling threat' to the administration. 'Who the hell does he think he is?' was Roosevelt's personal reaction.[14]

Coughlin thought he was the answer to the nation's problems. Government must turn to the teachings of Christ, he said, and listed sixteen principles of social justice some of which would require enormous government investment and administration. Apparently without recognising the contradiction, at the same time he opposed

Big Government which he said would lead the nation to fascism. It was his first dig at Roosevelt's New Deal and was not going to do much to heal the rift with the president. He realised that his stand was creating problems for the administration, but he believed that he was still an important adviser and personal friend of the president and gambled that the relationship would survive.

When it eventually dawned on Coughlin that he did not have as much sway as he thought, he reacted not by toning down his rhetoric but by stepping up his challenge to the nation's highest office holder. He would force the president to take notice of him and take on board at least some of his suggestions. Believing that he could count on the support of his loyal radio audience, he set up a new organisation, the National Union for Social Justice, based upon his sixteen principles, many of which were little more than exhortations rather than strands of policy. 'It is our intention to drive out of public life the men who promised us redress ... and have broken their promises,' he said. It was not so much a political party in its early manifestation, more a mass-movement pressure group.

Apparently Roosevelt was one of those he was referring to when, on 27 January 1935, he used his radio pulpit to accuse him of 'selling out the American people to the international bankers'. His address resulted in 40,000 letters being received by the Senate in opposition to Roosevelt's move to admit the United States to the World Court, a move that Coughlin said would lead to another war. When the vote came, Roosevelt suffered a humiliating defeat. Coughlin exulted in the following week's address, 'through the medium of the radio and the telegram you possess the power to override the invisible government.' Isolationism, always a popular policy, was given a significant boost and made it much harder now for Roosevelt to engage with other democracies to oppose European fascism. Coughlin's triumph was now seen as 'a bigger menace to the President and our government than ever'.[15]

Coughlin, never one to underestimate his own potential, now started a campaign to have the Federal Reserve restructured. He addressed a crowd of 23,000 mostly young people, each of whom paid fifty cents entrance fee, at Madison Square Garden on 22 May 1935 in which he claimed to be reviving 'the meaning of democracy as it was conceived by the fathers of this country'. He sent a warning to the Washington lobby of United States Steel Corporation, of the motor industry, the United States Chamber of Commerce and the American Association of Bankers 'whose feet clutter the steps of the White house and of the Capitol'.

The White House put out feelers to Coughlin to coax him back into a non-confrontational relationship. He seemed conflicted between haranguing the administration for two years of failure to challenge business and financial lobbies and a deep-rooted conviction that Roosevelt was the only salvation for the country. 'I support him today and I will support him tomorrow,' he said but, at the same time, warned his radio audience that the New Deal would result in a dictatorship.

By the end of the summer however, Coughlin's mood swings had seemed to settle on the side of hostility to the president. He called the New Deal 'un-American' and when he accused the President of breaking his promises, reconciliation seemed unlikely. Without saying as much, Coughlin was hinting that he may not support Roosevelt for re-election in 1936 and he now had a fellow Irish Catholic ally in Joseph P. Kennedy who headed the New Deal Securities and Exchange Commission. Roosevelt invited Coughlin and Kennedy to his private residence, Hyde Park, to clear the air but Coughlin had got a new financial backer, Francis Keelon whom he had met on an ocean voyage in 1932 and was on the point of forming a third political party. The Hyde Park meeting was the last opportunity that the two men would have to mend fences and they failed to take advantage of it.

Keelon was a self-made millionaire. His sister Joanna admitted to being afraid of his angry demeanour. She also told of meetings at Keelon's house where Jews were denigrated, Hitler was praised and a German flag was draped over the table. Often, she said, Keelon and Coughlin would be too drunk to make it to the local church to celebrate mass and so had a makeshift altar installed in the house.[16]

The country could no longer ignore European fascism and the press was starting to fill many column inches with discussion of how the threat of it was spreading to the shores of America. In 1936 American newspapers were full of stories about Nazis in America. If the facts did not quite match up to the sense of outrage that the press was trying to engender, then a little exaggeration of numbers of people involved was acceptable to meet circulation targets. It had been enough to see the emergence of the McCormack-Dickstein Committee. The main thread of articles was the extent to which organisations within the US were controlled from Germany. Hitler had been acutely aware of the negative aspects of widespread disapproval of foreign interference but this had not held the German Foreign Institute back to any noticeable extent. The exact degree of cooperation between the DAI and FONG is difficult to ascertain given that many German records did not survive the war and the German American movements had such poor administration and record-keeping.

In his 1936 book *The Coming American Fascism*, Lawrence Dennis argued that only a disciplined centralised state could challenge the collectivisation of the economy under the New Deal. He singled out Coughlin and his NUSJ as being the common banner around which the masses could unite in a fascist revolution to correct the trend towards Socialism. General Hugh Johnson took to the airwaves to defend the New Deal saying that Coughlin's approach made him and Hitler look like two peas in a pod except that Coughlin replaced the swastika with a cross. There followed a prolonged contest played out over the radio between the two sides in which many of Coughlin's supporters began to see him in a different light.

His hectoring broadcasts now made him sound more like the leader of an unruly mob. Even his friends began to criticise his stance by saying that his 'one-man organization [was] subject to the same personal dictation as Hitler's Nazis and Mussolini's Fascists.'[17] Coughlin defended himself but it was quite true to say that he had dictatorial powers over the NUSJ and when he said to Congress that 'I foresee a revolution' it was becoming hard for his audience to go along with him.

At its height the NUSJ boasted four million members but as the election of 1936 neared, Roosevelt still appeared to have enough support to retain the presidency with the only attacks that threatened to hurt his chances being from those who believed that he had extended federal power beyond its proper and constitutional limits.

The Catholic Church in America had also grown frustrated with Coughlin's blending of anti-Semitism and anti-communism with traditional Catholic theology. They were especially concerned with the violent outbursts against Jews and communists all across the East Coast states and his veiled praise of fascism as 'a little brown pill [that] banished unemployment, limited profits for the industrialists, liquidated debts and capitalistic exploitation'.[18] Communism, Coughlin said, was just one of the manifestations of the 'mystical body of Satan' which was his way of referring to Jews. He continued to attract huge crowds wherever he spoke. In Cleveland, 17,000 packed two halls and a theatre with the overflow blocking the street outside. In St. Paul, Minnesota, 8,000 turned out to hear him. Philip Cortelyou Johnson had also been drawn to Coughlin and acted on his behalf as a campaign organiser. Of one rally in Chicago, Johnson said that Soldier's Field had a picture of Coughlin 'sixty feet high' and it was so crowded that you couldn't move. The police, many of whom were of Irish descent, gave Coughlin a fanfare of sirens. When he spoke it was a thrill like Hitler. Johnson said, 'it was so intoxicating...the yelling and screaming'.[19]

The possibility of Coughlin running for president became an everyday subject of discussion in the press until someone pointed out that his Canadian birth ruled that out completely. That did not mean, however, that Coughlin did not have a part to play in the forthcoming election. Rumour was rife that he would form a third political party and speculation abounded over who would back him. Even if he didn't do that his influence was so great that both Republicans and Democrats were desperate for his endorsement. While his criticisms and support for individual policies of both parties left his members unsure which he supported, one thing was perfectly clear. Coughlin was now a bitter critic of the White House incumbent. Never enthusiastic about a third party, Coughlin revelled in the role of the maverick, above the grubby discourse and free of the responsibilities he would be burdened with as a political leader.

Coughlin's opposition to Roosevelt's New Deal brought him closer to the reactionary American Liberty League who had previously been the target of his most acerbic criticism at a time when he had been one of Roosevelt's most enthusiastic supporters. At the same time, Coughlin had chosen to flirt with the Republican candidate and former president Herbert Hoover whose party he now lauded as 'the only hope for saving America'.[20] Hoover's adviser, however, warned that getting close to Coughlin was like playing with nitro-glycerine but still they circled in the hope of gaining political advantage without incurring electoral damage. Secret meetings were held between Coughlin and Hoover

Another headache for Roosevelt was the prospect of Coughlin picking up the support of the man who had taken over leadership of Huey Long's political constituency after Long's death. This was one of Long's former bodyguards, the ordained Protestant preacher Gerald A.L. Smith described by the American journalist H.L. Mencken as 'the greatest rabble-rouser since Peter the Hermit ... the gustiest and goriest, the loudest and the lustiest, the deadliest and damndest ever heard on this or any other earth.'[21]

For a time, Roosevelt feared that Smith might forge an alliance with Father Coughlin and together they would harness the rural southern and urban Catholic vote in opposition to his presidency. He had little to fear, however, because Coughlin was wary of getting involved with Smith, a man he called a viper and a leech. There was a moment, however, when it seemed that a third man, Dr Francis E. Townsend, a sixty-something mild mannered physician, would be the catalyst that fused their ambitions. Townsend had proposed an Old Age Revolving

Pension Fund that would give everyone over the age of sixty a $200 per month pension to be paid for by a 2 per cent national sales tax.

The three men came together and formed the Union Party better known now as the Stop Roosevelt Party but, although they held common values or social issues, the differing characters of the three men made working together a fraught and tiresome issue. Coughlin had reversed his stance on the formation of a third party and now fully endorsed William Lemke as the Union Party candidate in the 1936 presidential election. Lemke was described as the face of middle-class America which did not endear him to Smith who saw him as completely devoid of charisma. Smith on the other hand, at a convention in Cleveland had the crowd in raptures. They stood and roared approval as, Bible in hand, he 'roared words of hate about Wall Street bankers [and] the New Deal social engineers'.[22] When Coughlin came to the rostrum straight after Smith it was clear that his voice, that had such force through the intimacy of radio, lacked Smith's power to move a live audience. While Roosevelt privately believed that the Union Party leadership would split over irreconcilable personal differences, he was not willing to take any chances and worked assiduously to undermine support for Coughlin in particular.

Coughlin was also losing the support of those who had been drawn to him because of his earlier support for Roosevelt and the New Deal and who now were not willing to make the same about-face that their leader had done. Aware of this, Coughlin toned down his personal criticism of Roosevelt portraying him as a victim of atheistic and communist advisers in his administration. The Lemke campaign itself lacked resources as much of the $700,000 kitty raised to finance the presidential campaign was being diverted for NUSJ use.[23]

When the votes were counted, the Union Party failed to get a single Congressional seat and overall polled 892,000 votes. Coughlin would call the Union Party campaign a 'horrible mistake'. He felt personally betrayed by his millions of listeners who had failed to turn out and vote for Lemke and declared that American government was now 'a one-party system'. 'When an upstart dictator in the United States succeeds in making this a one-party form of government, 'he said, 'when the ballot is useless, I shall have the courage to stand up and advocate the use of bullets.'[24] He went on the radio and declared the Union party defunct, but he would recover from his temporary setback and re-emerge with the support of a large number of members of Congress as well as that of the Vice-President John Nance Garner. He was far from being a spent force.

Chapter 6

BERLIN TAKES A FRESH APPROACH

> Why were intelligent men, considerable funds and energy employed on something as vainglorious and nonsensical as Deutschtum.[1]

Heinz Kloss was a young scholar who had been employed by the DAI in Stuttgart before the Nazis came to power. While he may have paid lip service to them after January 1933, he retained a strongly academic and cultural approach to his studies. Most of his work involved research into the historical background to German language, population and migration. He was to become one of the most important figures in disseminating the *Deutschtum* propaganda and in gathering information within the German American sections of the US He was by profession a historian of the new *Volksgeschichte* school. Born in 1904, he had studied economics at the University of Halle before joining the *Deutsche Akademie* (German Academy). His particular interest was in developing *Volkstumspolitik*, the folk-related propaganda emphasising historical and cultural links between Germany and the US In one sense he set out to show the important part played by Germans in the development of American society. In this, he applied a methodology developed by the *Volksgeschichte* historical school which included cartography, linguistics, statistics and anthropology to emphasise common heritage through 'blood' rather than nationality. Under the guise of research, his scholarly background gave legitimacy to his activities which were essentially aimed at reminding German Americans of their heritage as a means of binding them closer to the Reich.

When the Nazi Party came to power and looked across the Atlantic they had little idea about how their future relations with the US would play out and consequently had no explicit policy towards that country. All they had was a vague notion of a racially mixed society that had yet to define its national characteristics. Hitler's personal opinion was that it was a nation that would not overly concern itself with European politics but the various German communities in the US were considered to have played an equally important part in building up that country as had the British and it was necessary to remind and 'educate' German Americans about that. The problem for the Nazis was that the first German settlers in the late seventeenth century had been escaping from religious persecution and economic hardship and had tended to congregate in isolated groups of different regional backgrounds and religious groupings. Added to this separation of identities, the Germans had been one of the most enthusiastic ethnic groups in adapting to the ethos of Americanism. This was not surprising since the German nation had itself not come into existence until after the Franco-Prussian War of 1871. Before that, the German people had been just a collection of more than thirty Principalities. As a propaganda exercise, Germany had tried to remind German Americans of their 'blood ties' to Germany during the First World War which, after the US entered the war, had the opposite effect and tended to widen the gap.

This lesson was completely ignored by the Nazis who were entirely convinced by their own propaganda that 'blood ties' were the driving factor in defining a person's identity and claiming a personal loyalty. When the first post-war migration wave from Weimar Germany washed over the US it included many ardent Nazis who brought with them a strong affinity for this concept and naturally, when called upon to remind German Americans of their heritage, it was the doctrine of Nazism that they promulgated. When the Nazis took political control of Germany in January 1933 it was this small group of fanatics who clamoured to be acknowledged as the official Nazi movement in the US.

When FONG was formed in April 1933 it had been given accreditation by the NSDAP and pursued policies strongly associated with Nazi policies in Germany. It became known for its militancy and strong public presence excluding German Jews from its membership and organising a boycott of Jewish businesses in the US Its propaganda, which was notably aggressive, was supplied directly by Bohle's *Abteilung für Deutsche im Ausland*. This did not go down at all well with the US State Department who objected in the strongest terms to the involvement of German diplomats in activities organising German citizens on US soil. Many of the German diplomats, who had no affection for the Nazis, were actually embarrassed to find themselves embroiled in the dispute. They urged Berlin to modify its approach and tone down some of FONG's more aggressive and militant activities.

Berlin had become disillusioned with FONG after the Spanknöbel fiasco and the Gissibl-Schnuch affair and saw its ambitions to rally support for the NSDAP in the US under threat from the McCormack-Dickstein investigations. They desperately needed to improve their image in the eyes of the American public but they were now facing a hostile press on top of everything else. Naturally, Hess and Bohle did not want to lose the support that they had gained through FONG membership but needed to re-channel that into a more credible, more biddable, and less controversial movement.

Pressure was building from all sides for change or the whole movement risked crumbling into irrelevance despite evidence that there was still widespread support across the country. The German Consul General in New York, Hans Borchers, and the German ambassador in Washington, Hans Luther, were well placed to influence events and it was their view that FONG should be abandoned and all relations between Berlin and the US should go through the Embassy. Their experience of contact with German American communities convinced them that political propaganda should be replaced by an emphasis on cultural links. The 'melting pot' of American society was subjected to endless pressure for its various national groupings to abandon their cultural roots and become first and foremost Americanised. Borchers especially argued that bonds between German communities and their ancestral homeland should be strengthened by diverting funding from FONG into a concerted effort to revive German *kultur* and to foster a nostalgia for *Heimat* through art, film, theatre and lecture tours. From this would naturally follow a more sympathetic view of Nazism as nothing more menacing than a movement designed to reclaim Germany's place at the top table of nations.

Even though the relationship between FONG and Berlin was weakening by the day, Bohle tried to limit contact with its leaders but, at the same time, decided to take a closer look at its organisation and operation to see how best to develop it into a more useful entity possibly under a different guise and, crucially, under new leadership. The *Auswärtiges Amt* was almost ready to ditch FONG completely, but Bohle still believed that it had a part to play if properly controlled and he gave it one last chance. He chose for a fact-finding mission a relatively minor official Gustav Moshack, who had been in charge of the DAI America Department since 1933. The DAI had been set up in 1917 as little more than a card index of Germans abroad but had quickly turned into a research centre and information depository with the explicit purpose of maintaining contact with German emigrants, especially those from southwestern Germany. In the 1920s it had functioned as an agency that aided emigrants with information about work opportunities and German communities abroad but under the Nazis the organisation was greatly expanded and became an important source of information coming back in the opposite direction about political and economic conditions in foreign countries.[2]

Moschack made annual trips to the US which allowed him to set up a number of businesses under the auspices of the DAI and to build up a considerable range of contacts with official German bodies and German American communities in places such as Chicago, St. Louis, Pittsburgh, and Milwaukee. His objective was to bring together the many disparate German American groups under some sort of collective leadership that would take political guidance from the DAI in Stuttgart. Such leadership, he believed should be firmly rooted in the US with people who understood American culture and politics. Although the Steuben Society appeared to be well placed to take on this role, it was clear that it was too resistant to Nazi ideology to be of use.

Reports from German diplomats in US cities gave the DAI encouragement that there was scope for wide dissemination of Nazi doctrine. The consuls in New Orleans and Texas wrote of a pride felt by Germans there in the resurgence of Germany as a European power but it was difficult to channel that emotion into constructive measures that might further the Nazi cause. It was not possible to fire up these long-established communities with talk of the iniquities of Versailles, of which they had little knowledge and much less understanding. It was felt that perhaps greater emphasis should be placed on giving German Americans a better understanding of social and doctrinal developments in Germany taking place in the present time through a more sympathetic American press. There was opposition to this softer approach within the DAI, however, where it almost seemed as if there was a blind ignorance of the American scene when formulating policy. They deliberately chose to ignore much of the advice that it was given and allowed its intellectual efforts to be diverted from truth to fantasy in order to ingratiate itself with Nazis such as Gissibl, Schuster and Kappe who had so much influence in the dictation of policy.[3]

Approaches by the DAI to colleges associated with the German Protestant Church to distribute a document entitled German Youth in a Changing World were met with a mixed response. Less than half of the institutions bothered to reply. Their next approach was to support candidates for public office who were sympathetic to Germany, but this required hard cash which was in short supply during an economic depression. Moshack was also bluntly told that if he wanted rural Germans to respond to *Deutschtum* any delegates he sent to reach out to them should have a better understanding of local feelings and a more sympathetic willingness to listen rather than simply come along and deliver lectures on Nazism. In Pennsylvania, it was planned to open a research centre to gather information about how to galvanise the German Americans there.

*

When Goebbels was appointed to head the newly formed Ministry of Public Enlightenment and Propaganda (RMVP), he gained control over virtually every form of mass media in Germany. 'The national education of the German people,' he wrote in his diary, 'will be placed in my hands.' Going beyond his primary task of moulding the culture and public opinion of the German people, he saw the need to spread his message overseas, particularly to the US His strategy was, first of all, to broadcast a positive image of Nazi Germany to get the support of German-Americans and, in the event of war, to discourage them becoming involved.

One of the areas in which he saw great potential to disseminate Nazi propaganda was within American universities. The US government was also keenly aware of this potential and its inherent dangers for the country especially in the part played by student exchange programmes. John C. Metcalfe, who conducted undercover investigations into the activities of German American organisations, said of them that 'American students are being indoctrinated with the aims of fascism in Germany both abroad and at home to the detriment of democratic institutions in America.'[4]

At the end of 1933, Columbia University President Nicholas Murray Butler invited Hans Luther, Germany's ambassador to the US to speak on campus. Over 1,000 students protested outside of the auditorium where Luther was to deliver his speech. Returning from a visit to Germany in the following year, Dean Thomas Alexander expressed his approval of the 'wonderful' Nazi programme of sterilization that was 'throwing out the criminals and other undesirables.'[5] Columbia actually had a self-confessed Nazi, Friedrich Ernest Auhagen, teaching the German language on campus.

Harvard University also gave a platform to the Nazi ideology. President James Bryant Conant invited prominent Nazi figures onto campus. On 27 May German ambassador Luther was met by Boston Jews and anti-fascist groups when he arrived in Boston harbour on the Nazi warship *Karlsruhe*. These protestors were attacked and indiscriminately arrested by a police force numbering almost 200, some on horseback and wielding clubs. An editorial published by the *Harvard Crimson* called the demonstrators 'discourteous' and defended the police action. Several Harvard faculty members attended a ceremony to honour the men of the *Karlsruhe* at a prominent hotel in Boston.[6] Afterwards the ship's crew called their welcome in Boston 'the friendliest of any port'.[7]

In October, the Harvard Debating Council held a mock trial of Adolf Hitler for his part in the Night of Long Knives massacre. A panel of five Harvard professors found Hitler guilty on only two of four charges. Any reference to Hitler's oppression of Jews was ruled out as irrelevant. German departments at the University of Wisconsin and the University of Minnesota warmly welcomed Hans Luther in 1935 but it must be said that these visits were strongly opposed by many students. When Dr. Richard Sallet addressed the Germanic Club at Yale in December 1934, he called Nazi Germany a 'people's fellowship' that was 'inherently pacifistic'.[8] There can be no doubt that such events aided Goebbels' programme of projecting a positive image of the Third Reich.

Pro-Nazi student organizations such as the Paul Reveres maintained at least an underground presence at almost every major college in America. Sometimes they worked directly with German agents to distribute Nazi propaganda. At the University of California, for example, one pamphlet created by the Paul Reveres urged readers to force Jews from their homes and cities, concluding with the statement, 'let us all be American Hitlers.'[9]

*

The concept of *Deutschtum* was not one that had been invented by the Nazis. They had simply taken this concept of a sense of racial kinship amongst Germans outside the Reich, kept alive through use of the mother tongue and contact with the homeland. It was no more than the application of an idea they had been taught at school and through the classic literature of their race but its application to German efforts to galvanise German American feelings towards Nazism had been seriously questioned. 'It is unfortunate,' writes Arthur L. Smith, Professor of History Emeritus at the California State University, Los Angeles, that 'Germany encouraged the development of institutes such as the DAI that found their prestige and glory in the promotion of Deutschtum.' Smith wonders why 'intelligent men, considerable funds and energy were employed on something as vainglorious and nonsensical as Deutschtum.'[10]

The egregious error made by the DAI in its use of *Deutschtum* was to view German Americans through the same lens as German communities in Volga Russia and Latin America. These people had emigrated to areas that were culturally underdeveloped relative to the country they had left. They had brought with them capital, knowledge and experience which allowed them to become established as an elite with little incentive to assimilate into the local culture. This was decidedly not the experience of Germans who emigrated to the US where moves to become Americanised carried no loss of prestige.

On his first visit in 1934, Moshack travelled all across America visiting the many small groups that were loosely affiliated with FONG and found, contrary to what he had been led to expect, that pro-Nazi sentiment was strong and growing especially on the west coast where the Los Angeles-based Germanic Bund was thriving under the leadership of Ernst Rheydt-Dittmar. Crucially, Gissibl had tried to force this group to amalgamate with FONG, but the group had resisted and called on Moshack to protect its independence. This he was unable to do without becoming an agent of decentralisation when it was in Berlin's interests to amalgamate the German American movement under central control to prevent further deterioration of US-German relations.

At the same time, Haegele, who had failed to unseat Gissibl, still controlled the splinter group BANS and pestered Moshack to recognise it as the group around which any new movement would be formed but Gissibl and Schnuch, while not exactly popular, were still Berlin's first choice. Moshack's snub of Haegele persuaded Gissibl to send Schnuch to Germany to plead his case in person. He met Moshack who had returned from his six-week trip and set out the case for Berlin to reignite its support of FONG under Gissibl's leadership. With no real alternative in sight, Moshack pleaded Gissibl's case to Bohle but it was felt that internal difficulties would never be resolved as long as Gissibl remained in charge.

Relations between FONG and the DAI remained at an impasse but Moshack was working on a way forward. His mission to the US had proved to him that internal friction within the German American movement had been very much confined to New York City and it was this localised conflict that had caught the attention of the American press giving the impression that the whole country-wide movement was in disarray. Even German diplomats in the US were getting fed up with the constant bickering and uncertainty that was giving the press such a clear opportunity to attack the movement and was threatening to sap the enthusiasm of the membership.

Conditioned now to finding their bullying strategies effective elsewhere, the Germans were taken aback by the strong messages coming back from the US and took a moment to reconsider. America could obviously not be treated with the same arrogant contempt as Poland. Berlin's first response was to call on FONG to disbar members who were still German nationals to prevent it from appearing to be a branch of the NSDAP in the US and give it the appearance of being an American movement. Of course this had consequences. FONG lost a large part of its membership and many of the more enthusiastic Nazis returned to Germany. A new strategy was desperately needed to compensate.

Hess and Bohle were confident that FONG would simply crumble and make way for a new movement to be built on its still solid foundations with a more Americanised character but Gissibl was not so easily outflanked. He had, for more than a year, ever since the Haegele attempted coup, been assiduously recruiting American nationals to FONG in a bid to appease Berlin and retain control. Meanwhile Berlin had increased its support for 'American' anti-Semitic and anti-communist groups such as Pelley's Silver Shirts and the White Shirts of Iowa led by C.F. Fulliam. To increase its understanding of attitudes within the German communities, they arranged through the consular service for the writer Karl Goetz, who had made a deep study of German immigration in the US, to cross America, meet and lecture to audiences in cities and small towns. He was greeted enthusiastically wherever he went. In places he lectured to audiences in their thousands but some of the organisations he addressed, whose roots went well back into the nineteenth century, had fewer than a hundred members. All in all, he found that pro-German sentiment was still strong but there was little support for the Nazi movement. He found two distinctly different categories of pro-German Americans. There were those German immigrants who had retained their cultural identities much in the same way that the Volga Germans had. They lived in distinct communities and maintained German-language schools and German churches and there were others who had arrived later and expressed their German identity through membership of groups such as FONG. His tour resulted in an increase in German literature to these groups and subsidised travel for some to visit Germany and was taken as an indication that German Americans had not altogether been abandoned by Berlin. Reporting back to Bohle, Goetz made it clear that if Germany wanted to press ahead with its initiative to influence American public opinion, it had no choice but to channel its efforts through what was left of FONG which was the only organisation with country-wide connections.

What was needed was a movement that shied away from overt political action and emphasised instead the common bonds of 'blood' between German Americans and their ethnic 'cousins' in the Reich. This would be achieved through cultural initiatives similar to the *Dante Alighieri Society* that the Italians had set up in the 1920s to achieve similar goals to those now being pursued by the Germans. Their ambition was to establish a new propaganda campaign based on cultural ideas that German Americans could identify with. Kloss was the man they chose as political adviser and chief propagandist.

In 1927 Kloss had joined the DAI and was sent to the US to work for nine months. When he returned he took up a post in the research section of the Stuttgart headquarters. He looked at history to find a definition of just what a 'German' identity meant using linguistics which informed the Nazi doctrine of 'blood and soil'. What was the essence of 'Germanness'? Hitler had made abundantly clear that he claimed unlimited sovereignty over Germans abroad, even those who were, by birth, citizens of another country. Clearly if Kloss was going to apply this criterion to the US, he was going to have to battle against an American lifestyle that was increasingly dominated by mass media advertising and was fundamentally modernist. If German Americans had given themselves over to urban living and a multi-cultural society there was little he could do to entice them back with talk of *Deutschtum*. Traditional German foods, music, arts and crafts were quaint but struggled to compete with a government and establishment that was determined to mould all the different ethnic groups into one and call it American. Only the 'folk islands' of rural America offered hope of getting a response to Nazi overtures based on cultural heritage. The Nazis at home had altered the focus of social science teaching in schools and universities to encourage people like Kloss who saw social responsibility to the Reich as the new standard and the way forward to rescue Germandom from the destitution of Versailles.

Bohle planned to build a new German American organisation that targeted the whole German American community, from the crumbling ruins of FONG and, crucially, one that was acceptable to the US government. This required someone with broad vision and a clear idea of how to project a combined political, cultural and social ethos touching all sections of German American society. Kloss seemed to be the ideal choice, but he fell into the same trap by failing to appreciate the power of the 'melting pot' of American culture to obscure ethnic roots. He was, however, acutely aware of the difficulty in appealing to that generation which had arrived before the First World War during which they were conflicted by divided loyalties after the US sent its forces to fight in France. Survival as much as anything had forced them to choose loyalty to their new country even as they retained the traditions and customs of the old. It was this group, however, that it was essential to bring on board to get the numbers and legitimacy that would overcome the stigma of Nazism that FONG had been burdened with.

Any new German American organisation was going to be comprised of purely American citizens to show that it was not a puppet of Berlin but, to fulfil its brief and ensure the continued support of the Nazis, it would also have to educate its members about the social and cultural benefits they would derive from their close association with the Reich. It would need nationwide appeal and break out of FONG's reliance on east coast membership. One way forward was suggested by the German ambassador to Washington, Hans Luther. He had twice been Chancellor in the Weimar Republic and no great friend to the Nazis. His proposal was to tread a careful path based upon traditional diplomacy that Germany had followed before 1933 but he was up against a Nazi ideologue, Karl Strölin, the one-time chairman of the DAI and now mayor of Stuttgart. Strölin laid out his much more political ideas in a 'Memorandum Concerning the Political Activation of the American-Germandom'. He called for a new organisation separate from any connections to any German political institution but one that was vigorous enough to assume leadership of all German American groups in the US This group would then be the channel through which all contacts between the Nazis and the German American community would pass. As an essential part of his proposal, someone would be sent to the US to establish an effective network of informants, take charge of cultural exchanges and strengthen the bonds between German American citizens and their wider families in Germany. His ambition was to ensure that the US would never again enter into a war against Germany.

Much of what was in Strölin's report had been influenced by the work of Kloss and his colleague, Otto Lohr so Kloss was the logical choice for the mission. He drew up a map of all the 'German language islands' in the US where the German language was still spoken and worked on ways of binding them culturally with urban German communities to create a strong racially conscious group. He was acutely aware that the German immigrants, one of the largest ethnic groups in the US had not left distinct traces in American culture in the same way the Irish and Italians had.

The next step would be to make the German Americans aware of the larger worldwide German community.

Kloss argued that all German people shared 'a common essence, which united them, and which was manifested in the traditions, folkways, crafts, language and relationships' but he was employing wishful thinking by overemphasising the importance of German American organisations and achievements.[11] It was essentially seen as a programme of education but on ideological grounds relying on fact but still, in essence, propaganda albeit of a more subtle kind. The Germanness with which this new US grouping was to be made aware of was very much formulated along Nazi Party lines. Assumptions that were sufficiently prevalent as to be deemed 'common knowledge' were used as a foundation for theories and 'scientific facts' whose very legitimacy to shape public opinion was therefore questionable. Special attention was to be given to US-born Germans and naturalised citizens who would be 'reminded' of their German heritage. Special bi-lingual schools would be set up along with a research institute, publication of periodicals and lecture tours by experts, the most important being Kloss himself.

Kloss's research focussed exclusively on German American history encapsulated in his *On the Unification of the Germandom in America* written in 1935. It must be said, however, that this research was conducted with a pre-determined outcome in mind – to justify existing ideology. Kloss laid out the historical background according to *Volksgeschichte* principles but in a non-political frame. It was richly documented and aimed at an academic audience. His arguments pointed to a perception that the German communities in the US had not been accorded sufficient status as should have been their right given their contribution to the development of the American nation. He ignored the fact that early German colonists had little reason to hark back to their homeland in many cases having fled to avoid persecution by the German state because of their religious beliefs and practices. He was encouraged, however, by evidence that showed the German communities in the US had retained strong German identity but had historically lacked leadership, something that the Nazis were now ready to provide. All this was to be done outside the provinces of other German American groups in whom the Nazis had lost all faith.

Kloss' next publication, *Ethnic Minority Rights in the United States* argued that 'Americanisation' was an artificial construct that could not overcome ethnic loyalties. He cited the example of independent Dutch communities in Pennsylvania as being similar to the *Grossvolksinsel* Volga-Germans in Russia. The US, he said, was more like a 'balkanised' entity rather than a nation which flew in the face of the evidence that Germans had been quickly assimilated into the larger society even in states such as Ohio, Pennsylvania, Texas and Indiana where German influences were strongest.

He reinforced his arguments by drawing maps showing large parts of the American continent as being 'mainly' German, but his methodology was often suspect. For instance, he based much of his conclusions on analysis of German-sounding names and particular Nazi definitions of what 'German blood' was. One of his most egregious errors was to equate the German Americans with the German communities in eastern Europe that had been separated from the Reich after Versailles. He assiduously avoided referring to German Americans as 'Americans of German descent' preferring always to call them simply 'Germans'.

For the German home market, Kloss published information booklets in a joint venture, *Publikationsstelle Übersee* sponsored by the German Foreign Office and the DAI. Data about 'German folk islands' was of paramount importance since it would be used to identify those areas where a recruitment drive for agents and informants would be most productive. There was still a vast infrastructure of German cultural life including stores, cinemas, churches, clubs, and restaurants, while newspapers and radio shows featured public debates about the future of the German community in America.

Chapter 7

THE GERMAN AMERICAN BUND

> The representatives of the German-American Volksbund ... see in the overpowering decision of the German *Volk* an expression of the unity between Government and *Volk* in which we recognize the most sublime form of true democracy.
> Fritz Kuhn

Hess's call for all German nationals to resign their membership of FONG was taken up as a reliable means of bringing the movement to heel given that most of its leadership fell into that category. Should they refuse to remove themselves, Berlin would revoke their passports and even revoke their German citizenship rendering them stateless. Seeing that Berlin was serious, Gissibl appealed to German diplomats in the US and threatened to take his case to Hess in person but was shocked by the response from an agency that had at one time been so supportive. Go to Germany, said Consul Werner Jaeger in Chicago, and you will end up in a concentration camp.

Gissibl had returned from a visit to Germany in late 1935 with a clear-eyed determination not to let ten years of his life's work go to waste. He had appointed himself *Bundsleiter* (federal leader) at the Philadelphia convention in September but it was clear that his time in charge of FONG was coming to an end and he needed to find a successor if the movement was not going to become redundant. The man who put himself forward for the role was Fritz Julius Kuhn, born in Munich on 15 May 15 1896 who had become a naturalised American citizen on 3 December 1934.

During the First World War, Kuhn had served with distinction for four and a half years in a Bavarian infantry unit as a machine gunner then, following Germany's surrender in November 1918, he made his way back to Munich where he joined a Freikorps company under the command of Major-General Ritter von Epp. The Friekorps spent much of their time street fighting with communists and were a natural stepping stone to membership of the NSDAP. Kuhn was quite an imposing figure at five feet eleven inches tall and weighing more than 200 pounds. In 1921 he entered the University of Munich where he studied chemical engineering after which he emigrated to Mexico leaving his wife, Elsa (née Walther) in Germany.[1] Once settled in Mexico, he brought his wife over from Germany and a daughter Waltraut was born there. He worked as a chemist for four years before moving to New York where his wife gave birth to a son, Walter, and then the family moved again, this time to Detroit where Kuhn found work at the Henry Ford Hospital as an X-ray technician. In the summer of 1933, he joined FONG and quickly rose through the ranks to become leader of the midwestern division where he first came to Gissibl's attention for his veteran status, university education, impressive organizational talents and fiery rhetoric. His major drawback, however, was his poor mastery of English which he spoke with a thick, halting accent making him an easy target for ridicule. His personal life might be described as chequered. He was variously called a great liar, a thief, a forger, an adulterous womanizer, a braggart, a lout, and a boor. He liked nightclubs, liked drinking, and liked the company of women other than the one he married.[2]

Berlin had placed the nationality condition on FONG to restrain it because the core of this group contained mostly recent immigrants many of whom had not yet applied for US citizenship, but it was a crude strategy. Kuhn had inherited a country-wide movement that was on the verge of dissolution and if he was going to have any future as its leader he was going to have to preserve its membership and organisation somehow. He chose to believe that it had not been the membership of FONG that had disturbed Hess and Bohle but Gissibl's leadership and he saw that the edict had been narrowly focused for the specific purpose of getting rid of him. The answer was as simple as the problem. Create a new organisation out of the old one, the membership of which would not be bound by the Hess edict.

With Berlin having taken its eye off the ball, he quietly formed a new offshoot of FONG called the German Consumer's Cooperative (*Deutsche Konsum Verband* DKV) and encouraged all FONG members who were German nationals to join this new organisation leaving only American citizens in FONG. DKV actually had no structure apart from a membership and was largely a deception. Once the DKV recruitment was complete, their membership was then transferred to another new organisation called the Prospective Citizen's League which was 'open to all Americans of Aryan blood, German extraction and good reputation.'[3] Essentially this was a mechanism to allow Bund membership to German nationals who had begun proceedings to acquire American nationality. To placate Berlin, however, he did stipulate that all leaders of the Bund had to be American citizens and to the American press, he said 'We have nothing to do with Germany. We have nothing to do with German ambassadors or the German consul here. We get no orders from Germany and have no connection whatsoever with the German Government.'[4]

Kuhn had for some months been *de facto* leader of the movement and had served as editor of its weekly *Deutscher Weckruf und Beobachter* (Wakening Call and Observer) paper in Brooklyn but it was not until 29 March 1936, in Buffalo, New York, when he stood on the stage draped with German and American flags and addressed the annual convention of what was the remnants of the FONG, that he officially launched a new organisation called the German American Bund (*Amerikadeutscher Volksbund*), usually referred to simply as the Bund. Membership was open to all who had joined the Prospective Citizen's League, which had, up to that point, maintained a discrete distance from the Bund and even had separate headquarters.

Kuhn insisted on the precise wording of the title of the new organisation to reflect the importance of German heritage. His voice, commanding and full of resonance, had many of the qualities required of a populist leader. He understood the damage that internal quarrels had done to his movement and assured the audience that he would bring all that to an end. 'We are first of all Germans by race, in blood, in language,' he said.[5] The constitution of the Bund stated that it would 'defend the mother country [Germany] against all ill-will from any source [and] remain worthy of our Germanic blood, our German motherhood [and] our German brothers and sisters.'[6] At its height, the Bund would go on to have sixty-nine local units in nineteen states, twenty-three units in New York alone. Bund literature emphasized that it had been white Gentiles who had been the original European immigrants who settled the American wilderness, built the cities, and established the form of government and that the Bund was ready to serve as an auxiliary force to assist the police in the event of a communist insurrection.

Kuhn now applied his rather good business brain to installing a financially secure structure by imposing a series of fees and membership dues ($9) to be paid on an annual basis. Attendance at meetings called for a small admission charge, membership badges had to be worn before entry was permitted and, of course, these had to be bought. Kuhn had adopted Nazi style titles for the Bund hierarchy. Beneath him were three *Gauleiters* (department heads) who ran the East, Midwest, and Western districts of the US As in the Nazi structure in Germany, these districts were then broken down into *Gebiete* (States), *Kreise* (counties), and *Ortsgruppen* (cities or towns). Nazi style uniforms and insignia were adopted.

While most members wore only civilian clothing with membership pins, Nazi style uniforms of tan shirts with black ties, trousers, and a black belt with cross strap and insignia were adopted by some members. Later, they also had the option of a tailored jacket for formal occasions. It was tan with black sleeve bands, black collar halves, and epaulettes. Membership pins were often attached to the tie, while any military awards earned while in the service of Germany could be worn on the left front breast pockets.

Though the Bund often used the standard Nazi red, white, and black swastika flag, they also developed their own flag of a white background with four black-outlined Maltese red cross arms centred by a gold and black towering swastika radiating from a dome-enclosed 'AV'. Membership pins copied this same radiating swastika symbol to produce a dramatic effect. The AV, Nazi, and American flags flew side by side at many of the Bund meetings, rallies, and open-air marches. It was Kuhn's friends who were given exclusive rights to manufacture and sell Bund flags, uniforms and badges. Owners of retail outlets could buy certificates of membership that were expected to increase their trade with the rank and file. Kuhn held a controlling interest in the hugely profitable A.V. Publishing Company in Yorkville that published all Bund newspapers and periodicals.[7]

He established various programmes, such as the German American Business League (*Deutsche Konsum Verband* DKV) and the German American Vocational League (*Deutsch Amerikansiche Berufsgemeinschaft*) which helped members to obtain purchasing discounts, sell products, train for, and locate better jobs. This was especially helpful for those first-generation immigrants and their children who had fallen on hard times at the end of the Great Depression.

Upon taking the leadership role, Kuhn quickly focused on local interests. He told members 'In national as in local politics our considerations of the political situation are based on two viewpoints...the purely American standpoint, as American citizens, and the standpoint as an organization bound to the German folk which is to engage in political activity favourable to the German fatherland.'[8] Bund member Gustav Elmer appearing before a New York committee investigating subversive activities in June 1938 said 'The purpose of the Bund was to build a great American movement of liberation under the swastika, the common symbol of Aryan nationalism.'[9]

*

Kuhn believed the most receptive to such a message were the young and it was here that he set out to combine German tradition with American culture. The cover of the Bund's publication Fighting Germanness (*Kämpfendes Deutschtum*) featured a swastika and an American flag alongside a picture of Kuhn meeting Adolf Hitler at the Olympics and inside was an article by Colin Ross claiming that those with German blood will lead the United States into a new era. The issue contained collections of poetry, songs, and articles about local activity around the United States. The articles highlighted youth activity at Camp Siegfried in Yaphank, Long Island.

Camp Siegfried was one of more than twenty youth camps opened where boys and girls could stay for $5 a week and were taught a special version of German history emphasizing the Aryan character of the German race and where they could be 'freed from the sinister influences of Jewish Americanisation...to be strengthened and confirmed in National Socialism so that they will be conscious of the role which has been assigned to them as the future carriers of German racial ideals to America.'[10] The camps closely followed the example of Baldur von Schirach's Hitler Youth camps. Activities included hiking, drilling and singing and when the young people marched past they were given the stiff arm Nazi salute by their leaders. Kuhn saw the indoctrination of the young as an essentially, if not *the* essential, strategy of making the Bund a future viable power in American politics. The new vitality exhibited by the German economy also played a part in persuading many German Americans to look favourably on Nazism especially at a time when America was still struggling with high unemployment and widespread poverty.

The Bund inherited a number of properties that had belonged to FONG such as Camp Siegfried, Camp Nordland in New Jersey, Camp Efdende in Detroit, Camp Hindenburg in Wisconsin and Camp Deutschhorst near Philadelphia and, most importantly, an organisation with a ready-made administrative structure.

Camp Siegfried, by far the most important of these camps, was owned and operated by the German American Settlement League taking in young people who learned about camping, hunting, shooting, and even eugenics, and adults and locals who attended seminars on politics and local events. The camps were designed along the same lines as those that had been operated by the Ku Klux Klan with entertainment, bands, singing, games, gymnastics, and competitions. Much of their operation was in the hands of the *Frauenschaft*, the Bund's women's division. As the closest camp to New York City, Siegfried was developed as a showpiece where visitors from the Reich would be feted on the shores of Yaphank Lake in its fifty-four acres of wooded countryside.

What Camp Siegfried exposed above all else was the uncomfortable reality that Bundists were Nazi supporters and, at the same time, saw themselves as patriotic Americans. The Bund's greatest achievement was to enmesh patriotism towards two countries whose ideologies were in conflict. It embodied two strands of Nazi ideology in relation to 'Germanness' by appealing to both the *Volkist* tradition and the bringing together of all people of German descent scattered across the globe but it did so within local communities and neighbourhoods. Pervading all activities, however, was the celebration and dissemination of Nazi ideology. The young studied philosophy as taught in German schools and were taken on cultural trips to Germany. Returning students and grown-ups smuggled back with them Nazi uniforms. The camp served to instruct men, women and youth in the ways of the 'fatherland' and teach practical as well as political knowledge to its members.

The Long Island Rail Road 'Camp Siegfried Special' ran from Penn Station, Flatbush and Jamaica every Sunday to Siegfried where uniformed marchers greeted guests with *Heil Hitler* salutes and sang the Nazi National Anthem. Everywhere were Nazi flags and the buildings even had swastikas embedded in their stonework. On 15 August 1937, the DAI newspaper the *National Socialist Kurier* reported that 'in their summer camps young German Americans, who owe their duty to America and who are bound to Germany, learn to harmonise their duties as American citizens and their national and racial missions as Germans.'

The Bund was affiliated with the National Rifle Association (NRA) and, under the Second Amendment, fully exercised its rights to train the young in the use of firearms. Congressman Dickstein would later argue that 'the National Rifle Association of Washington D.C., is being used and abused by the members of the German-American Bund. This rifle association, which had at one time sent representatives to the Bund in 1938 to solicit members was recently exposed in the press when it was found out that this association had sold rifles to the members of the Christian Front, of which fourteen members were on trial.'[11]

The Bund sold alcohol at its camps. One witness who later testified to the FBI, said that 'They did appear to consume great quantities of beer and do a lot of marching and wearing of uniforms.'[12] While the consuming of beer was confined to camp property, marches and rallies were organized throughout Long Island in places such as Lindenhurst and Yaphank. On Thanksgiving Day 26 November 1936, 4,000 bottles of German wine were bought by the *Amerika-Deutscher Siedlungsbund*, the dummy holding corporation for the camp. It was purchased from Germany as part of the Nazi official relief campaign to assist German wine growers.[13]

As late as 2015, ownership of properties in Siegfried Park, as it became known, was still at the discretion of the German American Settlement League. The Park itself was still subjected to the original bylaws which stipulated that all buyers must be twenty-one years of age or older, of German extraction and of good character and reputation.

The National Youth Leader was Theodore Dinckelaeker of Long Island, New York. In preparation for a meeting in the Queensland Bauernschenke in December 1936, he said 'It is absolutely necessary for us to get hold of the American youth …It must be the duty of every German to support our work here …to help our youth …who someday will carry the mantle for German liberty to victory.'[14] 'German youth,' he said on another occasion 'must be brought up in the German language and must get a German education here. The best place to give them an education is in our Hitler Youth Groups.'[15]

On German Day 1937, three special trains were laid on to take people to Camp Siegfried. The official programme promised German open-air religious services, and a huge parade with a Reutli Oath to round off the day. This was an ancient oath sworn by Swiss peasants in the twelfth century to assassinate their tormentors. It was a clear indication of the trend towards instilling into young people mystical mumbo-jumbo in the way that fascist movements all across the world had done.

These Bund youth camps were not universally popular, however. Southbury was a peaceful farming community of about 1,200 people when Wolfgang Jung purchased 178 acres of land in the community's Kettletown district on 1 October 1937. Six weeks later residents noticed a large group of people clearing the site ready for construction of a camp named Camp General von Steuben similar to camps in Yaphank and Andover. Plans showed a youth hostel, a huge outdoor swimming pool and facilities for over 1,000 people A nearby abandoned road was scheduled to be altered to accommodate a branch line of the New Haven Railroad. Locals called a town meeting to discuss changing Southbury's zoning laws. Mass mailings went out to local neighbourhoods warning them of the danger in their community, and pastors at Southbury churches began preaching anti-Nazi rhetoric.

On Sunday, 5 December 1937, two Bundists, Gustav Kron and Richard Koehler were working on clearing the site when a police unit arrested and imprisoned them for violating Connecticut by-laws by working on the Sabbath. There was a massive turnout for the official meeting to be held at the South Britain Congregational Church a week later when new zoning laws were passed designating the land in Kettletown as appropriate for farming and residential use only. Constitutionally it was of dubious legality but it passed by a vote of 142–91. When charges against Kron and Koehler were dropped, the Bund announced that their Kettletown camp was not central enough and promptly sold the site.

The Bundists had been more welcome at Camp Nordland which was opened on 18 July 1937, when 10,000 German-Americans descended on Andover, a town with a population of 479 at the time. The Andover Fire Department raffled off a car at the opening ceremonies of the camp, selling over 1,500 tickets. This flood of money led most locals to tolerate the Bund even if they were not too happy about the wearing of swastikas and military uniforms, the large portrait of Hitler they displayed on the main wall of their recreation hall, and the parade of a group of Italian-Americans dressed as Mussolini's Blackshirts, who marched around giving the fascist salute.

Soon, local newspapers and town leaders began to criticise the Bund for its anti-Semitism and criticism of Roosevelt. State authorities warned the organizers of Camp Nordland that they were violating a New Jersey law that forbade the promotion of race hatred and race hostility. The Bund responded by delivering speeches at the camp in German rather than English. Apart from ideology, certain Bund activities at the Camp brought unwanted publicity. One Bund leader was arrested in Brooklyn for sexually molesting two high school girls at Camp Nordland. A 17-year-old girl testified that she and her friends were served liquor at the camp's bar, leading the town of Andover to deny renewal of the camp's liquor license.

The flag of the youth division of the Bund was a white Siegrune (lightning flash) in a black field. Each division had its own number in the top left-hand corner in the colour of its District (East – red, Middle West – White, West – Blue). The uniform of the boys' youth division was grey-brown shirt with two pockets and shoulder straps, brown kerchief, short riding breeches in the same colour as the shirt, black German army belt, black German Sam Browne belt and cap similar to that worn by the Hitler Youth. The girls wore white shirts with dark blue skirts, white socks and dark brown shoes. Both boys and girls were equipped with German army knapsack, German army auxiliary kits and German army canteens.

*

Kuhn appointed himself *Gauletier* of the Bund and, to avoid any continuation of the discord that had dogged FONG, in drawing up the constitution of the new organisation he reasserted the Leadership Principle (*Führerprincip*) based on the system in Nazi Germany where the leader principle was applied at all levels of society. Organizations and institutions there were, as far as possible, run by a single heroic leader rather than by an elected committee and that leader could demand unquestioning obedience. One of his first acts as leader was to try to reconcile the warring factions by offering a complete amnesty to the BANS membership but Haegele rejected his overtures. It mattered little because BANS was really too small for Kuhn to worry about and Haegele's rejection had, in fact, strengthened Kuhn's position by demonstrating the need for strong leadership to prevent the Bund falling apart altogether. This allowed him to appear before the membership as a saviour of the nation-wide German American movement and he faced only minimal opposition when he introduced major changes to consolidate his position. He made himself leader of the OD security force, each member of which was required to swear a personal oath of allegiance to him. The OD was the American equivalent of the German SS (*Schutzstaffel*) and was employed essentially to protect the leadership during mass meetings. OD men wore the basic shirt and breeches with a black overseas cap and a distinctive OD armband with embroidered or sewn-on insignia. They were present at all Bund events and rallies with instructions to ensure the safety of Bund members but were not permitted to carry weapons other than police batons. When it was suggested to him that the OD be disbanded because of its reputation for violence and its unfortunate similarity to the Nazi SS, Kuhn was adamant that the Bund 'stands or falls with the OD.'[16] This security force continued to train at special camps, parade in uniformed ranks through American streets and salute with a stiff raised right arm and was instrumental on a number of occasions in protecting Kuhn from assault when violence broke out at rallies.

Gissibl, Kappe and Schuster opted to return to Germany now that they could play no part in the new Bund leadership and set about establishing an organisation, *Kameradschaft USA* in Stuttgart under the auspices of the DAI. There was much concern over the many Germans who were expected to return to Germany in the late 1930s. German industry was desperately short of labour as its economy heated up under the Four-Year rearmament plan and young men were drafted into the military. Initially this organisation restricted itself to finding employment and housing for other Germans returning home from the US but, at the same time, both Gissibl and Kappe were working with Kloss and Moshack on projects relating to German American organisations in the US Both returnees were significantly more imbued with Nazi fervour than the DAI people and Gissibl, in particular, was keen to extend Reich influence within the American organisations.

Alongside this was the Ethnic German Office (*Volksdeutsche Mittelstelle* VDM) under Werner Lorenz, that had retained some contact with the Bund after 1937 and, in contravention of directives, refused to abandon German Americans to their fate. While the VDM was a much smaller organisation that the DAI, it had the advantage of being a purely Nazi creation and wielded political power way beyond its size.

The League for Germandom Abroad, (*Volksbund für das Deutschtum im Ausland*, VDA), had been formed in 1880 and was primarily involved with education and worked closely with the DAI. It had not been a strong supporter of Nazism and suffered a blow in 1937 when Bohle forced its leader Hans Steinacher into retirement and allowed the VDA to be absorbed into the VDM. Created in 1936 as an entirely Nazi entity and part of the Ministry of the Interior, the VDM had been charged with looking after *Volksdeutschen* who returned to Germany and wished to regain German citizenship but actually had a greater function in implementing Nazi policy abroad. The affection for and loyalty towards Germany exhibited by German Americans was exploited by the Nazis but it was acknowledged within the DAI that the usual Nazi propaganda would not be received well in America either by the German American communities or the US government. That did not, however, change the fact that their ultimate aim was to Nazify the German communities in the US Heinz Kloss had noted during his visits to the US that there was a strong anti-Semitic sentiment but bemoaned the fact that there was no 'ideological apparatus' to channel it. His views were at odds with those of people like Gissibl who seemed determined to impose iron control of the German American movements from Germany. This naturally had the effect of blurring the overall message.

The DAI could only ever be as good as the information it was getting from the US but, because of competing doctrines, it was difficult to get at the true facts. Facts which, in any case, were heavily biased because people like Moshack, whose opinion was highly valued, garnered their information almost exclusively from within the German American communities with no balancing view from the outside. This resulted in gross errors of judgement over the extent to which Nazi philosophy was viewed by US society as a whole. Gissibl was always too willing to interpret everything in relation to his own pro-Nazi prejudices and even Kappe persisted in giving a highly biased view of the support in the US for Nazi Germany even as late as 1941.

Kuhn took this opportunity to bring his own men in to run the Bund, people he could trust. Carl Nicolay had arrived in Brooklyn as a twenty-four-year-old in 1903 and made something of a name for himself as a songwriter, poet and journalist as well as being made *Ortsgruppenleiter* of the South Brooklyn Friends. He became an active member of the OD and took up a post in the Bund's press division. Others were Gerhard Wilhelm Kunze a mechanic and Hans Zimmermann, a waiter who had served in Ernst Röhm's Brownshirts. Richard Schmidt was, like Kuhn, a holder of the Iron Cross and had served as an engineer in the German navy. Anton Fuchs and Carl-Heinz Eymann were two more, both of whom later returned to Germany to fight in the war.

Berlin did not follow up on its threat to strip Bund members of German citizenship. Gissibl's departure was essentially what had been required and his replacement by Kuhn seemed rather less controversial. Getting the support of the German American community was still vitally important, however, and Kuhn was given time to show his colours. His strategy was to emulate the pageantry, if not the methods, of the NSDAP in Germany.

He placed great emphasis on giving the Bund a militaristic character with parades, uniforms, slogans, torchlight rallies, racial diatribes and a focus on himself as the supreme leader. To create an exciting atmosphere, many meetings were held after dark with martial music and rousing speeches in an effort to recreate the Nazi experience for his followers. His own personal virulent anti-Semitism and anti-Black views were well to the fore in all of his speeches.

Of special significance to Kuhn and indeed to the DAI was the idea of *Deutschtum* and the preservation of German culture throughout the world. It was implicit in the concept that people of German heritage, the *Volksdeutsche*, had dual obligations both to their country and to the Reich. One Bund publication put it like this: 'To be German does not mean to be a citizen of the old homeland, but rather it means to belong as a German, bound by the ties of our blood, to the solidarity of all the Germans on the earth. Thus the German is and remains our racial comrade, without regard to the citizenship papers which he may somewhere possess.'[17] The problem for Kuhn was that he wanted to consolidate his position and illustrate his importance by implying that he had a special relationship with the NSDAP hierarchy, including the Führer himself, but he realised that Berlin was anxious to play down the connection which was, in reality, much less substantial that Kuhn liked to make out. The reason for Berlin's reticence soon became obvious. Rather than establish an American identity, the Bund became more and more associated with events in Germany, especially the reported speeches of Hitler that were becoming ever more menacing and a threat to the peace of Europe. Press reports were giving many Americans the idea that the Bund was somehow a 'fifth column' of subversives working against the interest of the US The ramping up of Nazi anti-Semitic rhetoric and reports of intimidation and persecution of Jews in Germany and Austria further blackened the Bund's reputation.

The Bund was actually shunned by the majority of German Americans who saw Kuhn as a marginal figure. Despite describing himself as the man who united 'Germandom in America' he failed to reverse or even slow the trend that saw German immigrants living in America perceiving themselves as proud Americans who just happened to have German ancestry. Many of them simply tolerated the Bund and others remained members of it more out of respect for their ancestors rather than enthusiasm for Kuhn or for Germany's current politics. Despite the well-attended and well organised rallies, Kuhn's popularity was most keenly felt amongst the young who found the camps, rallies, uniforms and camaraderie an exciting escape from mundane living and an outlet for their youthful energy. John C. Metcalfe, a reporter who infiltrated himself into the Bund, later described, to a Congressional committee, youth camps where young people 'wore uniforms similar to those of the OD, marched in formation; learned German, and were tutored in the fundamental principles of National Socialism. American boys and girls sing hymns to Der Fuehrer and to the *Vaterland* they never have seen. Their youthful feet goose-step in a march of racial and religious hatred. The minds and souls of these 'babes in the woods' are a fertile field for the propaganda of the Bund.'[18] Each of these camps was owned by a puppet corporation responsible for the construction and maintenance of facilities but it was Kuhn himself who was often the titular head of these corporations.

It had come as something of a surprise to Berlin that the Bund had actually survived and apparently was gaining strength but it was difficult for Berlin to determine just how big the Bund movement had become. The way that records were kept at local level rather than in a central office made it likely that even Kuhn had no real idea of the membership numbers either which gave him licence to make them out to be greater than they actually were. He would constantly pestered Berlin with these exaggerated numbers when appealing for greater recognition of the Bund which, he told them had risen above the chaos of Gissibl's final years in charge. His avowed ambition was to create an American version of the NSDAP with all its trappings and place himself as the essential liaison between the Reich and the US but Berlin had still not recovered from the Gissibl and Spanknöbel years of upheaval and was in no mood to give him any encouragement in that role. They wanted a strong presence in the German American community, but the *Auswärtiges Amt* did not want Kuhn.

Response to his pleas for recognition were muted at best so if the mountain was not going to come to Mohammed, Mohammed would have to go to the mountain. He set up an 'Olympic Fund' raising enough cash to take him and 200 invited members to accompany him on a trip to the summer Olympic Games in Berlin. Proudly announcing that arrangements had been made for them to meet all the German leaders, Kuhn set sail on the *SS New York* on 23 June 1936 together with his followers, 50 of whom were from the OD, and arrived in Hamburg ten days later. They were met by Sepp Schuster, now working for the Labour Front in Germany who arranged for the party to take part in a march down the Unten den Linden on 2 August. Furthermore, arrangements had been made for Kuhn and four of his companions to meet Hitler in the Chancellery.

The five included Rudolf Markmann, Carl Weiler and the head of the Midwestern Department, George Froboese. Froboese later gave an account of what took place at the meeting with Hitler in the 1937 issue of the Bund's *Kämpfendes Deutschtum*.

> He shook hands with each of us, looked straight in our eyes and placed his hand on the shoulder of our Bund leader…He asked us about our comrades of German blood across the sea, thanked us for our strong opposition to the immoral press and its infamous lies, and inquired in detail about the future plans of our Bund.[19]

It was at this point that Kuhn presented Hitler with a $3,000 donation from the Olympic Fund to go towards the Reich's winter relief fund and gave him a special Golden Book (*Goldene Buch der Amerikadeutschen*) that had been prepared. It was an elaborately bound pictorial history of the Bund containing the signatures of 6,000 members.

Hans Dieckhoff, who became the German Ambassador to the United States in 1937, recalled speaking to Hitler about that meeting which they both agreed had been an unfortunate mistake. Hitler told Dieckhoff that he had only see Kuhn once to receive the donation and did not wish to see him again. Unfortunately, the two men had been photographed which gave Kuhn the opportunity to make more out of the meeting than had been the case even though it had been no more than a perfunctory meeting, one of many that Hitler was obliged to have with visitors from all over the world. A picture of the two shaking hands was circulated by the American media following the meeting and was often used by Kuhn to show that he had Hitler's support. The 6 August, 27 August, and 10 September issues of the Bund newspaper contained articles which implied that there had been more to Kuhn's meeting with Hitler than a quick handshake and that Hitler had given Kuhn instructions for future pro-German activities in the US It even went so far as to give the impression that Kuhn's championing of Alf Landon in the forthcoming presidential elections had been sanctioned by Berlin, a suggestion that the German Embassy in Washington was quick to play down. It also had the opposite effect of shocking many Americans out of their complacency by reminding them of the awful things that were happening in Germany.

The American press latched onto growing unease concerning the news emanating from Germany about Nazi persecutions and began referring to the Bund as 'a dangerous, foreign-born Nazi movement that was working with Germany to destroy American democracy.'[20] The Bund did itself no favours in this regard by working hard to make itself appear as a true Nazi party in order to convince people of its strength and legitimacy. It was relatively easy for American newspapers therefore, to condition the public by frequent use of the word Nazi when referring to Bund activities or personnel. This created the impression that the Bund was, to some extent, controlled from Berlin.

Evidence for this was produced by a confidential report concerning a meeting held at Michoud Restaurant in Stuttgart on the evening of 3 September 1937. A delegation of some forty Bund members who were at the time, attending the fifth assembly of the DAI were at the meeting along with a number of German officials and reporters. G.K. Hein and Hermann Schwinn both from Los Angeles District of the Bund and Wilhelm Kunze of Philadelphia were the main guests, dressed in black riding breeches, black boots, grey shirts, black ties and black Sam Browne belts. All three made speeches in German. The German guests included the German Foreign Minister Konstantin von Neurath and Ernst Bohle. The report of an unnamed source says that the conversation during the evening left no doubt that the Bund was 'under the influence, if not the direct control, of Bohle's *Abteilung für Deutsche im Ausland*.[21]

Schwinn later admitted that he and Hein had been at the meeting but that it had been a purely social affair with no Nazi officials present. He denied ever making public speeches or attending rallies or parades in any official Bund capacity or in uniform at the time.

Whatever the Bund leadership was willing to say in public about the extent of involvement with Berlin, members such as Stanley High who wrote to the *Saturday Evening Post* on 27 July 1939 were in no doubt what was required.

> Our whole program at this moment has just one aim, to unite all German Americans under one Bund banner and then bring national socialism to replace democracy in the United states…we must win the masses to our side. There will be bloodshed and fighting. We shall have to do our part…then will be the time to wipe out our enemies.[22]

Wisconsin was probably the most German of all the American states in the early 1930s. About 40 per cent of its population was either German born or first generation German American. They had come from places a wide apart as Pomerania and Austria, included both Protestants and Catholics, Jews, freethinkers, and socialists of various stripes. Its enthusiastic grasp of *Deutschtum* made Milwaukee, especially the northern part, the place for great schnitzel and sauerbraten, and it had a vibrant German-language press. The local Bund organisation was headed by a mechanical engineer from Hannover, George Froboese, who also became the Bund's Midwest regional leader. In southeastern Wisconsin, there were also Bund chapters in Kenosha, Racine, and Sheboygan.

As early as 1933, German fascists had begun harassing Wisconsin's Jewish community and distributing Nazi propaganda and infiltrated existing German American clubs, that were all part of the Wisconsin Federation of German-American Societies, in an effort to bring them under Nazi control. Under its president Bernhard Hofmann, an immigrant from Hamburg, the Federation had more than seventy member organizations. Bundists quickly caused trouble in the Federation. Some clubs withdrew in protest causing the Federation to ban displays of the German national flag – now with swastika. Using threats and intimidation, Bund members tried to find out who had voted against the swastika but, as a consequence, were promptly expelled from the Federation.

In the summer of 1937, the Bund opened Camp Hindenburg on the banks of the Milwaukee River near Grafton, where swastikas were proudly displayed alongside the American flag. Camp activities included picnics and political rallies. While at the camp children dressed in Nazi uniforms and learned military-style drill, including marching, inspections, and flag-raising ceremonies. Although the Bund denied it, children also received political indoctrination. Bund activities quickly brought protests from Milwaukee residents who called the Bundists 'an annoying clique of race fanatics and disrupters'. At Bund rallies there were often as many protesters as Bund members and outbreaks of violence were the inevitable result. Police arrested several protesters, but no charges were brought against them. The judge said that 'any group preaching revolutionary doctrines opposed to American democracy and founded on religious prejudices can expect trouble.'[23]

The OD would be in the vanguard of any paramilitary action against the government, but reports sent by FBI agents who had been infiltrated into the Bund did not suggest that these thugs would be much use for anything other than crowd control. At one training camp activities included marching and squad formation followed by 'two groups in a game of military hide and seek then the singing of "Hitler songs".

American labour leaders joined American Jewish organisations in expressing outrage when the Kuhn-Hitler picture was splashed all over the news media. Neither had Berlin been impressed by the version that Kuhn had given of the meeting. Despite having been feted by Gissibl during their visit, in his role at the German Foreign Institute, it was clear that Kuhn was struggling to make a favourable impression with Berlin whose reaction was articulated by ambassador Dieckhoff, as increasing concern over the 'stupid and noisy activities' of the Bund.[24] He recommended that what he called 'these philosophical adherents of National Socialism [whose] abrasive and tactless methods were reaping a harvest of hatred rather than converts' should be abandoned. An investigation by Dr Freytag of the American section in the *Auswärtiges Amt* soon revealed that the membership of the Bund was much the same as FONG had been and that there was very little difference between them. The solution was to champion an entirely new organisation which did not permit membership by German nationals and concentrate on cultural ties rather than political ones.

Diekhoff was also concerned by Kuhn's claims that he had met Göring and Goebbels during his Olympics visit, so much so that he launched an inquiry and concluded that, as already on other occasions, Kuhn had 'consciously deviated from the truth in order to strengthen his position with his adherents.'[25]

Kuhn would not agree to purging German nationals from the Bund fearing that it would wither away and isolate him personally from Berlin which, of course, was exactly what Berlin wanted. He was entirely over-dependent on these new German immigrants, many of whom had no real long-term ambition to stay in the US and become naturalised. His message had never been tempered to appeal to second or third generation Germans which Berlin had been especially concerned about influencing. Freytag suggested that the threat of withdrawing passports from German nationals who joined the Bund would be applied and this time would be implemented. NSDAP members in the US would be told in no uncertain terms to distance themselves from Kuhn and Kuhn would be barred from using Nazi emblems or insignia. The American State Department agreed with Berlin that the Bund was doing little to repair the damage done to American-German relations and applauded Freytag's approach to the problem. In return, Freytag requested that American press criticism of the Nazis be played down.

Dieckhoff was unrelenting in his criticism. His ambassadorial role was becoming ever more difficult and he unequivocally blamed that on the Bund which was having an entirely negative influence on relations. His report to that effect dated 7 January 1938 led to urgent talks in Berlin between Washington Embassy officials, the VDM and the *Auswärtiges Amt* political wing. The meeting accepted Dieckhoff's suggestion that Kuhn be given no encouragement if he went to Germany.

The restrictions that had been placed on the Bund were entirely unwelcome to Kuhn who felt he had no choice but to go and plead his case directly to Berlin which he visited once more in March 1938. Maybe he had been influenced by his own propaganda into thinking that he was more important to Berlin than was the case and that he would be given a sympathetic hearing but he was soon disabused of that notion. The closest he got to the German leadership was Captain Fritz Wiedemann, one of Hitler's aides who was, himself, rapidly falling out of favour with his boss. Kuhn pleaded his case for keeping German nationals in the Bund and complained that Berlin was making no effort to 'understand' the Bund. He asked for clarification over the general direction in which Berlin wanted the Bund to go forward. Wiedemann's position suggests that he was under instructions to give Kuhn little encouragement. He bridled at Kuhn's imputation of Berlin's culpability and basically told Kuhn to go back to the US, behave himself and stop causing trouble for the Reich. If he wanted to contact Berlin in the future he was to do so only through the VDM and nobody else.

Kuhn was chastened by his reception which had neither parades nor fanfare. He feared the worst but, in typical fashion, was working on ways to circumvent any restrictions Berlin placed on the Bund much as he always had done in the past. He would have to work quick, however. While he was in Germany, Berlin sent instructions to its Embassy in Washington to make it clear to Bund members in America that the threat of stripping German nationals of their passports if they remained in the Bund would be followed through immediately. There were plenty of new channels that had been opened up for Nazi propaganda to flow into the US, Berlin was happy to see the Bund collapse once and for all so that they could take full control of relations between the two countries.

When he returned home, Kuhn wasted no time in urging all Bund members to take out American citizenship and for those who chose not to, he created a movement Sympathisers of the German American Bund whose members, no longer in the Bund, would still be able to contribute to its funds. Dieckhoff furiously reported back to Berlin that Kuhn was flagrantly ignoring Berlin's wishes by telling Bund members that Berlin was bluffing again and would not really carry out its threat.

Kuhn had allied himself with the views of a number of other fascists by opposing Roosevelt's New Deal which they had renamed the 'Jew Deal'. George Deatherage, who had promoted himself as leader of the resurrected Knights of the White Camelia, was one of those who saw Roosevelt as having come under the influence of Henry Morgenthau, Bernard Baruch, Felix Frankfurter and Louis Brandies and other prominent Jews and depicted the New Deal as a huge Jewish-communist conspiracy. Increased criticism of the Bund was getting through to Kuhn at last, however, and he saw that it was time to make some concessions. The 'Sieg Heil' greeting was replaced by 'Free America', the design of the OD uniform was modified to make it less militaristic and Nazi songs were replaced by patriotic American ones, but its racist rhetoric remained undiluted.

Despite being somewhat restrained by lack of political support due to his exaggerated claims, Dickstein rode the wave of public anger at Kuhn's Berlin visit and called for an immediate inquiry into the Bund. He would not get the chance to make very much of it since, in May 1938, the McCormack-Dickstein Committee was transformed into the House Committee on Un-American Activities under the chairmanship of Texas Congressman Martin Dies, Jr. The committee was the latest in a line of similar groupings dating back to 1918 created to investigate supposed subversive activity by communist or fascist groups and individuals inside and outside of the Federal Government. Dies' proposal enjoyed support from both the left, which called for far-right movements to be investigated, and the right, which wanted to target communism and some aspects of the New Deal.

The FBI looked closely at Bund activities but, despite concluding that they were reprehensible, found nothing that could be construed as illegal. While Kuhn was openly urging Bund members to look to Berlin for leadership, he was breaking no laws. Dies' early investigations had convinced him that there were German citizens in the Bund membership and he called Kuhn up before the Committee in the summer of 1938 when Kuhn denied having any connection to the DAI. The publicity generated by the hearings and Kuhn's robust defence of the Bund encouraged a modest rise in membership and the prospects for the Bund overall seemed brighter than at any previous time. Estimates of Bund membership at this time vary wildly but it was difficult to actually define what a member was. In terms of people who made occasional financial contributions and attended the occasional meeting the figure may well have been in excess of 100,000 but if committed Bundists were counted that number would have been more like 25,000. If Reich Germans were excluded from that, which the DAI insisted should be the case then the number would be less than 10,000. It was suggested that Kuhn might have his American nationality revoked but the legal obstacles to that were significant. Bund finances were investigated by the tax authorities. Licences to sell alcohol were revoked. Police presence at meetings was beefed up. Bund members who worked in sensitive industries such as shipyards and aircraft factories were questioned. While Dickstein had focussed on the spread of Nazi propaganda by the Bund, Dies started using the word 'traitors'. Many unmarried Germans returned home, and it was not long before this exodus was felt as a severe drain on Bund finances and membership.

Kuhn found himself facing all sorts of oblique challenges to his leadership and was forced to deflect his growing number of critics inside the Bund by focussing on an outside menace. Naturally he chose to intensify vilification of the Jews and launched an invective that rivalled anything seen in Germany at the time. Hate campaigns became so intense that some of Kuhn's associates feared that it might incite some members to outright violence. The strong anti-communist message coming out of the Dies Commission also gave Kuhn a target to aim at as he aligned himself with attacks against Bolshevism. In September 1938, his newspaper *Deutscher Weckruf und Beobachter* carried a report of the Bund convention at which George Froboese said 'We will...stand like men before Hitler and thank him for saving Germany from that bloody and Godless Asiatic monster called Jewish communism.'[26]

Then, on 9–10 November 1938 came Kristallnacht, the 'night of broken glass' when a wave of anti-Semitic violence was unleashed all across Germany, Austria and the Sudetenland in Czechoslovakia. The rioters destroyed hundreds of synagogues and Jewish institutions. SA and Hitler Youth members across the country shattered the shop windows of an estimated 7,500 Jewish-owned commercial establishments and looted their wares. Jewish cemeteries became a particular object of desecration in many regions. This marked the first instance in which the Nazi regime incarcerated Jews on a massive scale simply on the basis of their ethnicity. American newspapers carried front page reports of the pogroms and continued follow up articles for several weeks. *Life* magazine was able to publish some images in its 28 November issue. On 14 November Roosevelt recalled the America ambassador. Berlin retaliated by recalling Dieckhoff. The pro-German Steuben Society made clear its position by roundly condemning Kristallnacht in the face of a wave of anti-German feeling that was sweeping across the US

Pressure was building against the Bund. One of Kuhn's difficulties was that he had so little knowledge of or grip on the control of the many Bund groups spread out all across the continent. On the west coast Bund groups were allying themselves with other organisations such as the KKK and the fascist Gold Shirt movement in Mexico and getting involved in street battles with communists and anti-Nazi groups. Other groups in Texas were virtually running their own organisation calling themselves Bundists but making up their own rules. Some states had Bund groups that were barely functional. Facing challenges from without and within, Kuhn clearly had a need to galvanise his movement and instil some centralised control if it wasn't to splinter completely.

Press criticism of the Bund was unrelenting and sparked a debate about first amendment rights pertaining to the freedom of speech and of assembly. The *Hamilton Daily News Journal* of 22 November 1938 argued that it did not give 'racist radicals' freedom to abuse it 'to the point where it becomes a menace'.[27] The *Washington Post* of 20 August 1939 called the Bund's OD guards at the Madison Square 'totally out of keeping with the atmosphere of a public meeting in a democratic country' suggesting that the Bund had overstepped the mark of what is acceptable in a free democracy. Ironically, it was liberals who bore the brunt of the *Washington Post*'s Dorothy Thompson invective for defending the Bund's rights calling the liberals degenerate, intellectually impotent and lacking in the first instincts of self-preservation. The *New York Times* may have been in her sights because of its defence of the Bund's constitutional guarantees that cannot be denied in a democracy. The New Jersey Supreme Court would later rule that the Bund's activities had not constituted a 'clear and present danger' to society.[28] The *Chicago Tribune* argued that the Bund's right to open discussion of issues was a strength of the US democratic system and any attempt to curb such rights would drive the organisation underground which would give it notoriety and allure as well as making it less subject to oversight and scrutiny.

Not all opponents of the Bund were content to protest within the confines of the law. In his book *Gangsters vs Nazis* Michael Benson tells of how one New York judge, Nathan D. Perlman, was so frustrated at the way the Bund was allowed to operate with impunity that he called on the services of the Jewish mobster Meyer Lansky to deal out some rough justice. Perlman suggested to Lansky that some of his men might break up Bund rallies and meetings with baseball bats, clubs and other street fighting paraphernalia but definitely no guns. 'You can do anything but kill them,' he said.

In honour of Hitler's 49th birthday, the Bund arranged to hold a rally on East 86th Street, Sauerkraut Boulevard, marching from Carl Schulz Park to the Yorkville Casino. Waiting for them at the Casino were Lansky and a bunch of his hoodlums including 'Mendy' Weiss, 'Bugsy' Goldstein, Harry 'Pep' Strauss, and Jacob 'Ice Pick' Drucker. They listened to speeches in a ballroom decorated with swastikas and pictures of Hitler then split up. With baseball bats and pool cues the gangsters attacked from three sides and although they were far outnumbered by the more than 3,000 in the audience, it wasn't a fair fight — most Bund members cowered in fear, while the gangsters dealt in violence every day. After beating one Bundist into semi-consciousness, Goldstein and Drucker threw him out of a second-storey window. He survived, but his leg was shattered. Afterward, the mobsters dropped their weapons and the American Legion hats they had worn. When the next Bund meeting was scheduled for White Plains, only about 250 of an expected 1,000 Nazis showed up, many still bearing injuries from the Yorkville fracas.

Perlman next turned to Chicago where he enlisted the help of Jake 'Greasy Thumb' Guzik, an associate of Al Capone to do a similar job.

The next time Chicago's Bund met, they were attacked by various tough Jewish boxers, including Jacob Rubenstein, who would later be known as Jack Ruby, infamous killer of Lee Harvey Oswald. In New Jersey he called on mob boss and bootlegger Abner 'Longie' Zwillman and Nat 'the Fighting Hebrew' Arno. We just loved to fight, said Arno.

In early 1939, Kuhn became embroiled in a scandal. Virginia Cogswell known as Georgia Peach, celebrated for her frequent appearance in gossip columns, tried to publish her diary in which she had written about her affair with him during which she says they had become engaged. Cogswell, who, according to newspapers, had been married nine times was said to be a previous winner of the Miss America contest but she had really only been the winner of a beauty pageant in Atlanta, Georgia when she had been Miss Virginia Overshiner. Asked in court if it was true, as reported in the press, that she had been married nine times, she admitted to having only seven ex-husbands.

Despite the Bund running perilously low on funds, Kuhn's answer to the increasing pressure on his leadership was to gamble and hold what he called a mass demonstration for true Americanisation, a huge Bund rally at Madison Square Garden to celebrate George Washington's birthday on 20 February 1939. The hall had a capacity of 22,000 and many accounts say that it was a sell-out but footage of the event clearly shows many empty seats. A more accurate estimate would put the number at around 20,000. Many protestors wanted the rally banned but the mayor of New York, Fiorello La Guardia defended the Bund's constitutional rights to go ahead with what would be the biggest Nazi rally in US history. The day before the rally, the *New York Times* published an article stating that the Bund was 'determined to destroy our democracy and to establish in its place a fascist dictatorship,' and followed that up with a statement by its editor asserting that 'the Bund would set up an American Hitler.'[29]

More than 1,700 uniformed police officers were on duty outside the hall with another 500 plain clothed officers mingling with the crowd inside. Around 100,000 protestors had gathered outside some of whom tried and failed to break through the mounted police cordon and enter the building. Inside the stage was set with a thirty-foot portrait of George Washinton flanked by stars and stripes banners and swastikas. Drums rolled and an honour guard of young men and young women marched in bearing the flags of the US, the Bund, Nazi Germany and Italy. There were introductory speeches including much reference to Jews and communists to warm the audience up, then Kuhn was introduced as 'the man we love for the enemies he has made' and he stepped up to the podium. Everyone in the hall gave the Nazi salute. He railed against 'slimy conspirators who would change this glorious republic into the inferno of a Bolshevik Paradise' and 'the grip of the palsied hand of Communism' pausing at intervals when the crowd responded with cries of 'Free America' the new Bund greeting that had replaced 'Seig Heil!' but with the same intonation and raised arm salute. 'If you ask what we are fighting for' he said, it is 'a social, just, white-ruled United States [and] labour unions free of Jewish domination.'

The audience burst into wild applause but at that moment, a young Jewish protester, Isadore Greenbaum, ran up to the podium and tried to attack the speaker. The newsreels captured the incident which was seen all across American cinemas in the following days. What they saw was a flurry of OD thugs descend on Greenbaum and beat him repeatedly as the crowd roared its approval until a squadron of New York policemen rescued him. The speech ended with a rousing rendition of the Star-Spangled banner and wild applause.

The Bund considered the rally to have been a huge success but it is indicative of its blinkered world view that it failed completely to see that the Greenbaum incident was the worst kind of publicity. It is probably fair to say that it was Greenbaum's action that defined the high point of Bund popularity because immediately after the rally which had attracted such a huge crowd of protestors the Bund went into a downward spiral of self-doubt and generated fresh determination on the part of the authorities to bring Kuhn down.

When the international press got hold of the story and gave it prominence outside the US, authorities stepped up their pursuit of Kuhn. In May, La Guardia set up a Special Tax Emergency Investigation led by District Attorney Thomas Dewey and William Herlands. They quickly discovered that the various corporations that Kuhn had set up to administer the Bund had violated many tax regulations. Kuhn desperately tried to put his house in order by paying some of the back taxes but when Dewey raided Bund offices in Yorkville and took away all the Bund's financial records, he found much more evidence. What Dewey found showed why Kuhn had been so eager to forestall further investigation of the accounts by claiming, without foundation, that Dewey had violated his constitutional rights. He was arrested in a Pennsylvania village and placed in the New York police line-up where he was arraigned in General Sessions Court on an indictment charging him with embezzling sums of money totalling $14,548.59 from the Bund. He pleaded not guilty and was held by Judge Cornelius F. Collins on bail of $5,000. His passport was seized, and a trial date set for 9 November 1939. Dewey, who obtained the indictment, said 'the indictment shows that Kuhn is just a common thief.' He added that it looked very much as if Kuhn was trying to flee when arrested.

There was concern in Germany that evidence presented to the Dies Committee about the level of support that Berlin was giving the Bund could only have been acquired through US government interception of mail and telephone calls. It was starting to get embarrassing especially alongside revelations about Kuhn's private life that involved a fair amount of night clubbing, jazz clubbing, drinking and womanising. Press coverage threatened to see the whole German movement in the US being tarred with the Bund's brush. German Americans were shying away from clubs and organisations that had even tenuous links with the Bund. When feelers were put out to see who might be willing to take over leadership from Kuhn, there were no takers. Kuhn's champion in Stuttgart, Gissibl, argued that Kuhn had learned his lesson and would henceforth be much more cooperative with the DAI and could bounce back if given sufficient support. When Kuhn's case came to court, however, much of whatever backing he had in Germany fell away.

This was a blow from which the Bund would never recover. Many in the Bund had known, or at least strongly suspected, that Kuhn had regularly diverted Bund funds for his own use but the Bund was so much under his personal control that when the annual convention was held in July he was re-elected as leader and authorised to take all necessary steps to defend the Bund against the charges laid against him. When he came to trial, Kuhn was charged with multiple counts of embezzlement. The case rested essentially on whether Kuhn had the right to spend Bund funds as he saw fit. Evidence showed that he had been a serial philanderer whose penchant for night-club entertainment was far removed from his public image.

His erstwhile 'fiancée' Virginia Cogswell, who was by now a drug addict, appeared as a witness. The *New York Times* described her as 'slim and chic in a tan and grey herringbone coat, brown hat with brown snood and wearing a huge yellow chrysanthemum'.[30] She claimed to have received two death threat in just the previous few days, but she also said that she had just recovered from ten days in bed with 'grippe'. She went on to testify that Kuhn had paid her medical bills of $60 at the Hotel Plymouth on 2 September 1938 with what she called 'federal money' but she denied ever having an affair with Kuhn and had only got involved with him when she was hired by the government to spy on him. It was claimed also at the trial that Kuhn had used $717 of Bund money to pay for the transportation of the furniture of one of his mistresses, Mrs Florence Camp, whom he called his 'golden angel sent from heaven', across the country. Kuhn defended himself by saying that he was just having fun. His wife, Elsa had left for Germany in 1938 but returned with their son to support him during the trial.

He was found guilty on two counts. One of the grand larceny of $717 from the Bund and the second of forgery when he had made a false entry in the accounts of $500. A number of other charges had been dismissed for lack of evidence. It was enough, however, to get him sentenced to two and a half to five years in New Yorks's Sing Sing correction facility where he was kept in solitary confinement for his own protection. In June 1941 he was moved to the Clinton Facility in Dannemora, New York.

Kuhn's imprisonment had revealed much about the links between the Bund and the DAI which caused the Institute to instruct all personnel to terminate all contact with the Bund 'in any form'.[31] A few days later at a secret meeting of the Bund's executive committee, Kuhn was expelled from the organisation. Bund creditors called in their loans, membership crashed and subscriptions to Bund periodicals fell dramatically. Leadership passed to Gerhard Wilhelm Kunze. He organised a few rallies in support of Kuhn but made no serious efforts for the Bund to finance an appeal to his conviction. Money raised ostensibly for that particular purpose was diverted for other ends.

Kunze's leadership was a disaster. He lacked the sort of popular support that Kuhn had enjoyed which was a critical factor given the independent mindset of many state organisations. Kuhn's supporters railed against his failure to appeal Kuhn's sentence. Bund finances were critically low and contributions were drying up. Politically it was losing whatever direction it had under Kuhn with members no longer sure of what it stood for. Anti-German feeling in the US was stoked up. Under Kunze's uninspiring leadership, the Bund continued to decline. He became obsessed with security of the movement and brought in strict requirements for new members. Ideologically he turned the movement more towards isolationism and played down the anti-Semitic message. Clearly his objective was to protect the movement from criticism and interference.

Holding a rally alongside the local Ku Klux Klan was probably not the best way to do that, however. A witness described the event: 'Flames from the wooden cross, forty feet high, crackled into the night throwing lurid shadows on the participants below, some of whom were dressed in hooded white robes, others in the grey uniforms of the German

American Bund. The scene took place at Bund Camp Nordland in New Jersey on 18 August 1940, when the Klan staged a monster anti-war, pro-American mass meeting jointly with the Bund. By mid-afternoon 3,500 Klansmen and Bundists had assembled. August Klapprott, the vice-president of the Bund, speaking with a thick German accent, said 'the principles of the Bund and the principles of the Klan are the same.' Enraged locals raided the camp and the organisers were forced to call the police for protection.[32]

A year later a bill came before the New Jersey legislature revoking the charter of the German American Bund Auxiliary, the owner of Camp Nordland. On 30 April American Legionaries raided the camp and dispersed the Bundists, confiscated some material they thought the FBI would like to see, permitted the press to photograph Hitler's portrait and the huge swastikas affixed to the roofs, and then they padlocked the place as a public nuisance. Camp Nordland would never open again.

When Kunze was called to appear before the Bund's executive committee to answer questions about his conduct in November 1941, it was discovered that he had fled to Mexico and the meeting voted to remove him from post. Along with twenty-three other members of the Bund, he would be convicted in the US District Court in Manhattan on 17 September 1942 of conspiring 'to counsel divers persons to evade, resist and refuse service in the land and naval forces of the United States'. On 11 June 1945 a 5 to 4 majority of the US Supreme Court reversed the convictions of all 24 co-defendants on the basis the prosecution had introduced insufficient evidence.

When Kunze had been removed, George Froboese had assumed the leadership but he too would meet a tragic end. After being subpoenaed to appear before a Southern District Federal Court in New York, on 16 June 1942 he was a passenger on the 09.15 New York-bound train and disembarked at Waterloo leaving all his personal belongings on the train. At around midnight that day, another incoming train spotted his body on the tracks. The nature of his fatal injuries suggested that he had been struck by one of the earlier trains. The circumstances of his death suggest that it was an act of suicide. That proved to be the final chapter for a Bund that in reality had been falling apart ever since Kuhn's imprisonment.

Kuhn was deported to Germany on 17 September 1945 where he was interned in Hohenasperg Fortress. He was released a year later but re-arrested in 1947 and put in Dachau internment camp. He escaped from there by once again promising marriage to a 32-year-old German civilian employee of the US armed forces. In a jury trial in April 1948, Kuhn was sentenced in absentia to ten years in prison. On 16 June 1948, he was arrested by the German police in the French occupied zone while trying to register a chemical laboratory. When presented to Munich police chief Franz Xaver Pitzer, Kuhn was asked about his past and ruefully replied 'Who could have imagined that it would all end like this.' He fell seriously ill in 1950 and died a year later.

Chapter 8

THE CHRISTIAN FRONT

> While I do not belong to any unit of the Christian Front, nevertheless, I do not disassociate myself from that movement.
> Father Charles Coughlin

Father Charles Coughlin suffered a major blow to his ambitions with the poor showing of the Union Party in the 1936 elections. He had seriously misread the public mood by railing against Roosevelt's New Deal which had benefitted so many of his radio audience. They may still have welcomed Coughlin's soothing voice over the radio in a world which was still far from secure and comfortable but his politics chimed less and less with the public mood. Even though America was still deep in recession and there would be more bumps in the road ahead, Roosevelt had given the people hope that they were on the right track and that, if they stuck with the plan, there would be benefits for all. Coughlin was far from being a spent force, however.

Much has been written about whether or not Coughlin can be called a fascist. He certainly had much contact with fascists and fascist movements both inside and outside the US Some came to the US to meet him and others he reached out to. Amongst the many prominent people who had recognised the political potential of Coughlin's popularity had been the German Chancellor Heinrich Brüning, who visited his church in Royal Oak in 1932, the very Reverend Hewlett Johnson, Archbishop of Canterbury who did the same in 1935, and William Aberhart, another preacher politician who became the premier of Alberta. The poet and anti-Semite Ezra Pound, whose enthusiasm for Italian fascism was well known and who would later be tried and imprisoned for treason by the US government, found much in common with Coughlin and started up a lively correspondence with him. The British novelist and fascist sympathiser Hilaire Belloc also had a significant influence on Coughlin when he met him in February 1938.

Coughlin, himself, had secretly written to Mussolini asking for his support for a campaign to restructure the world economic order in such a way as to reduce its reliance on the gold standard. Il Duce's advisers warned him not to get too involved with a man who had been 'frequently the subject of serious criticism'.[1] They did, however, recommend that the Italian government take note of Coughlin's Catholic following and commented on his apparent influence over a group in Congress who might be persuaded to take a pro-Italian line against Roosevelt's embargo against Italy after its invasion of Ethiopia in 1935. Coughlin later asked Mussolini, a man whose public support he craved, to contribute an article to his newspaper *Social Justice* to explain Italy's adoption of Germany's racial laws.

When the Spanish Civil War broke out, Coughlin praised Franco in the pages of *Social Justice* for being the 'Saviour of Civilisation', a title that he might well have thought suited himself just as well. One of the reasons that earned Franco that title was his disdain for democracy and Coughlin argued that the US would benefit from the introduction of a corporate state, in which democratic government would be replaced by groups each representing one aspect of the economy who would then decide policy. No longer should America be artificially divided in Republicans and Democrats, he said, would be ruled by representatives in Congress sent there by each of the economic groups. He bemoaned America's inability to deal with problems of government that the Fascist countries were already well on the way to solving.

Not content to dictate from the sidelines, Coughlin also became involved in a somewhat bizarre plot to intervene militarily against the Mexican government. In this he had solicited the support of Gerald Smedley Darlington Butler who was, for a second time, selected by an American right wing group to lead a military coup. As a member of the Marine Corps, Butler was no stranger to Mexico having worked there undercover for the Woodrow Wilson administration in 1914 as it planned an invasion to unseat General Huerta. It was for his services there that Butler was awarded the Congressional Medal of Honour.

On 8 August 1936, Butler walked into the FBI offices and reported that he had received a phone call from Father Coughlin asking him to take command of a 200,000-strong army and march on Mexico to topple the government there which was pursuing anti-Catholic policies. Coughlin told Butler that there was adequate financial backing. Butler was probably more amused than angry but he let Coughlin go on after gesturing to an aide to pick up an extension phone and listen in. Roosevelt would be taken care of if he tried to stop them, Coughlin said. That's treason, replied Butler but again left the matter open when Coughlin rang off. His earlier experience with Liberty League left him in no doubt that there were dark forces at play once again and at that point he had gone to the FBI. The matter was reported to Roosevelt who took it seriously enough knowing who had been behind the previous attempt to recruit Butler but because Butler did not get back to Coughlin there were no further developments in the matter.

One organisation that Coughlin went out of his way to link with was the British Union of Fascists led by Oswald Moseley. Twice he travelled to Britain, once in September 1937 and again the following year, to consult with Moseley on issues of common interest. Initially, the British government denied him entry, but Ruth Hannagan (Treglown) sponsored him and he was allowed into the country but confined to house arrest in her house outside Brighton. Despite the conditions of entry, Coughlin moved around the country with Hannagan. He later claimed to have travelled to France and Germany by private aircraft at this time but there is no evidence to support that ever happened. At some point he held two meetings with Moseley whose interest was radio. He had tried without success to establish a radio station in Germany to broadcast propaganda to British audiences. Coughlin instructed him in the techniques of speaking over the radio to create emotional responses from the audience. In return, Moseley authorised a number of articles for inclusion in *Social Justice* to be written on the 'Jewish Question'.

During the 1930s there had been a sharp rise in anti-Semitism in the US Fascist groups sprang up across the continent with the Black Legion, that grew out of the Detroit car manufacturing industries, being one of the most violent examples. Whilst not a direct offshoot from the Ku Klux Klan, many of the Legion's members were involved with both. The car plants in Michigan had attracted much of their workforce from the poor southern states and these migrants brought with them their racial prejudices. When the Klan suffered a sharp decline in popularity and became almost extinct due to a series of sex scandals in the mid-1920s many of its members looked for alternative outlets for their venom. As is usually the case, there were men ready and willing to exploit prejudice, rally bigots and lead them in a cause. In Bellaire, Iowa, it was a physician, and one-time Grand Cyclops of the Klan, called William Jacob Shepard who spawned a movement in 1925 whose members wore red-trimmed black robes with a skull and cross-bones motif and a black hood with holes cut out for vision.

Shepard had wanted his Legion to be a secretive organisation, but it was exposed after members brutally murdered Charley Poole in the spring of 1936. During the investigations into its activities, William Guthrie testified that a plot had been hatched, but never actioned, to breed a typhus bacillus in the cellar of his house. Another legionnaire Charles McCutcheon, a Health Department Bacteriologist at the Heman Kiefer Hospital in Detroit, would acquire the germs which would then be injected into milk and cheese in Jewish grocery shops.

Coughlin had never made a secret of his anti-Semitism but his adoption of a much more extreme version in the late 1930s had been described as a 'desperate gamble' to reclaim his lost popularity after his disastrous showing in the 1936 presidential election.[2] His broadcasts became increasingly infused with sentiments decrying usury, the practice of moneylending, which most listeners would have no trouble interpreting as an attack on Jews. Coughlin bamboozled his less-than-erudite listeners with his 'expert' dissection of history in which wars had been started by 'international bankers' for profit. Despite these overt attacks, he promoted himself as someone well versed in Jewish history and religion and as one eminently well placed to be 'a friend and champion of the Jewish people'.[3]

It was Coughlin's anti-Semitic pronouncements that brought him to the attention of the motor tycoon, Henry Ford, the only 'public figure who, once identified as an ally, did not at some later point become an enemy.' Ford had very strong anti-Catholic prejudices but even so Coughlin recalled their great friendship which, he claimed, saw them lunch together frequently. The man who brought them together was Ford's personal secretary, Ernest G. Liebold, a man who epitomised a Prussian military persona and a life-long supported of the new Nazi Germany. Heartily impressed by Coughlin's anti-Semitism, there is strong evidence, not least from the diary of Roosevelt's Interior Secretary, Harold Ickes, that Ford subsidised Coughlin's *Social Justice* newspaper.

After the demise of the Union Party, Coughlin suffered another setback when, on 21 January 1937, his patron Bishop Gallagher died of a throat infection and was replaced by Bishop Edward Mooney, a man who was markedly less sympathetic to Coughlin. He tried and failed to persuade Coughlin to tone down his anti-Semitism so resorted to demanding scrutiny of all Coughlin's radio broadcast scripts before he went on air. This was also doomed to failure because although Coughlin promised to comply with Mooney's request, in practice, he simply ignored them.

It was in 1938 that Coughlin publicly accepted as truth the *Protocols of the Elders of Sion*, a treatise that had been wholeheartedly endorsed by Ford, describing a Jewish plot to destroy Christianity. The publication had been proven to be a Russian forgery as far back as 1921 but that did not prevent Coughlin, who made no declaration about their authenticity, making repeated references to the *Protocols* as having an 'accord' with current events. He made it clear, however, that his animosity was not aimed at Jewry as such, whom he said should not be so sensitive about the issue, but just to a cabal of Jewish plotters who were working with communists to destroy American democracy.

On 20 November 1938, Coughlin made a sombre broadcast to discuss what the announcer called ' one of the most vital and burning questions of our day—the question of the Jew and of the Christian, and of persecution.'[4] This was in response to two events in German that had taken place just days before. The first was the rounding up and deportation by Nazi authorities of thousands of Polish Jews living in Germany and the second the infamous *Kristallnacht* when huge mobs rampaged through German cities attacking and killing Jews, smashing the windows of Jewish business premises and burning synagogues. Thirty thousand Jews were rounded up and thrown into Dachau, Oranienburg-Sachsenhausen, and Buchenwald concentration camps. Massive fines and taxes amounting to the equivalent of 400 million dollars were levied on Jewish community.

Coughlin responded to Kristallnacht on 5 December 1938 by writing an article in *Social Justice* entitled 'Background of Persecution,' which purported to set out an account of the horrors inflicted on the European people by Jewish Communists and Socialists. What was taking place in Germany, according to Coughlin, was a consequence of Jewish responsibility for the communist revolution which had brought about all the ills suffered by Germany since 1917. This was in fact an almost verbatim translation of a speech given by Goebbels.

In his radio talks, Coughlin added his voice to the protests at the excesses of Kristallnacht but then focussed on what he called a powerful minority who had 'broken the back of this generation's patience'. Claiming to speak as a 'student of history', he maintained that the German people were punishing those whom they saw as being responsible for all the injustices they had suffered since the end of the First World War but whose anger was regrettably preventing them from differentiating between good Jews and bad Jews. What he called 'the good Jews of America' should have no truck with Jewish-communist conspiracy. The radio station WMCA had felt compelled to announce prior to this broadcast that the views expressed by Coughlin did not necessarily reflect the views of the station. The announcer was quick to add, at the end, that, in the view of the radio station, Coughlin had made statements that they did not recognise as fact. In Germany, the Nazi propaganda machine was quick to claim that Jewish owned broadcasters in America were trying to silence Coughlin and that America was not allowed to hear the truth.

The Vatican found itself conflicted between giving Bishop Mooney authority to sanction Coughlin and trying to placate the Italian government. Mussolini's propaganda minister Roberto Farinacci had praised Coughlin as 'an apostle of Christianity' and someone who had shown how Catholics should respond to Nazism. In Germany, the editor of *Der Stürmer*, Julius Streicher called Coughlin a 'model fascist'.

Rather than ban Coughlin from any further broadcasts, however, WMCA simply wrote to him asking that the text of any future address be presented to them for approval in advance. In the event, Coughlin's next broadcast was cancelled. The *New York Times* correspondent in Berlin reported that Coughlin was being lauded there as a new hero of Nazi Germany. The German Foreign Minister Joachim von Ribbentrop reportedly sent his best wishes to Coughlin, a man whom, it is said, he held in high regard but German diplomats in Washington maintained a discrete distance from him in public.

With the prospect of war increasing daily, Coughlin was still finding support for his views. In July 1939, a nationwide Gallup poll organised by Fortune magazine found that 32 per cent of respondents believed that steps should be taken to 'prevent Jews from getting too much power in the business world.'[5] He campaigned on an anti-war ticket both blaming 'international financiers' and communists for trying to drag America into a European war. Britain and France were not morally superior to the fascist countries, he said, the Nazis were the only ones who saw clearly what was at stake and the only ones who were prepared to stand up to the Jewish-communist conspirators who finance revolution and war and dictate US policy. Referring to Coughlin, Roosevelt told the Ambassador to Britain Joseph Kennedy that if a 'demagogue' like Huey Long, meaning Coughlin, got their hands on power and campaigned on a ticket of anti-Semitism 'there could be more blood running in the streets of New York than in Berlin.'[6]

More seriously for Coughlin, the slide from his previous high-profile position saw him assailed on all sides by imitators who were making great efforts to recruit his followers to their own brand of political activism. His main rival would turn out to be the 39-year-old black-haired, grey-eyed, deep-voiced Gerald Burton Winrod, a man who didn't quite match up to Coughlin's personality but who, nevertheless, found favour with Berlin.

Winrod had left school as a teenager to become a travelling minister, a calling at which he was spectacularly successful. In Wichita, this self-educated fundamentalist Protestant preacher started an organisation called Defenders of the Christian Faith in 1925 one of whose fundamental messages was an absolute rejection of Darwinian evolution in favour of the Biblical creation narrative. His anti-Semitism shone through his preaching as when he referred to the Roosevelt administration in his newsletter, *The Defender* as being a 'biological' as well as a 'political' problem. It was not hard to see the anti-Semitic message. 'He is not one of us!' the article boldly declared.[7]

Winrod had made a three-month visit to Germany in 1935 when he met the publisher and Nazi propagandist Julius Streicher; when he returned he made no secret of his admiration for Hitler, whom he likened in print to Martin Luther calling Hitler 'law-abiding...a true man's man', and for Germany which he called 'the best country in Europe'.[8] His appeal seemed to grow in line with his pro-German stance. The German press heaped praise on him as someone in the mould of Streicher and it was reputed to be Nazi money that financed his takeover of the Capitol News & Feature Service of Washington, DC. *The Defender* which regularly reprinted material put out by *Weld-Dienst*, a Nazi propaganda agency set up in 1933 by Ulrich Fleischhauer, claimed a circulation of 110,000 alongside a mailing list that also did a steady trade in religious tracts.

It was Winrod's strong following in America's rural heartland that gave him encouragement to run for office on a Republican ticket in the 1938 US Senate elections in Kansas. If successful, he confidently predicted that he would run for the White House in 1940. Onward Christian Soldiers was blasted out from loudspeakers at every one of his rallies. He took a leaf out of Father Coughlin's book and made regular broadcasts across WIBW and KCKN radio networks, sometimes even twice in a single day as the election loomed.

Questions were asked about where the money was coming from to fund such a campaign. Roosevelt was wary of Winrod, having already been on the wrong end of Coughlin's diatribes. When the press got interested in Winrod's campaign, it rapidly became a big story with newspapers all across the country commenting on what the *Chicago Times* called an 'arch fascist' and the 'Kansas Nazi'.[9] Winrod threatened to get closer to the levers of power than any fascist before him. Republicans manoeuvred to derail his campaign. John D. M. Hamilton chairman of the Republican National Committee regretted that 'Once again intolerance has raised its head in the midst of our political picture...if Winrod is nominated...our party in Kansas will be on the wrong side of a vital issue. [He] has made noises like a fascist [and takes] slaps at Jews and Catholics.'[10] When the votes were counted Winrod had come third making inroads only in a few counties where Klan support was still strong. He tried to regain some traction for his movement but was increasingly met with violent protest whenever he spoke at meetings and rallies. Support for his brand of fascist politics was ebbing in the face of reports of rapidly escalating persecution of Jews in Nazi Germany and Austria after the Anschluss.

In 1937, as part of his redirected campaign, Coughlin had written in *Social Justice* that the economic ills of the US had been caused by 'the powers of anti-Christianity' and required Christians to form their own army to launch a crusade against the anti-Christian forces of the Red Revolution. In January 1938, he tried to recharge his political campaign and ward off competition from such as Winrod by forming a new organisation he called the Christian Front ostensibly to fight communism, but which also targeted what he called 'insidious enemies'.[11] Membership was restricted to non-Jews and the movement encouraged the boycotting of Jewish-owned businesses. Whether or not it was group policy, members armed themselves and acquired proficiency with their weapons at gun ranges and sports clubs. Very soon, Christian Front members were notorious for attacking and beating up Jews on city streets, calling themselves 'Father Coughlin's brownshirts.'

While he gave his wholehearted public support to the Christian Front, Coughlin maintained a discrete distance from it so as to be able to deny any responsibility for its anti-Semitic excesses. Local units of the Christian Front mingled openly with Italian Blackshirts and German Bund organizations. The headquarters of the Christian Front in Boston was paid for by a Nazi SS officer, Herbert Schultz, who had been sent from Berlin primarily to maintain surveillance on the former Chancellor of Germany now living in Boston, Heinrich Brüning. By the spring and summer of 1940, the leader of the Christian Front in Boston was meeting with Schultz and taking direction from him. The front itself was a rallying point for a myriad of small, often short-lived, organisations such as The Social Justice Distributors Club, Christian Order of Coughlinites, Crusaders for Social Justice, Crusaders for Americanism, the Flying Squads for Americanism, the American Nationalists, the Protestant War Veterans, the Committee for Defense of Constitutional Rights, 'The Greater New York Committee for Christian Action, the Christian American League, the Christian Merchants and

Consumers League, the German-American Business League, the Christian Phalanx, The American Brotherhood of Christians Congress, the Christian Labor Front, the Christian Workers Alliance, the Christian Minutemen, Christian Vigilante Front, Christian Pioneers, Christian Congress, Christian Defenders, Christian Defence League, most militant and vicious of all, were the Christian Mobilizers.

Joseph Ellesbury McWilliams was an accomplished public speaker who considered himself ideally suited to be the leader of the Christian Front but when Coughlin chose Jack F. Cassidy instead, McWilliams took umbrage and formed a splinter organisation calling itself the Christian Mobilizers. This movement differed little from its parent in that both developed ideologies based on Nazism with the same references to race and blood. The training of youth in military discipline through 'sports clubs' was also common to both.[12]

The Christian Front and Christian Mobilizers had recruited young people primarily from the Irish and German American working-class neighbourhoods. Their motivation stemmed from a heady brew of financial insecurity, social exclusion, religious background and racial, nationalistic pride. Kuhn had shared the stage with McWilliams and the Southern rabble rouser, George Deatherage, at a mass meeting where Bund troopers gave the speakers a guard of honour and where all gave the Nazi salute. Kuhn told the crowd, 'I am proud to be here and show through my presence and through the presence of Bund members that the German-American Bund stands shoulder to shoulder with the Christian Mobilizers.'

Coughlin started appearing at Bund meetings with the message that democracy had shown itself weak and unable to stand up to the conspirators and now dictatorship should be given a chance. This started a wave of rumours that the Bund and the Christian Front were discussing a merger, something that he vehemently denied. The rumours were clearly not unfounded, however. William Wernecke, a Bund member, did, in fact, have a number of meetings with Coughlin but they failed to find common ground and nothing came of them. Coughlin might well have simply been soliciting for Bund supporters to join the Front since the Bund as an organisation was rapidly disappearing. He was still very ambitious and saw himself working towards the day when he would have 'five million marching under the banner of a Christian Front'.[13]

In Philadelphia, which was swamped with anti-Semitic propaganda, Jews were attacked in the street and synagogue windows were smashed. A church with a Black population was also targeted there but the worst violence was in New York City where a sizeable part of the police force was of Irish descent with several hundred reputed to be members of the Christian Front. For months, Christian Front street meetings routinely exhorted crowds to liquidate the Jews in America. Thugs roamed the streets and subways insulting and attacking Semitic-appearing men and women. Brawls resulted in almost 250 arrests and 120 convictions. Taking the Christian Front as a guiding light, another, more sinister, movement emerged.

Led by William Gerald Bishop, the Country Gentlemen became one of the most organized and threatening anti-Semitic groups of the New Deal era. Almost half of their number were active or former members of the National Guard or other branches of the armed forces. Where the Front had been a mass movement whose tactics were in street protests and anti-Semitic agitation, this new variation stockpiled arms and manufactured improvised explosive devices to defend against what they believed was an impending communist revolution. Their plan was to explode these homemade bombs in Jewish businesses and communist offices within New York City hoping to incite communist revenge attacks and then hope that the governor of New York would call out the National Guard to crush the communists.

One member of the Christian Front, Claus Ernecke had arrived in the US in March 1927 and had lived for a few years quietly and unobtrusively earning a living as a salesman at the International Correspondence School. He signed up to join the 101st Cavalry of the New York State National Guard in 1931 but otherwise continued to live an unobtrusive existence. Then, in August 1939, he approached Denis Healy, a sharpshooter member of the National Guard to ask if he would agree to train members of the Brooklyn Chapter of the Christian Front in the use of firearms. Healy reported Ernecke's approach to the FBI who told him to play along with it, allow himself to become involved with the Front and, for a small financial reward, report back on their activities.

Healy was a colourful character who had lived in both Canada and Ireland as a child. His father had reputedly been a British undercover agent of the Royal Irish Constabulary and the young Denis seems to have been involved in the Irish War of Independence on the side of the Irish Free State. In the early 1920s he had arrived in the US where he joined up with the National Guard. When he had got back to Ernecke agreeing to help, he was shown the cache of rifles and Browning machine guns that the Front had accumulated. Ernecke now opened up to Healy about the purpose of the Christian Front but the FBI had planted listening devices in his house and heard every word he said. There were at least ten squads of Country Gentlemen, with twenty men each, in New York undergoing military training and planning to take over essential public utilities and communications, he said. They had fifteen thousand rounds of ammunition and there were caches of Enfield and Springfield rifles all over the city. Healy would now be taken to meet to Bishop.

Bishop, a tall blond man had told many different versions of his background. When he had been arrested in 1935 for illegal possession of a revolver and served a three-month sentence, he said his name was William Arneck born in Geneva in 1903 and had arrived in the US in early 1928 but there was no immigration record to support this. He gave an alternative version to the right-wing US newspaper *Common Sense* on 1 June 1966 when he wrote that he had been born in Salem, Massachusetts on 27 June 1900. In the years immediately prior to the First World War, he said that he and his mother had lived in England, France, Switzerland and Austria then after the war, he found himself as a refugee in England. From here he went to serve with Spanish forces in the Riff Wars before returning to the US in 1926. Clearly either a romantic or a deliberate obfuscator, he also claimed to have been involved in political activity in Mexico where he had been shot through the leg before settling in New York in 1923. He told his landlady that he had fought in a Canadian regiment during the First World War and then gone to serve with Lawrence of Arabia before fighting for Franco's forces in Morocco. To another he said he had trained at the prestigious Sandhurst military academy in Britain before serving in India. Another version, put forward by the FBI and, naturally, one that Bishop did not admit to, was that he was a German agent called William Bischoff who had been deported three times from Britain and three times from Belgium and later smuggled into the US Evidence uncovered by FBI agents suggest that he had, at some time, been in contact with Pelley's Silver Shirts.

Ernecke took Healy to meet Bishop and another man, Macklin Boettger, a burly, ruddy-faced volubly anti-Semitic squad leader of the Brooklyn Chapter. It was here that Bishop told Healy that he and a group of others had formed the Sports Club, an offshoot of the County Gentlemen organisation and it was these men who Healy was being asked to train. They met regularly at a camp just outside Narrowsburg where they practised at a rifle range. He was introduced to other leaders such as John Graff, the explosives expert, John Viebrock, Michael Vill, who claimed to have marched behind Hitler during his abortive Beer Hall Putsch, Edward Walsh and eighteen-year-old William Bushnell.

On the evening of 27 September 1939, Healy invited Bishop, Boettger and Ernecke to his house for dinner but agents had fitted listening devices. Amongst other things, Bishop told Healy that he had been assigned by the Committee for American Action to establish a military unit in New York. The next meeting was at Boettger's home and Healy reported back that it concerned preparations for a bombing campaign against the New York Jewish newspaper, the *Daily Worker* in order to 'terrify the Jews of New York City'.[14]

Meanwhile, John Cassidy had used his connections to Coughlin to force the resignation of the board of directors of the Christian Front leaving him in sole control and it was in this capacity that he now demanded action and addressed a gathering of some 400 at Prospect Hall in Brooklyn. After the rally, Healy was introduced to some men who belonged to the Irish Republican Army in New York who 'could make a bomb out of practically nothing' and who were keen to add their weight to Christian Front activities. Cassidy got a bit carried away and called for the assassination of 'about a dozen Congressmen' to show that they meant business. In the event of US entry into any European war, the Front would conduct a campaign of sabotage against the US war effort.

By 11 January 1940, Viebrock told a meeting that he had made nine bombs and planned the same number again. The group made fantastical plans to blow up railways, docks and bridges and take control of public buildings. The FBI had heard enough. However far-fetched these plans were and however unlikely it was that any serious action could be taken by Bishop's group other than small-scale structural damage they were not prepared to risk injury and death to innocent bystanders. Two days later Judge Grover Moscowitz of the US District Court issued warrants for the arrest of Bishop, Boettger, Viebrock, Ernecke, Vill, Graf and others on charges of conspiring 'to overthrow, put down and destroy by force the government of the United States'. FBI boss J. Edgar Hoover personally took part in raids on the home of Cassidy, Bishop and others that uncovered caches of guns ammunition and bomb-making equipment. A search of Cassidy's home yielded a full list of Christian Front members.

National newspapers revelled in the spectacle and gave many column inches to the trial. Coughlin was careful to distance himself from the Front but over 1,000 members of the New York Police Department admitted membership. In Ireland, the *Kerryman* newspaper called the arrest a British plot to cut off funds flowing from New York City to the Irish Republican Army.

While many of his followers called on Coughlin to disavow the Christian Front, he refused to do so 'While I do not belong to any unit of the Christian Front, nevertheless, I do not disassociate myself from that movement.' He said, 'I re-encourage the Christians of America to carry on in this crisis for the preservation of Christianity and Americanism more vigorously than ever, despite this thinly veiled campaign launched by certain publicists and their controllers, to vilify both the name and the principles of this pro-American, pro-Christian, anti-Communist and anti-Nazi group.' The trial became front page all across the US and even Roosevelt did a personal press conference to announce it. Coughlin stubbornly told his listeners, of which there were still a great many, that the trial was about the Communist puppet masters trying to snuff out a brave, dissenting voice fighting for liberty and Christianity and 'the picture printed in the papers made interesting and profitable publicity at the expense of facts and truth.'[15]

When the trial opened on 5 April 1940, both the FBI and the Catholic Church thought it better to keep Coughlin's name out of it as much as possible. Coughlin who had earlier been quoted as saying 'God bless Mr Cassidy and the Christian Front' was forced to distance himself further from the trial. He suggested that communists had even organised fake Christian Front groups whose aim was to discredit the movement. These sports clubs of which the defendants had been members were really nothing to do with the Christian Front movement, he said.

The Justice Department made several failed attempts to add around two dozen US Senators to the charge sheet for abusing congressional franking privilege. All the accused, some of whom were paid quite large sums of cash, made speeches in the House or the Senate urging the US not to get involved in any European war. When their speeches went into the Congressional record it automatically gave those representatives congressional franking privilege which allowed them to mail out, at government expense, unlimited copies of what they had said. This had been masterminded by George Sylvester Viereck who hit upon the idea of charging the American taxpayers for the privilege of allowing Nazi propaganda to be sent out under the name of various senators and congressmen into American homes cost free to the Germans.

Viereck had been born on New Year's Eve 1884 in Munich. His father was rumoured to have been an illegitimate son of Kaiser Wilhelm I, but his political inclination was towards socialism which got him a nine-month prison sentence in 1886. This convinced him to abandon leftist views and he emigrated to the US in 1896 with his wife and son. The young Viereck started writing poetry in a somewhat romantic, decadent style which was published in German-language newspapers and he gained a level of popularity for a while but quickly fell out of fashion.

His talent and fame had got him noticed by the White House, however, and he became active in cultural exchange programmes between the US and Germany. Then during the First World War, financed by Germany, he launched a periodical called *The Fatherland* promoting the German cause. When the US entered the war, he changed the name to *American Monthly* and toned down his rhetoric. Like many Germans he was incensed by the terms handed down to Germany after Versailles and took an early interest in Hitler's NSDAP, interviewing the man and printing it in his newspaper.

In the 1930s, Viereck became a highly paid publicist for the Nazi cause in America. German diplomats, including ambassador Dieckoff, relied upon him for his views on the state of US public opinion and congressional view of Germany and the European situation. He cultivated friendships with certain isolationist Congressmen, especially Hamilton Fish, Jr., of New York and Ernest Lundeen of Minnesota.

As required by a law enacted in 1938, Viereck registered as an agent of a foreign power, listing himself as an author and journalist. In late 1939 he would become instrumental in organising a 'Make Europe Pay War Debts Committee' which enlisted the aid of various Congressmen opposed to American intervention on behalf of the Allies. It was through this organisation that the issue of abuse of congressional privilege arose when congressmen mailed out hundreds of thousands of reprints from the Congressional Record espousing policies summed up in anti-war slogans like 'Europe for the Europeans; Asia for the Asiatics; America for the Americans.'

None of the politicians got anywhere near the courthouse. The two charges faced by the eighteen 'Brooklyn Boys' were conspiracy and theft of government property. The Justice Department had brought in the head of the criminal division from Main Justice in Washington D.C. indicating just how important this case was to the federal government but the prosecution case fell apart almost from the start. The local press had downplayed the seriousness of the charges by calling the defendants, average age thirty-two, the 'Brooklyn Boys'. The Catholic Church supported them volubly and it was noticeable that Helen Titus the spokesperson of the jury, which incidentally contained no Jews, was a cousin of one of Coughlin's advisers and a founder member of the Christian Front, Father Edward Brophy. Large crowds gathered every day to cheer the defendants.

More than fifty witnesses were called over a five-week period but it was Healy's testimony that was crucial to the prosecution case.

Defence counsel subjected him to eight days of cross-examination. The jury were shown motion picture evidence of the men shooting and marching at the Narrowsburg camp as well as sound recordings of them planning a campaign of sabotage in the event the United States entered the war against Germany. It was by stressing the extreme danger that the defendants posed to American democracy that actually worked against the prosecution. Amongst the evidence laid before the court details of plans to explode bombs in the premises of Jewish businesses and for the assassination of members of Congress with the intention of precipitating riots that would bring down the government. Defence counsels were able to pour scorn on what they called wildly exaggerated accusations that these few local men were really anything more than gun enthusiasts who might occasionally have got carried away with fanciful notions. Even if they had, it was argued, it was all in a good cause of defending America against the threat of communism.

After two months the trail reached its closing arguments. The defence claimed that all defendants were acting out of patriotism to defend the country against a potential communist insurrection. On 12 April the trial was adjourned because Healy had failed to appear, having collapsed during questioning through nervous exhaustion on the previous day. At the same time it was noted that one of the defendants, Ernecke, had also failed to respond when his name was called out in court. A search was conducted and Ernecke's body was found hanged in the cellar of 23 Parkside Avenue, a Brooklyn apartment house. He had reportedly told friends that since the trial had begun, he had received a number of letters containing death threats and had become very frightened and feared he would be murdered or kidnapped. The first police report suggested that a murder investigation be opened but that was later revoked when a doctor declared that he had committed suicide.

On 25 June, after six days of deliberation, the jury acquitted ten defendants on all counts, on two they could not agree and a mistrial was declared for the remaining five. The *New York Times* reported at the time that 2,000 people turned out in Brooklyn for a rally to celebrate the Christian Front defendants after the prosecution fell apart. It was as much a humiliation for the government as it was a cause for celebration for the defendants.

Little was known about the trial until a History professor, who was also a Jesuit priest, Charles Gallagher, had become intrigued by newspaper headlines he has seen in archives showing armed men holding heavy shotguns and rifles who had been put on trial for sedition. To him, the news reports of the time tended to portray these men as crackpots who were being dealt with by the authorities and shouldn't be taken too seriously. When he requested access to FBI files concerning the event, however, he was told that there was nothing on record. Further research uncovered what seemed to be an FBI case number. The existence of the files was eventually admitted but it still took many attempts to get it released. Gallagher found it to contain 2,500 pages, the third largest file in the FBI at that time. The file showed that in the autumn of 1939, about 100 Browning automatic rifles, described as one of the most lethal weapons on the battlefield, had been stolen from an armoury on Waltham Massachusetts.

Coughlin, meanwhile, organised the Christian Front as an anti-semitic militia with platoon-sized units waiting for his order to mobilise but Coughlin was careful not to be explicit about exactly what he expected of them. Despite this call for small units, the movement started holding mass events and street corner rallies, sometimes with up to 10,000 people at them. In Boston, the Christian Front chapter there was showing German military propaganda films with live translation from German to English for their audience. These propaganda films were designed to show the German military machine as invincible and encouraged the view that the US should on no account get involved in any European war.

When the US finally entered the war, Bishop was sent to Ellis Island as an enemy alien. On 22 July 1943 he was sent to Fort Lincoln in Bismarck, North Dakota and at the end of the war he was returned to Ellis Island and held with three hundred other German detainees. In October 1947 he was deported to Austria.

It is easy to dismiss these men as comic-book delusional fanatics with ambitions way beyond their capabilities, but events would show that they were far from being harmless. A few days after their trial ended in 1940, two bombs exploded simultaneously in the city, one inside the eighteenth floor of the German Consulate at 17 Battery Place and the other inside the offices of the *Daily Worker*. Another bomb, planted at the World's Fair in Flushing Meadows Park in New York on 4 July exploded while it was being deactivated killing two bomb squad detectives, Joseph J. 'Joe' Lynch and Ferdinand A. 'Freddy' Socha. The blast carved a hole in the ground five feet wide and three feet deep. Patrolman Emil Vyskocil, Detectives William Federer, Martin Schuchman, and Joseph Gallagher suffered serious injuries. An unprecedented reward was offered, with $1,000 coming from the police union and $25,000 from the city but no arrests were made. The British government sent an engraved silver dish to the widow of Joe Lynch 'in recognition of [his] gallantry'. She replied in a telegram to the King and Queen saying that she did not have a house to put it in and 'a basket of fruit to feed [her] children would be much better.' Nobody was ever arrested for the bombings and what remained of the Christian Front dispersed slowly thereafter after the US entered the war.

Chapter 9

DOING BUSINESS WITH THE NAZIS

> Business, like most institutions, is not given to serious thought on its role society or the disparities between its actions and its professions.[1]

In October 1936, the US Ambassador to Nazi Germany, William Dodd, wrote to President Roosevelt saying that 'more than a hundred American corporations have subsidiaries here [in Nazi Germany] or cooperative understandings'. In particular he noted that the US chemical corporation, DuPont, had links to IG Farben, which had huge investments in armament manufacture and was later implicated in slave labour practices and the Holocaust. A year later, the US State Department was happy to acknowledge that European fascism was advantageous to US business. When Dodd retired in 1938, he said 'Certain American industrialists had a great deal to do with bringing fascist regimes into being in both Germany and Italy. They extended aid to help fascism occupy the seat of power, and they are helping to keep it there.'[2]

The relationship between US companies such as Chase Manhattan Bank, Ford Motors, Dow Chemicals, Coca-Cola, Woolworth, Metro-Goldwyn-Mayer, Kodak, General Electric, Alcoa and IBM who did business with Nazi Germany has been well documented but a reference to it here will help to understand how the economies of the US and Germany were interconnected and why both governments were anxious not to see a breakdown. In the late 1930s it might be said that the ambition of US business was to make money and the ambition of Nazi Germany was to make war.

Perusal of the US business press of the 1930s shows that their periodicals were overwhelmingly opposed to fascism and Nazism but that had not always been the case. In the previous decade they had heaped praise on Mussolini as 'a fine type of business executive' and fascist Italy as 'the most credible development in human history'.[3] There was not the same press enthusiasm for the Nazis, however, as free speech was outlawed in Germany and the economy turned towards war industries and Hitler's drive towards autarky, or self-sufficiency, threatened to reduce trade with the outside world. US business press editorials, however, continued to see the slide to war from a purely business perspective and took no moral stance on the Nazi policies of internal repression,[4] but they were not unaware that 'war loans lead to war itself'.[5] This did not deter some writers from giving readers advice about how best to profit from the impending war, while James H. McGraw was quick to point out that 'to say industry...wants war is a vicious and deliberate lie'.[6] In February 1938, *Business Week* wrote 'Activity in the armaments business is going to soar to new heights [and] there is another opportunity for profitable business before the conflagration breaks out...prospects of profits; and war orders, like any other orders, produce a favourable state of confidence.'[7]

In the years prior to the outbreak of war between Germany and the US there were many linkups between more than twenty of the largest American firms and German industry. In a lot of cases these arrangements were simply continuations of associations that had been developed in the 1920s when US money had poured into Weimar Germany to rebuild its economy and help it pay reparations after the First World War. Bond yields of 7–8 per cent attracted $1.2 billion of US investment between 1924 and 1930. American bankers earned some $50 million as a result.[8]

A number of independent steel companies came together in 1926 to set up the United Steel Works under the German industrialist Fritz Thyssen. Thyssen was closely linked with the New York-based Union Banking Corporation, managed by American banker Prescott Bush, the father of the US President George H.W. Bush and the grandfather of President George Walker Bush. Bush was also a shareholder in a number of other companies connected to Thyssen including one that was involved in Nazi slave labour, the Consolidated Silesian Steel Company (CSSC).

The big US manufacturing firm ITT had bought a 25 per cent share in Focke-Wulf, the German aircraft producer, and was helping to produce military aircraft for the Luftwaffe and high-tech communications systems, even after Hitler had declared war on America in late 1941.

By 1939, Ford and General Motors' German subsidiaries had between them a 70 per cent share of the automobile market in Germany amassing huge profits. At the same time, more than sixty arms manufacturing companies in Germany were owned by American banks. Pratt & Whitney, Douglas and Bendix Aviation were freely selling military patents to the Nazis, with the full agreement of Roosevelt's government. As late as 1942, around a third of the Wehrmacht's 350,000 trucks in service were produced at Ford factories in the Reich. Between 1942 and 1944 the Ford plant in Cologne produced about 10,000 half-tracks for the German Army. A US Army report compiled by investigator Henry Schneider, on 5 September 1945, accused Ford manufacturers in Germany of being 'an arsenal of Nazism, at least for military vehicles', having acted with the 'consent' of the parent Ford company at headquarters in Dearborn, Michigan.

*

As many as fifty-three American companies were in some way connected to I.G. Farben, a company that had contributed 400,000 Deutschmarks to the Nazi election fund in 1933. Almost as soon as Hitler was established as Chancellor, Farben was rewarded by coordinating its business activities with the administration, an arrangement that was formalised in 1935 when Farben opened a central office for liaison with the Wehrmacht in relation to mobilisation, counter-intelligence, military security and secret patents. At the post-war Nuremberg War Trials, it was stated that 'Farben was integrated in the government planning and preparations for war and became one of Hitler's greatest assets.'[9] It became by far the largest supplier to the German war machine and took over a major part of the industrial plant of countries conquered by the Nazis during the war, utilising slave labour as well as building and running factories established inside concentration camps such as Auschwitz.

As early as 1933, one of the firms dealing with Nazi industry was DuPont who were perfectly aware of the anti-Semitic nature of the Nazi administration as shown by a report presented to Wendell R. Swint, director of DuPont's foreign relations department after a meeting with Farben officials which said 'The [Germans] discussed…the positive position of the government against the Jews'.[10]

There was no suggestion that US firms shared Nazi philosophy when they entered into agreements with German firms. It was purely business but the terms of agreements made between Farben and US companies were heavily biased in favour of the German firm who were able to control the flow of intellectual information and regulate the construction of manufacturing facilities. Often one US firm would be played off against another. This became critical in 1940 when it was found that of the twenty or so major items vital to armament manufacture, no less than fourteen were produced by companies involved with I.G. Farben. Had such arrangements been subject to public scrutiny at the time there is no doubt there would have been a significant reaction but deals were kept secret.

The biggest secret deal was between I.G. Farben and the Standard Oil Company of New Jersey concerning a process the Germans had developed for the manufacture of synthetic motor fuel from lignite and low-grade coal. When Standard's Frank Howard visited a manufacturing plant at Mannheim in 1926 it was immediately obvious to him that synthetic fuels would become a major competitor for his company. After long negotiations, the two companies reached an agreement whereby Farben would only supply synthetic fuel to Germany and Standard would stay out of the world chemical industry including within the US As part of the deal, Farben was allocated 2.2 per cent of Standard stock worth some $35 million.

That did not prevent them from working together on the development of the manufacture of synthetic rubber which would later make it 'possible for the Reich to carry on the war independently of foreign supply'.[11]

In 1938, Standard gave Farben complete technical data for the production of butyl rubber in return for Farben giving Standard similar information about buna rubber. Standard had also assigned control of patents for the methane steam process for the manufacture of ammonia which was a superior method of producing explosives. Farben subsequently refused to issue manufacturing licences to American firms.

The US military had requested Standard to develop 100 per cent-octane fuel for them, but Standard refused on the grounds that, under the terms of agreements with Farben, if they did so they would have to supply Farben with full technical reports of its use which the military would not agree to. At the same time, however, while Standard was adamant that they would not violate these agreements, they were negotiating with the German government to allow their 50 per cent-owned German subsidiary DAPG to bid for contracts under the German Four-Year Plan for rearmament. They were eventually granted a licence to build a plant with a capacity to produce 150,000 tons of 100 per cent-octane fuel each year for supply to both Germany and Japan.

Howard met I.G. Farben executives in the Hague in September 1939, weeks after the German invasion of Poland to 'work out complete plans for a modus vivendi which would operate through the term of the war, whether or not the US came in'.[12] In early 1940, Farben requested that Standard apply for patents in France and Britain to prevent them utilising Farben processes in their war effort.

In 1924, Standard Oil, together with General Motors and DuPont had invested in a company called Ethyl Gasoline Corporation for the manufacture and sale of petrol (gasoline) infused with tetra-ethyl lead. After initial catastrophes when workers at the refinery in Bayway, New Jersey went violently insane and twenty died as a result of lead poisoning. the US Public Health Service called for dilution of the additive and declared that leaded fuel posed no immediate threat to the public. In 1934, Ethyl asked for permission from the Chief of the Army Air Corps to provide capital for the construction of a plant in Germany to produce leaded fuel claiming that it would only ever be used for civilian use. They argued that not to do so would mean that the Germans would go ahead anyway and that 'General Motors [who had] important investments in Germany…and Standard Oil [who had] large investments in all phases of the petroleum business in Germany [would suffer] extremely unfortunate [consequences]' if they were denied permission. Ethyl went ahead and built plants not only in Germany but also in Italy. A Gestapo report of 1944 stated that 'since the beginning of the war we have been in a position to produce lead tetraethyl solely because, a short time before the outbreak of the war, the Americans had established plants for us ready for production and supplied us with all available experience.'[13]

*

When a squadron of SS burst into a city square and posted a notice demanding those listed to assemble the next day at the train station for deportation to the East, how had they compiled such a list? When Hitler came to power, one of its immediate priorities was to catalogue those of its citizens who were of Jewish blood, regardless of their assimilation, intermarriage, religious activity, or even conversion to Christianity. But to search generations of communal, church, and governmental records all across Germany, and later throughout Europe, was a monumental task. It required automation and the only system available and capable of doing it was the IBM punch card and card sorting system which was a precursor to the modern computer. This system would also be used later to help the coordination of the massive movement of European Jews out of their homes and into ghettos then along railways and into death camps. Racial census-listing was invented by the IBM subsidiary, Dehomag. Its systems recorded not just religious affiliation, but bloodline going back generations. They not only counted the Jews, they identified them.

Data processing had been around for more than a century but it was Herman Hollerith, an employee of the US Census Bureau who took it to a whole new level with his patents granted in 1884. His Tabulating Machine Company was set up in Washington D.C. in 1898 specialising in the development of punched card data processing equipment. The company successfully recorded the 1900 US census and then developed applications of its technology for use on many different branches of commerce in a number of different countries such as Brazil where it tabulated the 1917 census. Willy Heidinger, an acquaintance of Hollerith, licensed all of Hollerith's patents in 1910, and created Dehomag (*Deutsche Hollerith Maschinen Gesellschaft*) in Germany which was acquired through stock-purchase by Hollerith's original company, now called Computing-Tabulating-Recording Company (CTR) in 1923. In 1924, CTR changed its name to International Business Machines (IBM) and was now run by Thomas J. Watson.

At the beginning of 1933, the prize would be for Dehomag to get the contract to tabulate the June German census which would obtain information about the religion of every member of the population. Watson developed his punch-card technologies in line with the requirements of the census and was rewarded with a 1.35 Million Reichsmarks contract for the Prussian Census on 15 June 1933. Opening a new production facility in Berlin in the following year, Heidinger declared how proud he was that Dehomag's mission was to dissect 'cell by cell the German culture [and provide Hitler] with the material he needs for his examinations.'[14]

Dehomag eventually produced more than 2,000 tabulating machines for use inside Germany, and thousands more throughout German-dominated Europe. The machines were not sold, they were leased, and regularly maintained and upgraded by IBM technicians. Card sorting operations would be established in every major concentration camp as the Holocaust was systematically catalogued. IBM, however, did not just make the machines, they customised the card punching process until it complied with the exact requirements of the Nazi programme. Dahomag trained the Nazi officers and their surrogates throughout Europe, set up branch offices and local dealerships throughout Nazi Europe. They also regularly serviced the machines in the huge Hollerith Büro situated in the I. G. Ferben factory complex about two kilometres from Auschwitz III, in the Hollerith Service across from the parade plaza in Mathausen, or in the bombproof Hollerith Bunker just outside the gate at Dachau.

With huge new business opportunities opening up, Dehomag appointed Heidinger, Karl Hummel and Hermann Rottke as directors to bolster the German image to the authorities and shield from America the fact that Dehomag was still wholly owned and operated by IBM. As a result of its success in the Prussian census, Dehomag tabulating machines were to be found in all walks of German commerce from aviation to banking to motor manufacture with the introduction of the powerful new Dehomag D-11. On 1 July 1937, Watson was awarded the Merit Cross of the German Eagle Star, the second most prestigious decoration for a foreigner.

People and asset registration was only one of the many uses Nazi Germany found for high-speed data sorters. Food allocation was organized around databases, slave labour would be identified, tracked, and managed largely through punch cards. Punch cards even made the trains run on time and catalogued their human cargo. German Railway, the Reichsbahn, Dehomag's biggest customer, dealt directly with senior management in Berlin. Dehomag maintained punch card installations at train depots across Germany, and eventually across all Europe.

It was a mere formality when Dehomag was awarded the contract for the 1939 German census which, amongst other things, would collect detailed information about 'the ancestry, religious faith and material possessions [and] ethnicity, educational and financial circumstances' of all 80 million German citizens.[15] The results of this census showed 330,892 German Jews to whom the Nuremberg Laws were applicable. In the words of one Nazi statistician, 'In using [Dehomag's] statistics the government now has the road map to switch from knowledge to deeds.'[16]

When the Nazi death camps were established, each camp used the *Hollerith Abteilung* Dehomag machines to record all inmates allocating to each a five-digit Hollerith code that was tattooed onto their arm.

Hundreds of thousands of concentration camp prisoners across Europe were registered with standard pre-printed paper Inmate Cards, called *Haftlingskartei,* approved by IBM to be compatible for its punch card process. IBM control markings are shown on surviving cards.

The huge profits that Dehomag accrued from their German contracts were invested in property in the country. All other unallocated profits were allocated as royalties to IBM which were held within the company and so, crucially, incurred no German tax. When the US entered the war, Dehomag was taken over by the Nazis. Dehomag technology was exported to occupied Poland where it was utilised by a new subsidiary called Watson Business Machines to 'calculate exactly how many Jews should be emptied out of the ghettos each day' and to transport them efficiently on railways leading to the camps.[17] The Hollerith Department of Polish Railways also calculated the rate of deaths per square kilometre due to progressive starvation and other arcane facts compiled to satisfy the Nazis' lust for statistics.

By decrees of 24 and 28 June 1941 the German government blocked the assets of American companies' banks and by 11 December seized them putting them under the control of the Reich Commissioner for the Handling of Enemy Property (*Reichskommissar für die Behandlung Feindliehen Vermoegens*). According to the German Ministry of Justice the Reichskommissar was a trustee for the property of the enemy alien and that he must administer it for the benefit of the owner and that at the termination of the war he would relinquish control and the property would be returned to the owner with proper accounting. A custodian or Administrator (*Verwalter*) of the American property, usually a German director or manager of the firm or a lawyer was appointed by the Reichskommisar. The Administrators were given authority to carry out all transactions which would be for the benefit of Germany's war effort.

IBM set up an office in Geneva which, according to Werner Lier IBM's European manager in Geneva was the company's top officer in Europe, involved with virtually every transaction in every country throughout the war. Lier described the Geneva office as a nexus, which simply implemented the business decisions made by IBM New York. He went on to say that New York made all the decisions and his function was simply to monitor the business and keep the records. He described the functions of the Geneva Office as purely administrative.

Although IBM Geneva left a massive paper trail, it has been hard to unravel and decipher it. Deals and denials characterized virtually the length and breadth of IBM's wartime presence in Geneva. Murky transactions were fundamentally untraceable since they could filter through a maze of banks or their branches, many of them newly created by Germany and scattered across occupied and neutral countries. During the war years, IBM's own internal reviews conceded that correspondence about its European business, primarily through its Geneva office, was often faked. Dates were falsified. Revised contract provisions were proffered to hide the true facts. Misleading logs and chronologies were kept.

By late July 1945, IBM had lodged compensation claims for war damage. The total of $151,383.73 included $37,946.41 for damaged

Hollerith machines. It also called on State Department intermediaries to secure its bank accounts in Romania. At the war's end, IBM reclaimed Dehomag and all its assets and changed its name to IBM Deutschland.

By 1967, IBM was America's top company but gradually lost market share thereafter. By 2001 it came under scrutiny for its Nazi links and involvement in the Holocaust. On 22 June 2001, a Swiss Court ruled that a compensation suit filed against IBM by the Gypsy (Roma) International Recognition and Compensation Action could proceed. The presiding judge said 'The precision, speed and reliability of IBM's machines, especially related to the censuses of the German population and racial biology by the Nazis, were praised in the publications of Dehomag itself, the branch of respondent IBM. It does not thus seem unreasonable to deduce that IBM's technical assistance facilitated the tasks of the Nazis in the commission of their crimes against humanity, acts also involving accountancy and classification by IBM machines and utilized in the concentration camps themselves.' 'There was,' he said 'a great deal of evidence indicating that the Geneva establishment was aware that it was aiding and supporting [the criminal acts of the Nazis during the Second World War].'[18]

IBM has consistently stated through its spokesmen that it has no information about how its machines were being used in Europe during the Second World War.

Appendix 1

GERMAN AMERICAN BUND ORGANISATION

According to FBI file 100–9766 17 November 1941

Headquarters   178 East 85th Street, New York City

Officers   Gerhard Wilhelm Kunze   leader
                George Froboese   assistant leader
                Gustav J. Elmer   treasurer
                William Luedtke   secretary
                Wilbur Egan   attorney
                August Klapprott   eastern district leader

In 1937 there were three districts divided into smaller districts and sub-groups

District East (Gau Ost)   leader August Klapprott

District Westchester County
    Bronx
    New Rochelle
    Poughkeepsie
    White Plains
    Yonkers
    New Haven
    Stamford-Norwalk
    Rockland County

District Long Island
  Astoria
  South Brooklyn
  Glendale
  Nassau County
  Jamaica
  Lindenhurst
  Huntington

District Hudson County, New Jersey
  Hudson County
  Bergen County
  Passaic County
  Newark

District Philadelphia
  Philadelphia
  Trenton
  Reading
  Washington D.C.
  Baltimore

District New York City
  District Brooklyn
  District Staten Island
  District Buffalo
  District Schenectady

District Middle West (Gau Mittel West)   leader George Froboese

District Milwaukie
  Milwaukie
  Gary
  Hammond
  Kenosha
  St. Louis
  South Bend
  Chicago
  Fort Wayne

GERMAN AMERICAN BUND ORGANISATION

District Cleveland
  Dayton
  Cleveland
  Detroit
  Hamilton
  Pittsburgh
  Cincinnati
  Toledo

District West (Gau West)   leader George Froboese

District Los Angeles
  Los Angeles
  San Diego
  Santa Barbara
  San Gabriel valley
  District Oakland
  Oakland
  Petaluma
  Portland
  Seattle
  San Francisco
  Spokane
  Salt Lake City
  Concord

NOTES

Prologue

1. Radtke, Terry George, *Americanism and the Politics of Commitment*, (Rutgers State University of New Jersey, 1993), p.15
2. Seldes, George, *Facts and Fascism*, (Progressive Press, 2009), p.109
3. Pencak, William, *For God and Country: The American Legion, 1919–1941*, (Boston Northeastern University Press, 1989), p.73

Chapter 1 The Background to American Fascism

1. Steigman-Gall, Richard, *Star-spangled fascism: American interwar political extremism in comparative perspective*, (Kent State University, 2017), p.96
2. ibid
3. Steiner, H. Arthur, 'Fascism in America?', (*The American Political Science Review*, Vol. 29, No. 5, 1935), p.828
4. ibid, p.822
5. Steigman-Gall, p.102
6. Magil, A.B. and Stevens Henry, *The Perils of Fascism*, (International Publishers, 1938), p.56
7. Ribuffo, Lee, *The Old Christian Right: The Protestant Far Right from the Great Depression to the Cold War*, (ACLS History E-Book Project, 2008)
8. Bernard, William S., 'The Backgrounds of American Fascism', (*Social Science*, Vol. 13, No. 4, 1938), p.284
9. Conzen, Kathleen Neils, Gerber, David A., Morawska, Ewa, Pozzetta, George E. and Vecoli, Rudolph, 'The Invention of Ethnicity: A Perspective from the USA', (*Journal of American Ethnic History* 12, no. 1, 1992), p.8
10. Thaxter, Lucy, *An Account of Life in the Convent at Mount Benedict*, (unknown, 1843)
11. Boissoneault, Lorraine, 'How the 19th-Century Know Nothing Party Reshaped American Politics', (*Smithsonian Magazine*, 26 January 2017)
12. Thaxter
13. Tucker, Ephraim, *The Burning of the Ursine Convent*, (Worcester Society of Antiquity, 1890), p.40
14. *United States Catholic Historical Society* XII 1918, p.74
15. Bernard, p.286
16. Schaefer, R.T., *The Ku Klux Klan: Continuity and Change*, (Phylon, 1971)
17. Bernard, p.288
18. Steigman-Gall, p.106

NOTES

19   Jackson, C.O., 'William J. Simmons: A Career In Ku Kluxism', (*The Georgia Historical Quarterly*, 50(4), 1966), p.351
20   ibid, p.352
21   ibid, p.354
22   ibid
23   ibid, p.356
24   Jenkins, P., *'It Can't Happen Here'*: Fascism and Right-Wing Extremism in Pennsylvania, 1933–1942, (Pennsylvania History: A Journal of Mid-Atlantic Studies, 1995), p.35
25   Evans, Hiram W., 'The Klan's Fight for Americanism', (*North American Review* 223, 1926), p.52
26   ibid, p.38
27   Report in *Chronicle Telegraph* 27 August 1923
28   Judge J. Thomson, Oral; Opinion of the Court, in Equity, 1897 p.672
29   Loucks, Emerson Hunsberger, *The Ku Klux Klan in Pennsylvania*, (Forgotten Books, 2018), p.186
30   Allerfeldt, Dr. Kristofer, *Invisible Empire: An 'Imperial' History of the KKK*, (University of Exeter, 2014)
31   Ward, Harry F., 'The Development of Fascism in the United States', (*The Annals of the American Academy of Political and Social Science*, Vol. 180, 1935), p.55
32   ibid
33   Archer, Jules, *The Plot to Seize the White House*, (Hawthorne Books, 1973), p.192

Chapter 2 Friends of the New Germany

1   Diamond, Sander A., *The Nazi Movement in the United States*, (Cornell University Press, 1974), p.35
2   Wilbers, Christian, *Between Third Reich and American Way: Transatlantic Migration and the Politics of Belonging, 1919–1939*, (College of William and Mary, 2016), p.99
3   Hawgood, John A., *The Tragedy of German-America: The Germans in the United States of America During the Nineteenth Century and After*, (G. P. Putnam's Sons, 1940), p.302
4   Wilbers, p.116
5   Bungert, Heike, Heitmann, Jan and Wala, Michael (eds), *Secret Intelligence in the Twentieth Century*, (Routledge, 2003), p.36
6   Spivak, John L., *Secret Armies The New Technique of Nazi Warfare*, (Project Gutenberg, 2007)
7   Diamond, p.142
8   ibid, p.95
9   Smith, Arthur L., *The Deutschum of Nazi Germany and the United States*, (Springer, 2012), p.66
10 Smith, Arthur L., 'Kurt Lüdecke: The Man Who Knew Hitler', (*German Studies Review*, 26(3), 2003), p.604
11 Smith, *The Deutschum of Nazi Germany and the United States*, p.73
12 ibid, p.72
13 Grover, Warren, *Nazis in Newark*, (Routledge, 2017), p.26
14 Diamond, p.130
15 ibid, p.135
16 ibid, p.140
17 ibid, p.147
18 Grover, p.35

19 Diamond, p.172
20 jta.org/archive/Nazi-rebels-issue-beobachte-secede-from-national-friends
21 *New York Times* 20 December 1934 p.27
22 Diamond, p.174
23 Smith, Arthur L., *The Deutschum of Nazi Germany and the United States*, (Springer, 2012), p.84
24 Diamond, p.182
25 ibid, p.176

Chapter 3 William Dudley Pelley and the Silver Legion

1 Allen, Joe, 'Confronting the fascist threat in the United States in the 1930s.' (*International Socialist Review*, issue 85)
2 Harty, Kevin J., 'William Dudley Pelley, An American Nazi in King Arthur's Court,' (*Arthuriana*, Vol. 26, No. 2, 2016), p.70
3 Lebedoer, Suzanne G., 'The Man Who Would Be Hitler: William Dudley Pelley and the Silver Legion', (*California History*, Vol. 65, No. 2, 1986), p.127
4 Pelley, William Dudley, *The Door to Revelation*, (Pelley Publishers, 1939), p.19
5 Lebedoer, p.129
6 ibid, p.130
7 Centrell, Nick, *Rifles and Rhetoric: Paramilitary Anti-Semitism in the New Deal Era*, (Boston College University, 2015), p.57
8 ibid, p.62
9 ibid, p.60
10 Lebedoer, p.132
11 ibid
12 Sevareid, Eric, *Not so Wild a Dream*, (University of Missouri Press, 1995), p.70

Chapter 4 The New Deal

1 Shaw, R., 'Fascism and the New Deal', (*The North American Review*, 238(6), 1934), p.559
2 Goldfrank, Walter L., Fascsim and World Economy, (Barbara Hockey Kaplan, ed., Social Change in the Capitalist World Economy Sage Publications, 1978), p.75
3 Boaz, David, *Hitler, Mussolini, Roosevelt*, (Cato Institute, 2007) 0
4 Haider, Carmen, *Do We Want Facism?*, (John Day, 1934), p.123
5 ibid, p.243
6 Corey, Lewis, *The Crisis of the Middle Class*, (Covici Friede, 1935), p.280
7 ibid, p.283
8 Shaw, p.559
9 ibid, p.563
10 ibid
11 Flynn, John T. *As We go Marching On*,(Ludwig von Mises Institute, 2007), p.191
12 Garraty, John A., 'The New Deal, National Socialism, and the Great Depression', (*The American Historical Review*, Vol. 78, No. 4, 1973), p.910
13 Cupers, K., *Governing through nature: camps and youth movements in interwar Germany and the United States*, (Cultural geographies, 2008), p.15
14 *New York Post* 20 November 1934
15 newrepublic.com/article/164825/smedley-butler-marine-critic-american-empire
16 Lisio, Donald J., 'A Blunder Becomes Catastrophe: Hoover, the Legion, and the Bonus Army', (*The Wisconsin Magazine of History* Vol. 51, 1967), p.37
17 en.wikisource.org/wiki/McCormack-Dickstein_Committee p.4

18 Archer, p.14
19 ibid, p.16
20 en.wikisource.org/wiki/McCormack_Dickstein_Committee p.3
21 Wortman, Marc, 'Famed Architect Philip Johnson's Hidden Nazi Past', (*Vanity Fair*, 2016)
22 hueylong.com/programs/share-our-wealth-speech.php
23 Franklin D. Roosevelt, 'Recommendations to the Congress to Curb Monopolies and the Concentration of Economic Power, April 29, 1938,' in *The Public Papers and Addresses of Franklin D. Roosevelt: 1938 Volume, the Continuing Struggle for Liberalism* (New York)

Chapter 5 Father Charles Coughlin

1 Centrell, p.55
2 Warren, Donald, *Radio Priest,* (Simon and Schuster, 1996), p.1
3 Shenton, J.P., 'Fascism and Father Coughlin', (*The Wisconsin Magazine of History*, 1960), p.8
4 Mugglebee, Ruth, *Father Coughlin, the Radio Priest of the Shrine of the Little Flower: An Account of the Life, Work and Message of Reverend Charles E. Coughlin*, (Garden City Publishers, 1933), p.155
5 Warren, p.23
6 ibid
7 ibid, p.25
8 ibid, p.27
9 ibid, p.33
10 ibid, p.39
11 ibid, p.41
12 ibid, p.49
13 ibid, p.52
14 ibid, p.61
15 ibid, p.65
16 ibid, p.73
17 ibid, p.75
18 Centrell, p.45
19 Warren, p.76
20 ibid, p.79
21 Crane, Milton, *The Roosevelt Era*, (Boni and Gaer, 1947), p.193
22 *New York Times*, 17 July, 1936
23 Early to Roosevelt, 22 June, 1936, Official File 306, FDRL
24 Warren, p.93

Chapter 6 Berlin Takes a Fresh Approach

1 Smith, Arthur L., *The Deutschum of Nazi Germany and the United States*, (Springer, 2012), p.152
2 ibid, p.7
3 ibid, p.162
4 Investigation of un-American propaganda activities in the United States: Hearings on H. Res. 282, Second Session, Before the Special Committee on Un-American Activities. 78th Congress, 1938, 1133
5 'A Vicious Programme' *Columbia Daily Spectator*, 10 January 1934
6 Norwood, Stephen H., *The Third Reich in the Ivory Tower: Complicity and Conflict on American Campuses*, (Cambridge University Press, 2011), p.45

7   ibid, p.46
8   ibid, p.165
9   Spivak, John L., *Plotting America's pogroms: A documented expose of organized anti-semitism in the United States,* (PRISM: Political & Rights Issues & Social Movements., 1934), p.82
10 Smith, *The Deutschum of Nazi Germany and the United States,* p.152
11 Wilbers, p.58

Chapter 7 The German American Bund

1   Bernstein, Arnie, *Swastika Nation,* (St. Martin's Press, 2013), p.43
2   American Characters, BundesfÜhrer Kuhn, americanheritage.com/bundesfuhrer-kuhn
3   Diamond, p.220
4   Smith, *The Deutschum of Nazi Germany and the United States,* p.92
5   Diamond, p.218
6   Geels, James E., *The German American Bund: Fifth Column or Duetschtum?,* (North Texas State University, 1975), p.61
7   FBI file 100–9766 17 November 1941
8   Shaffer, Ryan, *Long Island Nazis; Local Synthesis of Transnational Politics,* (Department of History Stony Brook University, 2010)
9   FBI file 100–9766 17 November 1941
10 Diamond, p.241
11 Congressional Record – House," May 21, 1940, p. 10783
12 Nazi Activities in the United States," Federal Bureau of Investigation (New York Office) 23 May 1938, unpaginated
13 FBI file 100–9766 17 November 1941
14 *Deutscher Weckruf und Beobachter* 10 December 1936
15 FBI file 100–9766 17 November 1941
16 Diamond, p.214
17 FBI file 100–9766 17 November 1941
18 Hart, Bradley W., *Hitler's American Friends: The Third Reich's Supporters in the United States,* (St. Martin's Publishing Group. Kindle Edition), p.34
19 Diamond, p.255
20 Thrall, Mina, *'What For is Democracy?': The German American Bund in the American Press, 1936–1941,* (Chapman University, 2020), p.5
21 FBI report 65–381 29 June 1939
22 FBI file 100–9766 17 November 1941
23 How Milwaukee's German-Americans faced down fascism eighty years ago, Posted by Mark D. Van Ells 17 March 2017 *Milwaukee Independent*
24 Bell, Leland V., 'The Failure of Nazism in America: The German American Bund 1936–1941', (*Political Science Quarterly*, 1970), p.591
25 Diamond, p.266
26 *Deutscher Weckruf und Beobachter* 15 September 1938
27 'The German American Bund,' *Hamilton Daily News Journal* 22 November 1938
28 Thrall, p.26
29 'Bund Rally to Get Huge Police Guard', *The New York Times.* 19 Feb 1939
30 *New York Times* 18 November 1939
31 Smith, *The Deutschum of Nazi Germany and the United States,* p.111
32 weirdnj.com/stories/local-heroes-and-villains/camp-nordland-bund

Chapter 8 The Christian Front

1. Warren, p.108
2. ibid, p.132
3. ibid, p.136
4. ibid, p.155
5. Hart, p.86
6. Warren, p.165
7. ibid, p.139
8. Hart, p.82
9. 'Arch-Fascist seeks US Senate post,' *Chicago Times*, 5 July 1938
10. *Time Magazine*, KANSAS: Wilderness Voice, 1 August 1938
11. Hart, p.86
12. 'Nationalism and the Movement,' undated report (Summer 1939?), Archdiocese of Detroit
13. Quoted in the *New York Times*, August 21, 1939.
14. Centrell, p.86
15. pbs.org/wnet/exploring-hate/2022/03/09/ep-7-sedition/

Chapter 9 Doing Business with the Nazis

1. Kolko, Gabriel, 'American Business and Germany, 1930–1941', (*The Western Political Quarterly*, Vol. 15, No. 4, 1962), p.717
2. Shane Quinn, How Nazi Germany benefitted America's corporations, Global Village Space globalvillagespace.com/how-nazi-germany-benefitted-americas-corporations/
3. Prothro, James W., *The Dollar Decade: Business Ideas in the 1920s*, (Louisiana State University Press, 1954), p.204
4. Kolko, p.715
5. Editorial, 'If Europe Goes to War', *Factory Management and Maintenance*, 97 (September 1939), special supplement
6. McGraw, James A., 'Business Stands Against War', (*Business Week*, 7 October 1939), p.52
7. 'War's Delay Helps Business', ibid., 26 February 1938, p. 14.
8. Kolko, p.718
9. International Military Tribunal, *Trials of War Criminals Before the Nuremberg Military Tribunals Under Control Council Law No. 10* (15 vols., Washington, D.C., 1949–1953), VIII 1244.
10. George W. Stocking and others, *Cartels in Action: Case Studies in International Business Diplomacy* (New York: Twentieth Century Fund, 1947), pp. 500ff.
11. International Military Tribunal, 1265
12. Kolko, p.723
13. International Military Tribunal, 1279
14. Murphy, Harry, 'Dealing with the Devil', (*The History Teacher*, vol 53 no 1, 2019), p.173
15. ibid, p.174
16. The Atlantic April 2001 Hitler's Willing Business Partners Jack Beatty
17. Oliver Burkeman, *The Guardian*, 29 March 2002 IBM 'dealt directly with Holocaust organisers'
18. The Nazi Party: IBM & 'Death's Calculator', by Edwin Black. jewishvirtuallibrary.org/ibm-and-quot-death-s-calculator-quot-2 Downloaded 25/09/2023

SOURCES

Allen, Joe, Confronting the fascist threat in the United States in the 1930s. (International Socialist Review, issue 85)
Allerfeldt, Dr. Kristofer, *Invisible Empire: An 'Imperial' History of the KKK*, (University of Exeter, 2014)
Archer, Jules, *The Plot to Seize the White House*, (Hawthorne Books, 1973)
Bell, Leland V., *The Failure of Nazism in America: The German American Bund 1936–1941*, (Political Science Quarterly, 1970)
Bernard, William S., *The Backgrounds of American Fascism*, (Social Science, Vol. 13, No. 4, 1938)
Bernstein, Arnie, *Swastika Nation*, (St. Martin's Press, 2013)
Boaz, David, *Hitler, Mussolini, Roosevelt*, (Cato Institute, 2007)
Boissoneault, Lorraine, *How the 19th-Century Know Nothing Party Reshaped American Politics*, (Smithsonian Magazine, 26 January 2017)
Bradley, W., *Hitler's American Friends: The Third Reich's Supporters in the United States*, (St. Martin's Publishing Group Kindle edition)
Bungert, Heike, Heitmann, Jan and Wala, Michael (eds), *Secret Intelligence in the Twentieth Century*, (Routledge, 2003)
Centrell, Nick, *Rifles and Rhetoric: Paramilitary Anti-Semitism in the New Deal Era*, (Boston College University, 2015)
Conzen, Kathleen Neils, Gerber, David A., Morawska, Ewa, Pozzetta, George E. and Vecoli, Rudolph, *The Invention of Ethnicity: A Perspective from the USA*, (Journal of American Ethnic History 12, no. 1, 1992)
Corey, Lewis, *The Crisis of the Middle Class*, (Covici Friede, 1935)
Crane, Milton, *The Roosevelt Era*, (Boni and Gaer, 1947)
Cupers, K., *Governing through nature: camps and youth movements in interwar Germany and the United States*, (Cultural geographies, 2008)
Diamond, Sander A., *The Nazi Movement in the United States*, (Cornell University Press, 1974)
Ells, Mark D. Vann, *How Milwaukee's German-Americans faced down fascism eighty years ago*, (Milwaukee Independent, 17 March 2017)
Evans, Hiram W., *The Klan's Fight for Americanism*, (North American Review 223, 1926)
Flynn, John T. *As We go Marching On*, (Ludwig von Mises Institute, 2007)
Garraty, John A., *The New Deal, National Socialism, and the Great Depression*, (The American Historical Review, Vol. 78, No. 4, 1973)

SOURCES

Geels, James E., *The German American Bund: Fifth Column or Duetschtum?*, (North Texas State University, 1975)

Goldfrank, Walter L., *Fascsim and World Economy*, (Barbara Hockey Kaplan, ed., Social Change in the Capitalist World Economy Sage Publications, 1978)

Grover, Warren, *Nazis in Newark*, (Routledge, 2017)

Haider, Carmen, *Do We Want Facism?*, (John Day, 1934)

Hart, Bradley W., Hitler's American Friends: The Third Reich's Supporters in the United States, (St. Martin's Publishing Group. Kindle Edition)

Harty, Kevin J., *William Dudley Pelley, An American Nazi in King Arthur's Court*, (Arthuriana, Vol. 26, No. 2, 2016)

Hawgood, John A., *The Tragedy of German-America: The Germans in the United States of America During the Nineteenth Century and After*, (: G. P. Putnam's Sons, 1940)

Jackson, C.O., *William J. Simmons: A Career In Ku Kluxism*, (The Georgia Historical Quarterly, 50(4),, 1966)

Jenkins, P., *'It Can't Happen Here': Fascism and Right-Wing Extremism in Pennsylvania, 1933–1942.*, (Pennsylvania History: A Journal of Mid-Atlantic Studies, 1995)

Kolko, Gabriel, American Business and Germany, 1930–1941, (The Western Political Quarterly, Vol. 15, No. 4, 1962)

Lebedoer, Suzanne G., *The Man Who Would Be Hitler: William Dudley Pelley and the Silver Legion*, (California History, Vol. 65, No. 2, 1986)

Lisio, Donald J., *A Blunder Becomes Catastrophe: Hoover, the Legion, and the Bonus Army*, (The Wisconsin Magazine of History Vol. 51, 1967)

Loucks, Emerson Hunsberger, *The Ku Klux Klan in Pennsylvania*, (Forgotten Books, 2018)

Magil, A.B. and Stevens Henry, *The Perils of Fascism*, (International Publishers, 1938)

McGraw, James A., *Business Stands Against War*, (Business Week, 7 October 1939)

Mugglebee, Ruth, *Father Coughlin, the Radio Priest of the Shrine of the Little Flower: An Account of the Life, Work and Message of Reverend Charles E. Coughlin*, (Garden City Publishers, 1933)

Murphy, Harry, *Dealing with the Devil*, (The History Teacher, vol 53 no 1, 2019)

Norwood, Stephen H., *The Third Reich in the Ivory Tower: Complicity and Conflict on American Campuses*, (Cambridge University Press, 2011)

Paxton, Robert O., *The Anatomy of Fascism*, (Vintage, 2005)

Pelley, William Dudley, *The Door to Revelation*, (Pelley Publishers, 1939)

Pencak, William, *For God and Country: The American Legion, 1919–1941*, (Boston Northeastern University Press, 1989)

Prothro, James W., *The Dollar Decade: Business Ideas in the 1920's*, (Louisiana State University Press, 1954)

Quinn, Shane, *How Nazi Germany benefitted America's corporations*, (globalvillagespace.com/how-nazi-germany-benefitted-americas-corporations/,)

Radtke, Terry George, *Americanism and the Politics of Commitment*, (Rutgers State University of New Jersey, 1993)

Ribuffo, Lee, *The Old Christian Right: The Protestant Far Right from the Great Depression to the Cold War*, (ACLS History E-Book Project, 2008)

Schaefer, R.T., *The Ku Klux Klan: Continuity and Change*, (Phylon, 1971)

Schaffer, Ryan, *Long Island Nazis: A Local Synthesis of Transnational Politics*, (Department of History Stony Brook University, undated)

Seldes, George, *Facts and Fascism*, (Progressive Press, 2009)
Sevareid, Eric, *Not so Wild a Dream*, (University of Missouri Press, 1995)
Shaffer, Ryan, *Long Island Nazis; Local Synthesis of Transnational Politics*, (Department of History Stony Brook University, 2010)
Shaw, R., *Fascism and the New Deal*, (The North American Review, 238(6), 1934)
Shenton, J.P., *Fascism and Father Coughlin*, (The Wisconsin Magazine of History, 1960)
Smith, Arthur L., *Kurt Lüdecke: The Man Who Knew Hitler*, (German Studies Review, 26(3), 2003)
Smith, Arthur L., *The Deutschum of Nazi Germany and the United States*, (Springer, 2012)
Spivak, John L., *Secret Armies The New Technique of Nazi Warfare*, (Project Gutenberg, 2007)
Spivak, John L., *Plotting America's pogroms: A documented expose of organized anti-semitism in the United States*, (PRISM: Political & Rights Issues & Social Movements., 1934)
Steigman-Gall, Richard, *Star-spangled fascism: American interwar political extremism in comparative perspective*, (Kent State University, 2017)
Steiner, H. Arthur, *Fascism in America?*, (The American Political Science Review, Vol. 29, No. 5, 1935)
Thaxter, Lucy, *An Account of Life in the Convent at Mount Benedict*, (unknown, 1843)
Thrall, Mina, *"What For is Democracy?": The German American Bund in the American Press, 1936–1941*, (Chapman University, 2020)
Tucker, Ephraim, *The Burning of the Ursine Convent*, (Worcester Society of Antiquity, 1890)
Ward, Harry F., *The Development of Fascism in the United States*, (The Annals of the American Academy of Political and Social Science, Vol. 180, 1935)
Warren, Donald, *Radio Priest*, (Simon and Schuster, 1996)
Wilbers, Christian, *Between Third Reich and American Way: Transatlantic Migration and the Politics of Belonging, 1919–1939*, (College of William and Mary, 2016)
Wortman, Marc, *Famed Architect Philip Johnson's Hidden Nazi Past*, (Vanity Fair, 2016)
Historical Records and Studies, (United States Catholic Historical Society XII 1918, 1918)

INDEX

A.V. Publishing Company, 113
Abbot, Thomas Rankin, 22, 23
Aberhart, William, 137
Alexander, Thomas, 102
American Brotherhood of Christians Congres, 145
American Business League, Deutsche Konsum Verband DKV, 113
American Civilian Conservation Corps, 71
American Legion, ix
American Liberty League, 76, 80
American National Socialist Bund, Bund Amerikanischer Nationalsozialisten BANS), 51, 104, 118
American Nationalists, 144
American Protective Association, APA, 10
American-German Comradeship, 52
Arneck, William, 147
Arno, Nat 'The Fighting Hebrew', 131
Ascoli, Max, 69
Avery, Sewell, 76

Baruch, Bernard, 127
Behn, Martha, 36
Belloc, Hilaire, 138
Bishop, William Gerald, 146, 147
Black, Supreme Court Justice Hugo, 18
Black Legion, 6
Blackburn, Alan, 81

Boettger, Macklin, 147, 148
Bohle, Ernst, 124
Bohle, Ernst Wilhelm, 40
Borchers, Hans, 41, 45, 100
Brandies, Louis, 127
Brink, Werner, 50
Brinkley, Dr John S., 56
Brooks, Sidney, 57
Brophy, Father Edward, 150
Brüning, Heinrich, 137
Bushnell, Prescott, 155
Bushnell, William, 147
Butler, Major General Smedley Darlington, 26, 51, 73–81, 102, 138–139
Butler, Nicholas Murray, 102
Buzzell, John R., 8
Byrd, Senator Robert, 18

Camp, Florence, 134
Cassidy, Jack F., 145
Christian American Crusade, 6
Christian American League, 144
Christian Congress, 145
Christian Defence League, 145
Christian Defenders, 145
Christian Labor Front, 145
Christian Merchants and Consumers League, 145
Christian Minutemen, 145
Christian Mobilizers, 145
Christian Order of Coughlinites, 144
Christian Party, 58
Christian Pioneers,, 145

175

Christian Vigilante Front, 145
Christian Workers Alliance, 145
Church of the Christian Democracy, 55
Clarke, Edward Y., 19, 20, 21, 25
Clarke, Robert Sterling, 74–76
Committee for Christian Action, 144
Committee for Defense of Constitutional Rights, 144
Conant, James Bryant, 102
Corey, Lewis, 68
Coughlin, Father Charles Edward, 86–97, 137–145, 148–149, 152
Coulter, Mildred, 37
Country Gentlemen, 146
Crowe, James, 11
Crusaders for Americanism, 144
Crusaders for Social Justice, 144
Cyr, Paul, 83

Deatherage, George, 127, 145
DeBlanc, Colonel Alcibiades, 13
Debs, Eugene, x
Dennis, Lawrence, 81, 94
Dewey, Thomas, 85, 132
Dickstein, Samuel, 42
Dieckhoff, Hans, 123, 125, 126, 127, 129
Dies, Martin, 128
Dillon, John J., 22
Dinckelaeker, Theodore, Jnr., 116
Dodd, William, 154
D'Olier, Lieutenant Colonel Franklin, ix
Domaszewski, Professor Alfred von, 35
Doyle, Bill, 73
Drucker, Jacob 'Ice-Pick', 130
Durrschmidt, Georg, 31

Elmer, Gustav, 114
Emerson, Colonel Edwin, 31, 39, 40, 42, 46, 55, 56, 57, 61
Epp, Major-General Ritter von, 111
Ernecke, Claus, 146, 148, 151

Ethnic German Office, Volksdeutsche Mittelstelle VDM, 119
Evans, Hiram Wesley, 20–25 passim, 36
Everest, Wesley, x
Ex, Alfred, 33
Eymann, Carl-Heinz, 120

Farinacci, Roberto, 142
Fechner, Robert, 71
Feder, Gottfried, 66
Federer, William, 152
Fish, Hamilton, 150
Fish Committee, 89
Fisher, Fred, 88
Fisher, Geiorge B., 56
Fisher, Lawrence, 88
Flying Squads for Americanism, 144
Flynn, John T., 70
Ford, Henry, 59, 89, 140, 141
Forrest, Nathan Bedford, 14
Frank, Leo M., 17
Frankfurter, Felix, 127
French, Paul Comley, 77
Friedersdorff, Frank von, 33, 34, 36–41 passim, 46–52 passim, 100, 101, 104–105, 110, 118–120, 122, 125, 133
Friends of Germany, 39, 40, 42
Friends of the New Germany, FONG, 40–52 passim, 94, 99, 100, 104–107 passim, 110–114 passim, 118
Froboese, George, 122, 124, 129, 135
Frost, Jonathan P., 17
Fuchs, Anton, 120
Fürholzer, Edmund, 31, 32

Gallagher, Bishop Michael, 88, 140
Gallagher, Joseph, 152
Garner, John Nance, 97
Gau-USA, 39
German American Business League, DAWA, 46, 50

INDEX

German American Historical Society, GAHS, 28
German Consumer's Cooperative, Deutsche Konsum Verband DKV, 111
German Foreign Institute, Deutsches Ausland Institut, DAI, 33, 50, 52, 94, 98, 101, 103, 104, 106, 107, 109, 115, 119–120, 123, 128, 133
German-American Business League, 145
Gissibl, Andreas, 33
Gissibl, Fritz, 33
Gissibl, Peter, 33
Glasser, Walter, 50
Goldfrank, Walter L., 62
Goldstein, Bugsy', 130
Graff, John, 147
Greenbaum, Isadore, 132
Grey, Edward T., 57
Griebl, Ignatz Theodor, 45–46
Griffith, D.W., 16
Gulden, Royal Scott, 57, 60, 61
Guthrie, William, 140
Guzik, Jake 'Greasy Thunb', 130

Haag, Lucien C., 84
Haegele, Anton, 49, 50, 51, 104, 105, 118
Haider, Carmen, 66, 67, 68
Hamilton, John D.M., 143
Hanfstaengl, Ernst Wilhelm, 45, 48
Hannagan, Ruth, 139
Hanson, Ole, x
Hayes, President Rutherford B., 14
Hayes, Virgil, 57
Healy, Denis, 146, 147, 148, 151
Hein, G.K., 123
Herlands, William, 132
High, Stanley, 124
Hoffmann, Theodor, 49, 51, 52
Hofmann, Bernhard, 124
Hollerith, Herman, 159
Hoover, Herbert, 32, 39, 64, 90, 91, 96

Hoover, J. Edgar, 77, 148
Howard, Frank, 157
Hummel, Karl, 160

Ickes, Harold, 140
Industrial Workers of the World, IWW, x

Jaeger, Werner, 110
Jefferson, Charles, 16, 19
Johnson, Alex, 21
Johnson, General Hugh, 70
Johnson, Philip Courtelyou, 81
Johnson, President Andrew, 12
Johnson, Reveren Hewlett, 137
Jones, Calvin, 11

Kappe, Walter, 34, 36, 40, 41, 43, 46, 47, 49–52 passim, 101, 118–120
Keelon, Francis, 94
Kemp, W.W., 57
Kennedy, John, 11
Kennedy, Joseph P., 94, 142
Kiep, Otto, 42
King, Alvin O., 83
Kloss, Heinz, 98, 106–109, 119
Knights of Mary Phegan, 17
Knights of the Flaming Sword, 22
Knights of the White Camelia, 13, 14
Know Nothings, 9
Koehler, Richard, 117
Köppen, Johannes, 71
Kron, Gustav, 117
Ku Klux Klan, KKK, 11
Küchler, Käte, 28
Kuhn, Fritz Julius, 110–114, 118, 120–123, 125–129, 131–136, 145
Kunze, Gerhard Wilhelm, 120, 123, 134, 135

La Guardia, Fiorello, 131
Lansky, Meyer, 130
League for Germandom Abroad, Volksbund für das Deutschtum im Ausland, VDA, 119

League for the Liberation, Fraternity of the Liberation, 54
League of German Girls, 71
Lemke, William, 97
Lester, John, 11
Liebold, Ernest G., 140
Lincoln, President Abraham, 11
Lohr, Otto, 107
Long, Huey, 81–85
Lorenz, Werner, 119
Lüdecke, Kurt G.W. (Conrado), 35–38 passsim, 46
Lundeen, Ernest, 150
Lusitania, 28
Luther, Hans, 52, 100, 102, 103, 107, 143
Lyman, Theodore, Jnr., 8
Lynch, Joseph J., 152

MacGuire, Gerald C. 'Jerry', 73–78, 81
Manger, Paul, 39
Markmann, Rudolf, 122
Maurer, James, x
Mayne, David C., 60
McCord, Frank O., 11, 12
McCormack, John W., 42
McCormack-Dickstein Committee, 38, 41, 43, 45, 48, 49, 56, 57, 77, 78, 80, 94, 100, 127
McCutcheon, Charles, 140
McDermott, Patrick 'Paddy', 23
McGraw, James H., 155
McWilliams, Joseph Ellesbury, 145
Meister, Willi von, 39
Mensing, Frederick, 41
Metcalfe, John C., 102, 121
Ministry of Public Enlightenment and Propaganda, RMVP, 102
Mooney, Bishop Edward, 140, 142
Morgan, J.P., 26, 76
Morgenthau, Henry, 92
Morse, Samuel F.B., 6
Moscowitz, Judge Grover, 148

Moseley, Oswald, 139
Moshack, Gustav, 100, 102, 104, 119, 120

National German-American Alliance, Deutsch-Amerikanischer Nationalbund, NGAA, 28
National Party, 82
National Socialist German Workers' Party, NSDAP, 32–52 passim, 79, 99, 100, 105, 111, 120, 121, 122, 126, 150
National Socialist Teutonia Association, Nationalsozialistische Vereinigung Teutonia, Free Society of Teutonia, Teutonia League, 33, 34, 36, 37, 38, 49
Native American Association, 8
Neurath, Konstantin von, 124
Nicolay, Carl, 120
Nieland, Dr Hans, 37
Niswender, Donald, 58

Oberholtzer, Madge, 24
O'Keeffe, Mother St. Augustine, 8
Order of '76, 57, 60
Ordnungsdienst, OD, 41, 43, 44, 118, 120, 121, 122, 125, 127
Overshiner, Virginia, 131
Owsley, Alvin, ix

Pavy, Judge Benjamin, 84
Paxton, Robert, 4, 5
Peach, Georgia (Virginia Cogswell), 131, 133
Pelley, William Dudley, 53–61 passim, 87
Perlman, Nathan D., 130
Pew, J. Howard, 76
Phagan, Mary, 17
Plug Uglies, 9
Pont, Irénée du, 76

INDEX

Poole, William 'Bill the Butcher', 9
Pound, Ezra, 137
Procht, Gerhard, 50
Protestant War Veterans, 144

Radio League of the Little Flower, 89
Raskob, John J., 76
Reed, Richard, 11
Republican Union Leagues, 13
Rheydt-Dittmar, Ernst Wilhelm, 104
Richards, George A. (Dick), 88
Rickenbacker, Eddie, 88
Ridder, Bernard, 42, 43
Ridder, Viktor, 42
Rip Raps, 9
Robinson, W.L., 25
Rohe, Mies van der, 63
Roosevelt, Lieutenant Colonel Theodore "Ted", Jnr., ix
Ross, Colin, 114
Rottke, Hermann, 160
Rubenstein, Jacob (Jack Ruby), 131

Sallet, Dr. Richard, 103
Schacht, Hjalmar, 39, 66
Scheurer, Adolf, 39
Schirach, Baldur von, 71, 114
Schivelbusch, Wolfgang, 63, 64
Schlitter, Oskar, 50
Schmidt, Richard, 120
Schnuch, Hubert, 49, 49, 50, 100, 104
Schrader, Frederick Franklin, 39
Schuchman, Martin, 152
Schuster, Josef (Sepp), 34, 36, 40, 41, 49, 50, 51, 101, 118, 122
Schuster, Sepp, 41
Schwinn, Hermann, 36, 123, 124
Scott, Sarah C., 56
Second Great Awakening,, 7
Sevareid, Eric, 59
Shaw, Roger, 68, 69
Shepard, William Jacob, 139
Silver Legion of America, Silver Shirts, 55–61 passim, 67, 86, 105, 147

Silver Shirts, 6
Simmons, William J., 16
Sister Mary John, 7, 8
Slaton, John, 17
Sloan, Alfred P., 76
Smith, Al, 76
Smith, Gerald Lyman Kenneth, 1
Socha, Ferdinand A., 152
Sons of the Sires, 9
Spanknöbel, Heinrich (Heinz), 36–47 passim, 100, 122
Spanknöbel, Martha, 39
Speer, Albert, 63
Spivak, John L., 78–80
Sprecht, Karl, 36
Steinacker, Hans, 119
Steiner, H. Arthur, 2, 4
Stephenson, David C., 24
Strasser, Gregor, 66
Strauss, Harry 'Pep', 130
Streicher, Julius, 142, 143
Stresemann, Gustav, 30
Strewst, Hans, 41
Strohlen, Theodor, 50
Strölin,, Karl, 107
Sturmabteilung,, SA, 34
Supreme Order of the Star-Spangled Banner, 9
Swastika League, 38
Swint, Wendell R., 156

Thaxter, Lucy, 7, 8
The Greater New York Committee for Christian Action, 144
The Social Justice Distributors Club, 144
Themlitz, Paul, 36
Thompson, Dorothy, 130
Thyssen, Fritz, 155
Titus, Helen, 150
Toal, Paul von Lillienfield, 56, 61
Townsend, Dr. Francis E., 96
Tugwell, Rexford, 64
Tyler, Elizabeth, 19, 20, 21, 25

Union Defence Guard, UDG, 59
Union Party, Stop Roosevelt Party, 97
United German Societies of Greater New York, UGS, 38
Ursine Convent, 7
USS Buford, 10

Viebrock, John, 147
Viereck, George Sylvester, 39, 149–150
Vill, Michael, 147
Vyshocil, Emil, 152

Walsh, Edward, 147
Walter, Reinhold, 48

Waring, Dorothy, 60
Watson, Thomas J., 159
Weiler, Carl, 122
Weiss, Dr. Carl, 84
Weiss, Mendy', 130
Whitney, Thomas R., 9
Wiedemann, Fritz, 126
Wilson, Thomas E., x
Winrod, Gerald Burton, 142
Works Progress Administration and Public Works Administration, 71

Zachary, Roy, 58, 59
Zimmermann, Hans, 120
Zwillman, Abner 'Longie', 131